D1756183

AMERICAN PHILOLOGICAL ASSOCIATION

TEXTS AND COMMENTARIES SERIES

Series Editor
Sander M. Goldberg

Sallust's *Bellum Catilinae*, Second Edition
J. T. Ramsey

A Commentary on Demosthenes' *Philippic* I: With Rhetorical
Analyses of *Philippics* II *and* III
Cecil Wooten

Cicero's *Pro L. Murena Oratio*
Elaine Fantham

Cicero's *Pro L. Murena Oratio*

Introduction and Commentary by
Elaine Fantham

OXFORD

UNIVERSITY PRESS

Oxford University Press is a department of the University of Oxford.
It furthers the University's objective of excellence in research,
scholarship, and education by publishing worldwide.

Oxford   New York

Auckland   Cape Town   Dar es Salaam   Hong Kong   Karachi
Kuala Lumpur   Madrid   Melbourne   Mexico City   Nairobi
New Delhi   Shanghai   Taipei   Toronto

With offices in

Argentina   Austria   Brazil   Chile   Czech Republic   France   Greece
Guatemala   Hungary   Italy   Japan   Poland   Portugal   Singapore
South Korea   Switzerland   Thailand   Turkey   Ukraine   Vietnam

Oxford is a registered trade mark of Oxford University Press
in the UK and certain other countries.

Published in the United States of America by
Oxford University Press
198 Madison Avenue, New York, NY 10016

© 2013 by the American Philological Association

Library of Congress Cataloging-in-Publication Data
Fantham, Elaine, author.
Cicero's Pro L. Murena oratio / Elaine Fantham.
pages cm — (American Philological Association texts and commentaries series)
ISBN 978-0-19-997453-5
1. Cicero, Marcus Tullius. Pro Murena. I. Title. II.
Series: American Philological Association texts and commentaries series.
PA6279.M8F36   2013
875'.01—dc23   2013021156

1 3 5 7 9 8 6 4 2

Printed in the United States of America
on acid-free paper

Contents

Acknowledgments

After writing three commentaries on Latin poets I thought I knew how and what to write about Cicero's *Pro Murena*, a speech I have always loved. But I hadn't taken on board all the disciplines necessary to do justice to Cicero's wit and manipulation of argument (and facts!) so as to make the speech enjoyable to modern students who are far more sophisticated in political thinking, but rather less comfortable in Latin than I was at their age. Any student interested in modern democratic politics in North America or the United Kingdom will recognize how little the standards of careerists have changed or improved.

This commentary would never have reached the press without the unstinting and tactful-but-truthful help of two distinguished scholars and good friends, Bob Kaster and Sander Goldberg, at different stages. I owe them an immense debt of gratitude for the labor and judgment they applied to making it a better piece of work and, I hope, a better teaching tool.

In addition I had most useful help and advice from Kevin Lawson, whose recent experience of teaching introductory and intermediate Latin to university students alerted him to the kind of grammatical comment that would be appropriate; Kevin also read meticulously through my draft text, and I am most grateful to him.

I was also able to benefit from the detailed reports and suggestions of the series' referees, Bob Cape and Jon Hall, both experts in Ciceronian rhetoric, and Francis X. Ryan's scrupulous and helpful comments on senatorial careers and procedure.

I hope I have done justice to their suggestions; any errors persisting are my own, whether inadvertent or perverse.

Elaine Fantham May 2012

Cicero's *Pro L. Murena Oratio*

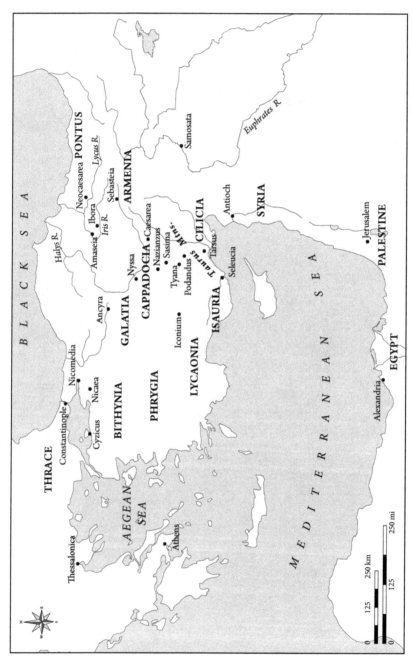

Anatolia and Northern Mesopotamia. After R. Syme, *Anatolica*, A. R. Birley, ed. 1995, Oxford: Oxford University Press.

Introduction: *Pro Murena*

The sheer political and social interest of Cicero's defense of L. Licinius Murena urged me to attempt this commentary so as to make it accessible to students, both those concentrating on Roman history and those studying classical languages and literature in general. In recent years, our students have shown a particular interest in the history of the later Roman Republic, not least because many important and original books have been published about Cicero and his age. Many students, however, including some of the most talented historians, have not had the chance to learn Latin in high school and need additional help with grammar and idiom to make full use of their gifts. It is my hope that if students after their third year of studying Latin give patient attention to the glosses and explanations of language provided in this speech and commentary, they will make a linguistic breakthrough and go on to read other texts—letters, biographies, historical monographs like those of Sallust and Tacitus—with relative ease and considerable enjoyment and be released from the straitjacket of syntactical comments. To those who do not need this kind of help, I appeal to their patience and generosity of spirit.

In November 63 BCE, Cicero rose to his feet in the open public forum to defend Licinius Murena in the standing court for electoral corruption. His chief argument was that the safety of Rome itself and survival of its republican constitution were at deadly risk unless Murena was acquitted and able to enter his consulship on 1 January 62. Who was Murena? Who were his accusers? What were the charges against him and the political circumstances of this trial?

The historical value of Cicero's defense extends beyond the person of this typical Roman military officer and would-be politician. It is a wonderful source for Roman popular values and a not entirely unbiased assessment of the prejudices of elite Romans in determining their sons' choice of career path. Their preference was for the career of an army officer or one as an advocate and political speaker, but there were less popular options, for example pursuing the skill of a jurisconsult (legal adviser) or the unworldly vocation of a philosopher. Cicero himself had made his name as an advocate before rising to the highest political office as consul for 63 BCE. As consul, he would summon a meeting to recommend legislation or explain senatorial action, speaking *ad populum* or *in contione*, as he did in the Second Catilinarian speech or in the Third Catilinarian, when he revealed the evidence of the Allobroges. These speeches were delivered shortly before and after he spoke for Murena. And as consul, again, he would address the Senate concerning the issue under consideration, as he did in the original form of the Fourth Catilinarian. But when Cicero writes to Atticus two years later (*Att.* 2.1.3, January 60), he does not include the defense of Murena (as he does the defense of Rabirius Postumus on trial before the Roman people) among the ten "consular" speeches he was sending to his friend and potential publisher. He was consul when he made Murena's defense, but he did not speak as consul. This was "only" a judicial speech.

If he had not omitted the *pro Murena* as a trial brief, the hectic nature of political life in and after the Catilinarian crisis would itself be sufficient to explain why Cicero does not dwell on this speech in his later career. Both speech and trial are strangely detached from the context as provided by ancient historical sources. Neither conventional ancient (and modern) discussions of Cicero's consulship nor narratives like Sallust's monograph on the conspiracy of Catiline or Dio Cassius's continuous history or Appian's *Civil Wars* mention the episode (though Murena is named incidentally as a commander in Appian's *Mithridatic Wars*). Even Plutarch, who twice alludes to the trial, cites only isolated anecdotes without context. One of his two allusions (*Cic.* 35) reports that Cicero performed below standard in delivering his defense because anxiety to surpass Hortensius, who had appeared earlier for the defense, had caused him insomnia. This is unconnected with Plutarch's other, better known, allusion to Cato's reaction when Cicero mocked his Stoic absolutism: "What an amusing consul we have" (*Comparison of Demosthenes and Cicero* 1.4). It would appear, then, that Plutarch knew the episode from a source that dwelt on Cicero's vulnerability and loss of nerve.

As it is, the defense of L. Licinius Murena has survived the middle ages by a thread, or rather by a single medieval manuscript, now lost (see "III. Text" below). What kept it alive and warrants our own concern for this speech is its rhetorical skill, parrying the charges of highly esteemed figures like Cato and glossing over Murena's (probable) guilt. With its variety of material and witty mockery of the technicalities of law and impracticality of Stoic absolutism, the *Pro Murena* was a model for students of eloquence, as the twenty-four references and quotations in Quintilian's *Institutio*—as many as the references to all four speeches *In Catilinam*—indicate.

I. HISTORICAL CONTEXT

We can date the trial of Murena and this speech from internal evidence to the weeks just after 9 November 63, but we have no idea why it took the prosecutors Sulpicius and Cato several months after the election to bring their charges. Presumably the team would have needed some weeks to obtain documentation from tribal headquarters about electoral bribery through *divisores*, the provision of free seats at the games and public meals, and the hiring of political followers and escorts (*sectatores*), but it is not in Cicero's interest to indicate any details of such allegations. Rome in Cicero's day was permeated with electoral corruption, and just as we are still surrounded by examples of bribery, coercion, and the exceeding of legitimate election expenses in even the most democratic countries, so the level of electoral manipulation in Rome makes it difficult to work up indignation about whatever Murena's infringements may have been. What do we know about Cicero's client, and his political and military career?

1. The defendant

T. R. S. Broughton (MRR 2: 80–81)[1] summarizes Murena's career:

> **L. Licinius L.f. L.n. Murena** (RE 123): Leg. Lieut. 73–69, pr. urb. 65, procos. Gallia Cisalpina and Transalpina 64–63, cos. 62.

That is, our Murena, listed in Pauly-Wissowa's *Real Encyklopädie der classischen Altertumswissenschaft* as Licinius 123, was son of L. Licinius Murena (RE 122) and grandson of L. Licinius Murena (RE 121).

He served first as a staff officer to his father and then as legate to Lucullus in the Mithridatic war, 73–69 BCE, returning to be elected praetor in 65 BCE and allotted the urban praetorship. After his year at Rome, he went as propraetor or proconsul to govern the two Gauls and was elected consul for 62 BCE.

In attempting to trace Murena's family and early career there is only intermittent evidence beyond Cicero's own reportage in the speech itself. Murena's father, paternal grandfather, and great-grandfather had all risen to the rank of praetor, no doubt on the strength of their competence as military men. Thus his father fought under L. Lucullus and was entrusted by him with two legions and a command against Mithridates Eupator of Pontus, extended when Sulla returned to Rome. It was the elder Murena who renewed the fighting in the "Second Mithridatic War" starting in 84 BCE. At the head of a notoriously undisciplined army

---

[1] MRR = *Magistrates of the Roman Republic*, T. R. S. Broughton, APA publication, vols. 1–2, New York 1960, also vol. 3, 1991. In this introduction and the commentary, I list each individual's number in the RE entry under his *gens*, here Licinius 123. Murena's father (Licinius 122) was praetor by 88 and legate to Sulla in 87 (?) and 86–84 and served again as propraetor in 84–81 and legate from 70?–66. Our Murena's grandfather (Licinius 121) was praetor in or before 101 BCE.

(including the maverick force of the disgraced Flavius Fimbria) he pursued open aggression at the expense of the Greek cities like Amisus, which he besieged, no doubt in part to keep his army from mutiny by providing them with loot, and in pursuit of the undeserved triumph which he was awarded in 81 BCE (Appian *Mithr.* 14; Plut. *Luc.* 15, McGing 1986: 132–36) but did not live to celebrate. Young Murena seems to have served on his father's council of junior officers and acquired his military experience at this time. (See Magie 1950: vol. 1, chpts. 8, 9, and 14).

After his father's death, Murena reappears as a legate to Lucullus (RE Licinius 104) in the "Third Mithridatic War" (74 or 73–68 BCE; see MRR 2: additional note 106–9) and is prominent in the fighting in Armenia during the long campaign against Mithridates's son-in-law Tigranes in Lucullus's last years of command in 70–69 BCE (Plut. *Luc.* 25–26). Murena was put in charge of 6,000 infantry at the siege of Tigranocerta (*Luc.* 27). But following his success late in 70 BCE, Lucullus turned eastward in what had now become a separate campaign against Tigranes, but met with increasing resistance from his own forces. He was a difficult commander, and his maneuvers in hitherto unknown parts of Armenia must have confused and alienated his troops. Certainly his young brother-in-law P. Clodius turned against him, instigating a mutiny of his forces at Nisibis in Armenia (Tatum 1999: 44–46), but Clodius was probably motivated as much by the quest for popularity as by personal spite.

Back in Rome, hostile factions in the Senate began to reassign some of Lucullus's provinces (Asia, Cappadocia) away from him, and once the *lex Manilia* of 66 BCE had transferred the overall command in the eastern Mediterranean to Pompey, political scheming in Rome and disloyalty within Lucullus's own army (Dio 36.16, 2–3) forced him to abandon his campaign (Plut. *Luc.* 35–36) while partisans of Pompey at Rome obstructed Lucullus's administrative settlement and request for land to reward his discharged veterans. He needed domestic allies, and we should allow for the possibility that Murena, after his praetorship of 65 BCE and year as governor of Transalpine Gaul, was standing for the consulship in Lucullus's interest as well as his own.[2] Certainly, Lucullus in turn led the opposition to Pompey's requests for additional military support (Plut. *Luc.* 42) and according to Plutarch (mostly based on Lucullus's memoirs), Cicero himself acted as a friend and political ally of Lucullus, whom he treats with tact and courtesy even in his address to the people advocating a new overall command for Pompey (66 BCE).

2. The prosecution

Murena's two leading prosecutors, Ser. Sulpicius (RE 95) and M. Porcius Cato (RE 20), were among the most serious and significant figures in contemporary political life, so let us pause first to consider their accusations and then to review their lives. Michael Alexander offers both a general discussion of how we retrieve the lost prosecutions of Cicero's day (2002: 1–54) and a short chapter on *Pro Murena* itself (121–27). Our only evidence for this case has to come from Cicero's speech, although Cicero's co-defenders Hortensius (RE 13) and M. Crassus may have answered other points made by the prosecution. Indeed, this speech is unusual in indicating (at the end of §57) that Cicero himself has omitted some responses to the junior prosecutors' technical evidence of excessive electioneering. But if we read the speech with careful suspicion, we are in the same position as Alexander for detecting what charges were made. A sample is the charge of being a dancer (§13), which must surely have been embedded in other, more alarming accusations of moral frivolity during Murena's youth. Only his expert knowledge of the Ciceronian corpus and the entire record of prosecutions during the late republic enables Alexander to offer a more seasoned assessment with insight into what Cicero has chosen not to debate.

---

[2] Wiseman 1971: 120, 139 rightly stresses the importance for his electability of Murena's military record and association with the campaigns of Lucullus, who was present in court to show his support (cf. *Mur.* §20). Murena also gained significant citizen votes from his recruiting in Umbria while governor of Cisalpina and Transalpina (cf. Adamietz 1989: 176). Did Rome already expect trouble from the Allobroges? The next governor was the military man Pomptinus. In 60, the province was designated as consular.

Ser. Sulpicius was ten years older than his fellow-prosecutor Cato, but despite his reputation for integrity, carried much less authority: he did not reach the consulship for another eleven years (51 BCE). This must have been a matter of personality; Sulpicius was probably a low-key speaker, more scrupulous than unsophisticated people could appreciate. Yet he had successfully held the praetorship and already earned public respect as a legal advisor. Cicero shared this respect, as is clear from two later occasions on which he mentions Servius: in his *Brutus*, a history of Roman oratory (46 BCE), where Servius (*noster Servius*, 150–53) is praised for his study of jurisprudence with Aquilius Gallus and Lucilius Balbus, which had given him a command of dialectic and the law; and in the ninth *Philippic* oration, commemorating Servius's death as an envoy to Antony in 43 BCE and proposing that the consuls should honor him with a bronze pedestrian statue on the Rostra. We come to know the mature Servius in more detail from Cicero's correspondence and from the subsequent formation of Roman law by his pupils and their successors. When Caesar invaded Italy in January 49 BCE, Servius tried like Cicero to keep his neutrality, and Cicero's letters treat Servius as a model for what he felt he should do. On Caesar's victory, neither man was willing to compromise himself in the Senate, but Caesar trusted Servius and made him governor of Achaea, a position where he could mediate on behalf of Pompeian survivors seeking amnesty. It was Servius who reported to Cicero the assassination of M. Claudius Marcellus (RE 229) on his departure from Greece in 45 after Caesar had pardoned him. We have this letter (*Fam.* 4.12) and the more important letter of consolation to Cicero after the death of his daughter Tullia (*Fam.* 4.5), one of the most humane documents of the Roman Republic.

Sulpicius's candidacy for the consulship of 62 was to be expected and needs no explanation beyond normal ambition to live up to the model of a successful career. But why resort to prosecuting Murena? Maybe Murena was so flagrantly guilty of malpractice that prosecution was inevitable? Sulpicius had probably agreed with Cato that he and Silanus should collaborate as candidates and work together as consuls—not for a political goal but perhaps to counter vested interests such as those of the Asian tax companies. And he would have been encouraged by the success of Torquatus and Cotta in 65 BCE, when they were made consuls at a supplementary election after achieving the bribery convictions of the "successful" candidates Autronius and Sulla. Clearly he did not believe his charges against Murena would increase the risk of Catiline (who had fled the city) either being made suffect (a substitute for a consul who died or was disqualified during his year of office) or seizing power by a coup. Murena himself may have hoped to earn as consul the governorship of a province that would bring him military glory or economic enrichment, but there is no evidence that either Sulpicius or Murena had any significant political agenda.

The most prominent member of the prosecution was **M. Porcius Cato**. Brought up as an orphan by his mother's family and influenced by his elder half-sister (and future mother of Brutus) Servilia—who would marry her own daughters to Silanus (but why?), to Cassius, the future conspirator, and to Lepidus, the future triumvir—Cato was clearly an obstinate and assertive child (see Plut. *Cato Min.*) and first made his name in politics as quaestor in charge of the treasury, which he purged and reorganized. In 63 BCE he was prompted by hostility to Metellus Nepos and Caesar (incoming praetor) to stand for the tribunate and notoriously introduced a populist grain law to fight the *populares* with their own weapons. It was Cato who turned the Senate around to impose an (unconstitutional) death penalty on the Catilinarians in the debate only a month after our trial, reversing the tendency to mildness that Caesar had stimulated by his speech as praetor-designate (Sall. *Cat.* 52.2–36 [Cato] reacting to 51.9–43 [Caesar]). From 63 BCE to his death, Cato followed policies opposed to Caesar, but while Clodius would drive Cicero out of Rome in 58 BCE in retaliation for these executions, he did not dare to attack Cato. Instead, he offered him the potentially lucrative commission to wind up the finances of Cyprus, where the last Ptolemy had ruled, bequeathing the territory to Rome. This kept Cato away from Rome for two years from 58–56 and gave him a motive not to challenge Caesar's legislation of 59 BCE. On his return Cato stood for election as praetor for 55 BCE, but with his brother-in-law Domitius was driven from the election field by violence. He was however elected praetor for the following year and in due course was a candidate for the consulship of 51 BCE. He pursued contradictory policies with and against Pompey, but at the beginning of 49 BCE urged Pompey to declare a state of emergency and take up arms against Caesar.

During the actual campaigns, Cato took no part in combat (he was marginally too old, but this was a principled refusal to fight against fellow citizens); instead, he was garrison commander or admiral in Syracuse, Dyrrhachium, Corcyra, and finally at Utica in Africa. After the final defeat of the anti-Caesarian forces at Thapsus, Cato negotiated the evacuation or pardon of the Romans under his command, then committed a flamboyant suicide (April 46 BCE). From then on, the dead martyr to liberty became more influential than he had ever been while alive, and his legend as a Stoic saint began to take shape with eulogies by Brutus (M. Iunius Brutus, RE 53) and Cicero and biographies by lesser friends, which formed Plutarch's sources for the *Life*.

C. Postumius is named by Cicero along with Servius as *familiari meo, ornatissimo uiro* (§54). He was a recent or continuing candidate in the praetorian elections. As a man of 40 during the sixties, he may well have been killed or eliminated from politics in the Civil War.[3] A younger **Ser. Sulpicius** is also mentioned, *adulescenti ingenioso et bono*, and he is recorded in a junior magistracy in 42 BCE (he is thought to be the father of the poet Sulpicia). These two junior prosecutors, Postumius and the second Ser. Sulpicius (identified in *Mur.* 56 as *sodalis filius*) have been recognized by David (1992: 565–68 and 879–80) as associated members of Sulpicius's family. Postumius (i.e., his gentile name, not the cognomen Postumus) was perhaps the brother of Sulpicius's wife, Postumia. While Postumius was old enough to be a candidate for the praetorship, Sulpicius (perhaps the moneyer of 74 BCE) was still a young man. The assignments of these *subscriptores* for the prosecution were in any case minor: a review of lists of *divisores* and

---

[3] The only C. Postumius in MRR is a *monetalis* of 74 BCE (see above, MRR 2.608). Broughton, following the Mss of our speech, lists the junior prosecutor of Murena as C. (Curtius) Postumus, MRR 2.558, but see the important addendum at 3.171–72.

unauthorized monies (*de pecuniis deprehensis*, §54) and in Sulpicius's case, of equestrian centuries who had received them.

3. Corruption and electoral malpractice

After the death of Gaius Gracchus, the scattered evidence for
events leading to the Jugurthine war leaves the impression that
senators and magistrates were becoming increasingly unscrupu-
lous in their abuse of money to manipulate power and commands.
Before considering bribery by candidates for election, we should
take into account the widespread practice of Roman commanders
accepting or demanding money from client kings and potential
successors in return for using Rome's military to put them in
power. The most extreme case was Jugurtha, the bastard son of
Micipsa of Numidia, favored because of his service under Scipio
Aemilianus. Jugurtha would murder one of the named heirs
(Hiempsal) and attack the other (Adherbal). When the tribune
Memmius was prosecuting the influential Aemilius Scaurus (RE
140) and had Jugurtha brought to Rome on a safe conduct to
support his evidence of bribery, a bribed tribune interposed his
veto, and Jugurtha was prevented from speaking. But it was
Jugurtha's protection of the assassin Bomilcar and subsequent
escape from justice, condoned by the Roman elite, which led to his
famous comment that Rome was a city for sale and marked for a
swift downfall if it found a purchaser (Sall. *Jug.* 35.10 *urbem
venalem ac mature perituram si emptorem invenerit*).

On the other hand, Polybius (ca. 200–ca. 118 BCE), in praising
the incorruptibility of mid-republican Rome, stresses Roman
severity and condemnation of any kind of bribery.

> At Rome nothing is considered more disgraceful than to
> accept bribes and seek gain from improper channels. For
> no less strong than their approval of moneymaking by re-
> spectable means is their condemnation of unscrupulous
> gain from forbidden sources. A proof of this is that at Car-
> thage candidates for office practice open bribery, whereas
> at Rome death is the penalty for it.

Among the Romans those who as magistrates and legates are dealing with large sums of money maintain correct conduct just because they have pledged their faith by oath. Whereas elsewhere it is a rare thing to find a man who keeps his hands off public money and whose record is clean in this respect, among the Romans one rarely comes across a man who has been detected in such conduct.

(Plb. 6.56 4 and 15, tr. Paton LCL)

Scholars have long debated when Polybius wrote this comment. He was already fairly old when the Romans repatriated him after ca. 150 BCE; how long did he continue writing? Unless he was deceiving himself, he can hardly have written this unqualified praise after 120 BCE.

The same decade provides the earliest evidence for prosecutions for electoral bribery/malpractice in a permanent tribunal (*quaestio perpetua*) analogous to Gaius Gracchus's tribunal for provincial extortion. Cicero reports two trials of 116 BCE, in which Rutilius Rufus (RE 34), a high-principled Stoic and candidate for the consulship, charged his successful rival Aemilius Scaurus (RE 140) with bribery; when Scaurus was acquitted, he in turn charged the defeated Rutilius (cf. Alexander 1990: 34, 35), who was also acquitted.

Non ille solum qui repulsam tulerat accusavit ambitus designatum competitorem, sed Scaurus etiam absolutus Rutilium in iudicium vocauit.

Not only Rutilius who had been defeated accused the elected consul of electoral corruption, but Scaurus, even when acquitted, called Rutilius into court.

(Cic. *Brut.* 113)

This was not the only prosecution before the court. Marius (RE 14), who seems to have been involved in chicanery at every stage in his quest for office, was prosecuted for bribery after his election as praetor and narrowly escaped condemnation (Alexander 1990: 19, the sources being Val. Max. 6.9.14 [from Livy?] and Plut.

Marius 5). There is no evidence for the law setting up this court, but it is generally assumed (Gruen 1968: 124–25) to be a new measure in 116. If no cases of *ambitus* are reported during two generations before the prosecution of P. Autronius and P. Sulla in 66 BCE, this is most likely because major wars and two revolutions (Marius in 88, Sulla in 82) absorbed the attention of historians. We should probably read the flurry of reported accusations at this time as a true reflection of increased bribery brought on by the growing greed of politicians and availability of surplus wealth.

We are accustomed to look cynically at the elaborate rules that limit the amount of money accepted from special interests by modern political parties, whether for individual candidates' use or at the central office. Established parties have now become expert in maximizing the money they can legally take in from persons, corporate entities, and lobbyists, whose function it is to win the support of these parties for their organization or policy or country. But this kind of corruption is not the same as distributing money to buy the votes of individuals and groups. As Lintott (1990) has shown, it was routine in republican Rome for candidates to spread money among their traditional supporters in the electorate.[4] Members of tribes or neighborhoods (*vici*) and regular tribal officials called *divisores* were appointed to distribute funds within these units. It was a different matter for candidates to buy the goodwill of unrelated citizens with theatre seats and food and pay for their services. Yet men did not think of their own largesse (*largitio*) as bribery. Bribery was what the other candidates practiced.

To some extent this was a matter of degree. A certain level of *largitio* was tolerated, and practiced, by the political class, but there was a point where it unbalanced the finances not just of rivals, but of the "market." The election campaigns of 54 BCE present a fine example, and at the same time offer a bird's-eye view of another electoral contest. Writing to Atticus (*Att.* 4.16.6), Cicero reports that there were four consular candidates, two patricians,

---

[4] On electoral campaigns, see Yakobson 1999; on procedure, see Staveley 1972; and on the progress of junior magistrates through the *cursus*, see Wiseman 1971, Lintott 1999.

only one of whom could be elected; Cicero remarks ambiguously "you know Messalla's resources." Scaurus is facing a prosecution (for bribery?) but has his generous games as aedile in his favor. Of the plebeians, Domitius Calvinus has powerful friends and has won favor by his show (*munus*), and Memmius is backed by Caesar's soldiers and benefits from Pompey's influence. This gives an idea of the factors that affected chances of success, but a second letter at almost the same time reports (*Att.* 4.15.7) *ardet ambitus* "bribery is running riot." The candidates had borrowed such astronomic sums that the interest rate doubled! This year would end in multiple prosecutions and without incoming consuls.

Less extreme examples of bribery probably provoked Piso's law of 67 BCE and the amendments to it proposed by Cicero as consul of 63 BCE. The *lex Calpurnia* had penalized the hiring of escorts, the wholesale distribution of free seats at the games, and the indiscriminate distribution of meals. Its exact terms are not recorded, but Cicero's modifications in the *lex Tullia* show that the earlier law excluded offenders from the Senate, banned them from future candidacy for office, and fined them heavily. Adamietz argues in the introduction to his edition of *Pro Murena* (1989: 27) that the need was not to strengthen the law, but to find ways of proving guilt and distinguish accepted or acceptable inducements from what was forbidden. In this same year 63, Cicero's own *lex Tullia*, introduced under pressure from Sulpicius (§46–48), increased penalties for candidates and bribery agents (*sequestres*) and changed temporary exclusion from political life into the penalty of exile. The motive was said to be fear of Catiline's increasingly lavish handouts, but Murena too had been enriched by his military service, and it is likely that Sulpicius was trying to counter the role played by Murena's wealth in the election.

The highly colored reports (originating in Cicero's *De consiliis suis*) of the alleged first Catilinarian conspiracy to assassinate the consuls of 65 BCE are suspect, given that the electoral campaign of fall 64 BCE, in which Cicero competed against Antonius and Catiline, passed off without significant violence. Both of Cicero's rivals seem to have been relying on unprecedented scales of bribery, and he was no doubt elected because the electorate believed his accusations of bribery and planned violence. Certainly, when Cicero entered office on 1 January 63 BCE his main concern was unrelated to Catiline. The new tribunes, in December 64 BCE, collectively put forward an extraordinarily radical bill known to us only through Cicero's published speeches in *De lege agraria*, which denounced it in two *contiones* and one speech to the Senate, along with two supplementary explanations (*apospasmatia*) proposed for his list of consular speeches in *ad Atticum* 2.1.3. Servilius Rullus (RE 80), with the Pompeian supporters Labienus (RE 6) and Ampius Balbus and most of the tribunician college, proposed to have ten commissioners with praetorian rank selected by 17 of the 35 tribes in order to appropriate public lands in Campania for distribution to Roman citizens and veterans, and to sell or subject to land tax estates belonging to Mithridates and other land that had become Roman public property since 88 BCE, the year Rome was awarded Egypt on the abdication of Ptolemy Alexander.

Complicating the interpretation were a number of clauses ostensibly exempting Pompey's extensive new conquests from consideration. Even without those territories, such widespread estates would have provided the commissioners with enormous patronage. They would also seem to be taking out of Pompey's control land he would need for his veterans' settlement. The most plausible of conflicting explanations of the bill's hidden purpose would see it not as explicitly directed against Pompey but as seeking to make him dependent on allying with its proposers on their terms (see Sumner 1966). The predominant reading makes Caesar himself, who was already acting in Pompey's interests at the time, into the *éminence grise* behind the bill. In any case, Cicero's harangues won the day, and the bill was aborted.

Elections for the higher magistrates (consuls and praetors) were due to be held in July, and there is no evidence that the elections of 63 were delayed beyond one day. *Murena* §48–53 implies that Catiline was still considered a candidate, but there seems to have been no repetition of the fierce campaigning and conspicuous bribery of 64 BCE. In fact, there is no record of bribery during the months from July to November, and it seems to have played no role in the ensuing events, to which we now turn.

The interest of our sources (chiefly Sallust) indicates a shift toward the replacement of bribery by violence, with rumors that Catiline was beginning to stockpile weapons in private houses and assign regions of the city to appropriate supporters. Bold in his sweeping assessments of political corruption, Sallust is not concerned to provide a convincing timetable for the impending revolution. Just as Sallust assigns surprisingly little activity to the conspirators in the second half of 64 BCE and first half of 63 BCE, so several months elapsed after the elections of 63 BCE before talk of a conspiracy began to be taken seriously by the Senate (Ramsey 2007: 17). Sallust gives this impression without dating it, and the next public event in Ramsey's helpful outline (19–20), the Senate's emergency decree of October 21, seems to have been a reaction to growing rumors of violence and uprisings planned by Catiline inside and outside Rome, scheduled for late October. Two weeks later, after a rumored attempt to assassinate Cicero himself (Sall. *Cat.* 28.1–3), Cicero denounced Catiline in the Senate (the First Catilinarian speech, November 8) and before the people (Second Catilinarian, November 9), seeking to drive him from Rome. Cicero had no formal powers to do so: the nearest precedent is the action of A. Gabinius (RE 11), who as consul in 58 publicly expelled (*contione relegavit*) Lamia to a distance of more than 200 miles from the city of Rome. This may have been in conformity with senatorial custom. In any case, Catiline presumably felt it was in his interest to leave the city.

4. Domestic affairs and election patterns in the years leading up to 62 BCE: First phase

In the elections for the year 62 BCE, conducted some time after July 63 BCE, Cicero presided over a contest of four candidates that included L. Sergius Catilina (RE Sergius 23), until Cicero drove him from the city by his denunciation in the Senate on 8 November. The three others were Ser. Sulpicius Rufus (RE 95), Decimus Iunius Silanus (RE 163), and L. Licinius Murena (RE 123). Of these, Silanus and Murena were announced as elected, that is, each of them obtained more votes than Sulpicius. From the order of speaking by the consuls-designate in the Catilinarian debate of 3 December, it is clear that Silanus obtained a majority of the voting units sooner than Murena (and Catiline, who goes unmentioned in the reports.) There was probably reason to charge both consuls with *ambitus* (bribery beyond what was legally authorized), but Cato at least, the driving spirit behind Murena's prosecution, had sworn in advance not to prosecute Silanus, his brother-in-law, on grounds of kinship.

What was the usual pattern? We might usefully start in 66 BCE, when Catiline, returning from his time as governor of the province of Africa, was denied permission to stand by the consul Volcatius Tullus (RE 6), since he was under threat of prosecution for provincial abuses. The election for 65 BCE had four candidates, but the two initially elected, P. Autronius Paetus (RE 7) and P. Cornelius Sulla (RE 386), were charged and convicted under C. Calpurnius Piso's (RE 63) new bribery law and went into exile—an exceptional event. They were replaced at a supplementary election by the two other candidates, L. Manlius Torquatus (RE 79) and L. Aurelius Cotta (RE 102), and despite rumors and disruption on the first day of 65 BCE, these two men entered office uneventfully and remained the consuls of the year. But the extreme circumstances may have deterred candidates from standing for election for the year 64 BCE. An early letter of Cicero (*Att.* 1.1, written in July 65) speaks of *illi qui nunc petunt*, mentioning Caesar (Sex. Iulius Caesar, RE 143), who was regarded as a dead cert, while Thermus was believed to be competing with Silanus. Cicero thinks it will be in his interest for Sex. Caesar to be elected with Thermus. In fact, Thermus does succeed and became consul for 64 BCE along with Sex. Caesar.[5] The same letter offers detailed information about a larger field of potential candidates for 63 BCE. P. Sulpicius Galba was apparently the only candidate already canvassing and was getting a cold response (*prensat unus Galba, sine fuco ac fallaciis more maiorum negatur*). Besides Galba, expected to compete with Antonius and

---

[5] For the identification of this Thermus with the C. Marcius Figulus otherwise attested as Caesar's consular colleague, see Ryan 1995b.

Cornificius, others mentioned are Caesonius, Aquilius Gallus (RE 23, the distinguished jurist and praetor of 66), Catiline—"a certainty if it is dark at noontime"—and the radicals Ti. Aufidius (RE 12) and Lollius Palicanus (RE 21).

When we first study the sources for this decade, we are inclined to assume that Cato embodied virtue and Catiline epitomized vice, but Roman politicians were much more flexible in their estimates. Consider Cicero's *ad Atticum* 1.2, written just after the birth of baby Marcus, when Cicero was beginning his run-up year for the elections.

> Hoc tempore Catilinam, competitorem nostrum, defendere cogitamus. Iudices habemus quos volumus, summa accusatoris voluntate, spero, si absolutus erit, coniunctiorem illum nobis fore in ratione petitionis, sin aliter erit, humaniter feremus.

> At this time we are considering defending our fellow-candidate Catiline. We have the jury we want and the greatest goodwill from the accuser. I hope that if he is acquitted, he will cooperate more closely with us in our approach to candidacy, but if not, we will take it philosophically.

Of course, defending (*etiam alienissimos, Mur.* 8) was Cicero's specialty, but Cicero may be looking beyond the trial to the possibility of collaboration with his rival. In the end, Cicero—who cynically notes that he will accept Catiline's condemnation *humaniter* ("philosophically")—did not participate, but Catiline was acquitted anyway (Alexander 1990 §212).

By 64 BCE, the list—like that of candidates putting themselves forward in U.S. primaries—would have shrunk, according to the argumentum of Asconius's commentary on Cicero's (fragmentary) speech *In toga candida*, leaving only Galba and Catiline as patrician candidates, C. Antonius (RE 19) and the Catilinarian C. Cassius Longinus (RE 58) as *nobiles* (from families which had recently held office), and Q. Cornificius (RE 7) and Licinius Sacerdos (RE 157).

Solus Cicero ex competitoribus equestri erat loco natus;
atque in petitione patrem amisit. Ceteri eius competitores
modeste se gessere, visique sunt Q. Cornificius et Galba
sobrii ac sancti viri, Sacerdos nulla improbitate notus;
Cassius, quamvis stolidus tum magis quam improbus videretur post paucos menses in coniuratione Catilinae esse
eum apparuit et cruentissimarum sententiarum fuisse auc-
torem. Itaque ii quattuor prope iacebant.

Catilina autem et Antonius, quamquam omnium maxime
infamis eorum vita esset, tamen multum poterant. Coier-
ant enim ambo ut Ciceronem consulatu deicerent, adiutoribus usi firmissimis M. Crasso et C. Caesare. Itaque haec
oratio contra solos Catilinam et Antonium est.

Cicero was the only candidate of equestrian rank, and he
also lost his father during the canvass. His other rivals
behaved like gentlemen, and Q Cornificius and Galba
showed themselves sober and virtuous men; Sacerdos was
not known for any misbehavior and Cassius, though at the
time he seemed stupid rather than wicked, was exposed a
few months later as part of Catiline's conspiracy and the
proposer of the most bloodthirsty measures. So those four
were ignored.

But Catiline and Antonius, though their lifestyles were
the most scandalous of all men, still had great influence.
Both of them had conspired to oppose Cicero's attempt on
the consulship, relying on Crassus and Caesar as their
strongest backers. So this speech is only directed against
Catiline and Antonius.

                                    (Asconius 82–83C)

Most scholars now recognize that this statement does not implicate
M. Crassus (RE 68) and Caesar (RE 131) directly in the Catilinarian conspiracy. Cicero's speech was prompted by the veto of the
tribune Mucius Orestinus (RE 12) against a proposal in the Senate
to pass a more severe bribery law (*aucta etiam cum poena*) and
dated by Asconius to only a few days before the actual election. No
doubt Cicero's speech in the Senate helped reconcile the

electorate to voting for the outsider Cicero along with Antonius as the lesser of the two remaining evils.

One other point needs to be made here. Neither during the election campaign nor after the election did candidates make public speeches to state their policy or partisan associations.[6] There were no fixed "parties" and most politicians had no policy. They could speak to a *contio*, a meeting of citizens, only when invited by the presiding magistrate, and they spoke in the Senate only when addressing the question put by the chair.

5. The immediate context of Murena's trial: Last phase

Pro Murena begins by recalling to the jury and audience the day that Cicero as presiding officer had announced the election returns (perhaps three months before) and drawing a parallel between Cicero's own prayers to the gods at that time that this event might bring fortune to the Roman people (*ut ea res mihi fidei magistratuique meo populo plebique Romanae feliciter eveniret*), and the present prayer to the same immortal gods for the same consul to remain in office and retain his standing (*salus* = civic rights). There can be no more powerful talisman than invocation of the gods and of the Roman people, and if we did not know that this was the third and last of the speeches for the defense of Murena, we would have accepted this renewal of his solemn prayer as the proper opening for such a major political defense.

On the day of the elections, Cicero as presiding officer had announced the successful candidates as D. Silanus and L. Murena. Why did the prosecution of Murena by the unsuccessful candidate Ser. Sulpicius Rufus, supported by Cato and two younger family associates, take so long to get underway after the election? It was of course a requirement that candidates whose application (*professio*) had been accepted could not be prosecuted on criminal charges once they had entered office, but they could be tried

---

[6] Compare *Commentariolum* §53 attributed to Quintus Cicero, *nec tamen in petendo res publica capessenda est neque in senatu neque in contione*. ("As a candidate, you should not tackle political issues either in the senate or assembly.")

after their election—the window of opportunity was very narrow. It is clear from internal evidence that this trial was held when Catiline had already been expelled but his supporters had not yet embarked on their new conspiracy to provoke a revolt of the Allobroges. Murena's acquittal must have preceded the senatorial session of 3 December, but his story is not integrated into the Catilinarian developments by any of the sources, and several detailed accounts of Cicero's consulship, like that of Mitchell (1979) do not even mention Murena. Apart from some assistance to Caesar early in 62 when Caesar was threatened by conservative enemies for his radical behavior, Murena himself is not heard of again.

And when all had been said and done, what was the point of being consul? For a year the two consuls would preside over the Senate in alternate months. They could shape an agenda and the one holding the *fasces* in January could determine who of the surviving ex-consuls should speak first, but for a conventional politician the position did not offer real power. (Only radicals like Caesar used their consulship to force through popular legislation against the will of the Senate). The rewards came after, with the highly independent position of proconsular governor often lasting for several years and entailing the control of a province which either offered good prospects of victories over native tribes (even Cicero celebrated his victory over the Pindenissitae of the Taurus mountains) or territorial conquest or, in a settled province, immense wealth through abuse of privilege in billeting or taxing provincials. It was Caesar's extended provincial command in the two Gauls that won him his lasting military glory and also the immense wealth to finance a new Forum.

II. THE SPEECH: RHETORIC AND ELOQUENCE

Modern publicity and media, political and commercial, have given rhetoric a bad name and a narrower usage denoting whatever is cheap and insincere, but ancient rhetoric was a discipline that enabled speakers to construct their speeches effectively, both in the argumentation and psychological orientation of the whole and in individual sentences. Good speaking had to be well argued, but also involved *psychagogia*, Aristotle's term for emotional persuasion aimed at the prejudices of jurors and audience.

The *Pro Murena* was in fact the last of three speeches *pro Murena*, and as Cicero says, following Hortensius and Crassus obviously affected his plea. Though there is no reason to believe his claim that this made his task any harder, responsibility for closing out the case for the defense undoubtedly presented the advocate with special challenges and opportunities:

> mihi durior locus est dicendi datus cum ante me et ille [Hortensius] dixisset et vir summa dignitate et diligentia et facultate dicendi Crassus. Ego in extremo non partem aliquam agerem causae sed de tota re dicerem quod mihi videretur. (§48)

As with the *Pro Caelio* and other cases, this speech, as the last component of the defense, did not need the conventional format of introduction (*prooemium*), statement of charges (*propositio*) and the main issue deriving from them, the narrative of relevant actions and events (*narratio*), a digression (*egressio*), and the pathetic *peroratio*. Only the last element is appropriate to Cicero's role as final advocate. Cicero restates the issues as *reprehensio vitae* (Murena went in for dancing!), *contentio dignitatis* (a comparison of the standing and political records of Murena and Sulpicius), and *ambitus crimina* (§54). In last position, this speech naturally incorporated the emotional peroration picturing the tragic exile and undeserved sorrows of his honorable client. But what made the speech famous were its digressions: one on the relative merits of a military as opposed to a civil life (and incidentally of rhetoric versus jurisprudence), the other on the folly of Stoic rigor and extremism.

The actual charges of violating restrictions of the canvass were pretty dull and would not have provoked any moral indignation among the worldly jurors or casual audience. Cicero's main need is therefore to diversify and maintain the high moral and patriotic tone of his speech, something he does superbly. Besides choosing the actual content, he did this by varying the form and focus of his arguments, shifting from one addressee to another (the formal addressees are the jurors, but much of the speech is apostrophe, or retort, to the prosecutors Servius and Cato). He could also vary the tense of his statements and psychological content of his speech acts. Reproaches for past actions (notably §44 *petere consulatum nescisti*), warnings over consequences, and threats or promises for the future, challenges to the prosecution (§33 *illam pugnam navalem parvo certamine commissam arbitraris?*; §34 *hunc tu hostem Cato contemnis?*), and recall of the jury's obligations because of their *fides* and power (§2, §86–87) could be used to break out of simple narration, and direct or indirect quotation, like the *sermocinatio* (conversation) of §45, as diversion from his own voice.

I will approach the analysis of *Pro Murena* through the conventional structure of ancient rhetorical manuals, which we can observe in the anonymous *Rhetoric for Herennius* and Cicero's own *On Invention*, both composed in the 80s BCE, when Cicero was still a student.

1. Figures

Teachers of rhetoric spent most of their time on the figures: **figures of language** (imposing patterns on words); **tropes**, entailing the transfer of a concept from one field to another ("The <u>hand</u> that rocks *the cradle* rules <u>the roost</u>" is a multiple set of tropes, i.e. synecdoche and metonymy of hand for mother and cradle for baby); and finally **figures of thought**, the most interesting kind of rhetorical tactic—the conversion of a simple statement into, for example, a rhetorical question ("can it be doubted that . . .?") or the replacement of a statement with the denial of its opposite. And of course there is nothing to stop the same clause or sentence from containing both figures of language and figures of thought, verbal patterning and logical play, like antithesis or paradox.

Let me give some examples. **Figures of language** (often referred to as figures of speech) include paired synonyms, like the paired superlatives of §7 (*sapientissimus et ornatissimus . . . gravis-sime . . . acerbissime, familiaritatis necessitudinisque*) and the double patterning of parallel elements (*et debuisse confiteor et praestitisse arbitror*). Cicero may even use three parallel units, as in *aut ab amico aut a gratioso aut a consule postulandum*. It was a traditional Latin pattern to introduce three parallel units with anaphora of a key word and build a slightly longer final unit, but the expansiveness of this sentence is effectively cut short by the pungent and powerful cola (minimal phrases) that follow: *abiit illud tempus; mutata ratio est*. Antitheses may pivot on key words: *contra honorem . . . tantum debuisse, contra salutem nihil debere* (I owed you this much against his election, but no action against his political survival).

The *Pro Murena* is rather Isocratean in its delight in word balance and word-play: *me contra amici studium pro amici periculo dicere* (§10) or the contrast in §28 of *cum peteres consulatum* with *cum Murenam ipsum petas*; likewise Isocratean are the symmetrical balanced antithetical clauses (cf. §22 repeatedly). In chapters 32 and 34 we see the power of anaphora: §32 *Mithridates, quem L Sulla . . . cum bello invectum totam in Asiam cum pace dimisit, quem L. Murena, pater huiusce . . . repressum magna ex parte non oppressum reliquit* and in §34, *si bellum hoc, si hic hostis, si ille rex contemnendus fuisset neque tanta cura senatus et populus Romanus suscipiendum putasset, neque tot annos gessisset neque tanta gloria L. Lucullus, neque vero eius belli conficiendum exitum tanto studio populus Romanus ad Gnaeum Pompeium detulisset*. The flamboyant demonstratives resume with renewed emphasis on *tot: per tot annos tot proeliis tot imperatores bella gesserunt* and another echo from *bellum confectum iudicarit in bellum confectum arbitraretur*.

This kind of thing is not subtle, but the Isocratean symmetries create a sense of measure and balance that tones down emotion in what Cicero will call the middle or moderate style (*Orator* 75–90). Variety is created by introducing other modes of discourse like *sermocinatio*, the imagined exchange of formulae in the praetor's court (§26) or gossip in the forum (§45 *videsne tu illum tristem, demissum? iacet, diffidit, abiecit hastas . . . scis tu heri accusationem cogitare, inquirere in competitores, testes quaerere. Alium fac iam, quoniam hic sibi desperat*), or again the parodic summary of Zeno's *praecepta* (§61) and Cato's imaginary defense of his decision to prosecute (§62). *Pro Murena* is actually unique in the variety of "languages" it incorporates.

Quintilian, who knows the speech so well, cites it only twice for tropes. The first citation picks out the antonomasia of §60 (*non multa peccas, inquit ille fortissimo viro senior magister*) alluding to Chiron as aging teacher of Achilles, for as Quintilian says (8.6.30) *neutrum enim nomen est positum et utrumque intellegitur*. The second citation (8.6.49) is double, pertaining to the extended allegories of *Murena* §35–36, where the image of the tide-tossed Euripus and that of a wind storm turning around popular favor combine the appeal of simile, allegory and metaphor (*similitudinis allegoriae translationis*). Cicero keeps the metaphors of tide and storm apart, but Quintilian takes this opportunity to warn against changing metaphor in midstream, as an *inconsequentia rerum foedissima*. But the speech draws extensively on analogies with human activities, such as acts of sale (§3), merchant captains welcoming newcomers into harbor (§4), instrumental musicians (§29), and briefer allusions to charioteers and trick riders (§46, 57). There are vivid single-word metaphors, identifying the jurors as steersmen at the *gubernacula rei publicae* (§74, 83) or evoking single combat (*abiecit hastas . . . plaga* §48, *securim iniecisse* §48, *gladiator* §50, 83). Metaphors are drawn from actual warfare: *deicere, deturbare* of dislodging defenders in a siege §79: *vallatum* §49, of Catiline surrounded by his bodyguard, and *signifer* of his role as standard-bearer §50. So also in the apocalyptic account of Catiline's fifth column we find first the Trojan horse, then the terrorist themselves hidden *in speculis et insidiis* (§79).

More unusual is the transference in *scaena competitrix* (§40), where the fancy stage of his rival's theatre competed with Cicero's aedilician shows, or Catiline's play on fighting house-fires not with water but by demolition (*non aqua sed ruina* §51). The proverbial *securim . . . iniecisse* (§48), like shooting oneself in the foot, occurs first here in republican Latin but is found again in Petronius 74 and Apuleius (Otto 1890, s.v. *crus*).

We might also consider Cato's imputed harangue against public meals as *adlici benevolentiam cibo* and *lenocinium a grege delicatae iuventutis* as a typical moral philosopher's analogy, for in fact, the highly developed *ethos* of the speech, its establishment of a moral foundation from which to judge Roman society, is its most conspicuous feature, more conspicuous than its rhetorical embellishment or even its splendid wit. The *Pro Murena* is steeped in social and historical content, taking the listener out of the narrow field of the charges into a wider world. It is exceptional in the range of historical exempla and in the nuances of social distinction. There is material from every phase of Roman history starting with the secession of the plebs to the Aventine in §15. Cicero's intimate knowledge of consulships from the three preceding generations includes the careers of Q. Pompeius (cos. 141 BCE), M. Aemilius Scaurus (cos. 115 BCE), and the unexpected feats of Philippus, Catulus and Scaurus (Scaurus again, §34), the new men Marius (cos. 107 BCE), Didius, and Coelius Caldus (coss. in 98 and 94 BCE, and the most recent "new men" before Cicero himself), and from a less-well-known period, the radical scribe Cn. Flavius, whose publication of the legal calendar at the end of the fourth century broke the jurists' monopoly (§25). Cicero reacts to Sulpicius's supposed contempt for wars with mere Greeks and Asiatics by offering a proud survey of Rome's great *triumphatores*, who celebrated over two centuries of triumphs over Greek enemies, from Manius Curius against Pyrrhus of Epirus to Flamininus, Fulvius Nobilior, Aemilius Paulus, Metellus Macedonicus, and L. Mummius over Macedonia and mainland Greece.

But most conspicuous is Cicero's focus on two figures: Cato the censor, great-grandfather of the prosecutor, and Scipio Aemilianus, born the son of Aemilius Paulus and adopted by Africanus's delicate son (who had no children or political career).[7] Often presented as antagonists by modern historians, Cato and Aemilianus were in most respects allies, agreeing in the end that Carthage should be destroyed. Cato married his son to Scipio's birth sister Aemilia,

---

[7] For Scipio and his "circle," see Astin 1967, appendix VI; for Cato the elder, Astin 1978.

while another sister was married to Aelius Tubero. Cicero built up an idealized picture of Scipio and his circle, Laelius (cos. 140 BCE), Philus, Sulpicius Gallus, and young men more gifted in moral philosophy than political strategy, like Tubero, condemned for misplaced economy in his contribution to the public funeral banquet (§75). All these men would feature in his *De republica* (54–51 BCE) and *Laelius: De amicitia* (§46). Indeed, it is remarkable how closely the historical references in *Pro Murena* anticipate the *Brutus*, Cicero's fully developed history of Roman oratory, composed more than fifteen years later.

Cicero takes pains to introduce Panaetius, the accommodating Stoic associate of Scipio and his circle (§66), as a desirable counterpoint to the rigidity of Zeno (§61), and he tells parallel anecdotes about the overwhelming authority of Cato and Scipio as prosecutors (§58–59), but he also sets up Cato the elder as a model for the young Cato (now in his early 30s and tribune-designate for 62 BCE), using a culinary metaphor to suggest that the younger man would be improved by seasoning with his ancestor's wit (§66 *si illius comitatem et facilitatem tuae gravitati severitatique asperseris non ista quidem erunt meliora . . . sed certe condita iucundius*), a splendid example of Cicero's infuriating habit of annexing another man's kin and using them against him (Treggiari 2003).

The speech draws out the implications of these famous exempla in support of two claims: the preeminence of military glory and the value of outsiders (new men like himself) to Roman political life. If Murena was not himself a new man (even his great-grandfather had been a praetor), he was still to some extent an outsider, and this may have made it harder to defend him. Clearly, Sulpicius had treated Murena's social standing contemptuously (§15 *contempsisti L. Murenae genus, extulisti tuum*), and Cicero was able to use this to provoke hard feelings against Sulpicius among the equestrians and humbler census class of the jury. Even while pretending to assimilate Sulpicius to himself (§16 *quare ego te semper in nostrum numerum adgregare soleo quod virtute . . . perfecisti ut cum equitis Romani esses filius, summa tamen amplitudine dignus putarere*), Cicero is playing on the social subdivisions and snobberies of the senatorial class, but he will also expand on the role of humbler citizens in electioneering.

2. Rhythm

It is harder to develop an instant response to the rhythmic power of Cicero's *clausulae*, spread across and within periodic sentences, but intensifying toward the end of both period and peroration. *Clausulae* often begin at word boundaries, for instance *ēssĕ vĭdĕātūr* (§15, 36), *laūdĕ cĕlĕbrātūr* (§16), but the distinctive rhythm may also begin inside the second or third word from the end of the period, such as *desperāssĕ vĭdĕātūr, habērĕ vĭdĕātūr* (§44). We find it easy to recognize these *clausulae*, all versions of the resolved cretic (in which one of the long syllables is substituted by two short syllables, $-\cup\cup\cup$) plus trochee or spondee ($-$ x), because meter and word accent coincide: most of Cicero's favored *clausulae* were composed of these feet, for instance cretic ($-\cup-$) plus spondee ($--$), two cretics ($-\cup-/-\cup-$), or two trochees ($-\cup-$ x), because of this coincidence.

The prayer-like first period of *Pro Murena* is full of such *clausulae*: *renuntiavi* ($\cup-\cup-$x), *eveniret* ($-\cup-$x), *obtinendum* ($-\cup-$x), *suffragiisque consentient* ($-\cup--\cup$ x: double cretic), *concordiamque afferat* ($-\cup--\cup$ x: double cretic). Or if we turn to the close of the speech and start at §89, compare *res maximas gessit* ($-\cup--$x), *conspectuque privat* ($-\cup-$x), *exsulem videat* ($-\cup-\cup\cup$ x: cretic plus resolved trochee), *suae calamitatis* ($-\cup\cup\cup-$x), *maestumque visistis* ($-\cup--$x), *promitto et spondeam* ($--\cup--$x).

3. Psychological manipulation (Gk. psychagogia)

Cicero presented the orator's tasks as *docere* (proving the case), *conciliare* (winning good will), and *movere* (swaying the emotions, equivalent to Platonic and Aristotelian *psychagogia*). *Conciliare* covers the art of winning over the audience, so it is difficult but essential to assess the orator's task of appealing in political and social terms to his diverse audience. While the jurors would comprise senators and the wealthy knights from the municipalities (along with the third component of jury panels, the next-lower census category of *tribuni aerarii*), the spontaneous audience would range from the elite and their dependents to the poor or unemployed *tenuiores*, who gained their self-esteem from their role of supporting candidates by their mere presence. Cicero must avoid offending politicians of the conservative core, supporters of Lucullus, but also younger, more radical partisans of Pompey. Murena's relationship with Lucullus (who was in the audience; see §20) had to be handled most discreetly, as Cicero held the balance between his own sympathy for the retired commander and his full knowledge of the immense public partisanship for Pompey. We can assume that a majority of the audience would be irritated by the unworldly and inconsistent severity of Cato,[8] and Cicero evokes this potential resentment by his stories of the prosecutions launched by the too influential Aemilianus and Cato the elder. But even a marginal allusion like that to Lanuvium probably reflects Cicero's concern for the audience: Murena's home town Lanuvium had sent a delegation (§90), which would be flattered by the attention Cicero paid them.

Any political speech generated this kind of tightrope walking, but Cicero has two effective weapons as he approaches the end. All his Roman audience will respond to the fear of arson and being murdered in their beds, and most of them will also be moved by the risk of public disorder and consequent personal ruin if their new consul were overthrown. The emphasis of Cicero's speech suggests that he counted on public concern for security overriding interest in the technical guilt of the defendant: it is not surprising, given the fine distinctions of legislation, that the Romans were more interested in the consequences of the trial than its basis in fact, that is the degree to which Murena had in fact violated current electoral law.[9]

---

[8] Some examples: Cato's declaration that he would not prosecute his brother-in-law Silanus for bribery; his proposal of the grain law in 62 BCE; his organization of bribery on behalf of his son-in-law Bibulus to elect him as a check on Caesar for the consular elections of 59 BCE; and his voting of a twenty-day supplication for Bibulus in 50 BCE.

[9] See the disagreement between Zetzel 1994 (review of Craig 1993) and Riggsby 1997.

III. TEXT

I have reproduced the Oxford Classical Text of A. C. Clark (1908), which has not been superseded.

The modern text of *Pro Murena* depends on a few fifteenth-century copies made from the Italian humanist Poggio Bracciolini's transcription of the lost *Vetus Cluniacensis*, a manuscript attested in the twelfth-century catalogue of the Abbey of Cluny and brought to Italy by Poggio in 1415. At about the same time, a French scholar carefully transcribed the *Pro Roscio* and *Pro Murena* in what we now have as Paris 14749 (Ste. Victoire 91). The original was obviously damaged or illegible in a number of passages, which none of the copyists could correct (cf. Clark vi), nor have recent editors provided plausible conjectures. Most notable of these gaps is a lacuna before §73, which probably extended for half a page. There are also some minor variations where the speech is cited by Quintilian, and I have cited these to illustrate them, but his text changes nothing from the consensus of the main humanist manuscripts. This is probably why there has been no new edition since Clark's Oxford Classical Text of 1905; certainly Adamietz, the most learned editor of our generation, has made only very modest choices or suggestions in doubtful passages.

For details, see L. D. Reynolds and M. D. Reeve in Reynolds 1983: 88–91.

M. TVLLI CICERONIS
PRO L. MVRENA
ORATIO

SIGLA

Σ = cod. Paris 14749, olim S. Victoris 91
B = Excerpta Bartolomaei de Montepolitiano, quae in cod.
      Laur. LIV. 5 inveniuntur
A = cod. Laur. XLVIII. 10 'A.D. 1415' a Ioanne Arretino
      scriptus (Lag. 10)
π = cod. Perusinus E. 71 'A.D. 1416' scriptus
Φ = cod. Laur. LII. 1 (Lag. 65)
χ = cod. Laur. XLVIII. 25 (Lag. 25)
ψ = cod. Laur. (Gadd.) XC sup. 69
ω = cod. Laur. XLVIII. 26 (Lag. 26)

s = cod. Monacensis 15734
w = cod. Guelferbytanus 205

Schol. = Scholiasta Gronovianus

M. TVLLI CICERONIS

PRO L. MVRENA ORATIO

QVAE precatus a dis immortalibus sum, iudices, more
institutoque maiorum illo die quo auspicato comitiis centu-
riatis L. Murenam consulem renuntiavi, ut ea res mihi fidei
magistratuique meo, populo plebique Romanae bene atque
5 feliciter eveniret, eadem precor ab isdem dis immortalibus
ob eiusdem hominis consulatum una cum salute obtinendum,
et ut vestrae mentes atque sententiae cum populi Romani
voluntatibus suffragiisque consentiant, eaque res vobis po-
puloque Romano pacem, tranquillitatem, otium concordiam-
10 que adferat.   Quod si illa sollemnis comitiorum precatio
consularibus auspiciis consecrata tantam habet in se vim
et religionem quantam rei publicae dignitas postulat, idem
ego sum precatus ut eis quoque hominibus quibus hic
consulatus me rogante datus esset ea res fauste feliciter
15 prospereque eveniret.   Quae cum ita sint, iudices, et cum 2
omnis deorum immortalium potestas aut translata sit ad
vos aut certe communicata vobiscum, idem consulem
vestrae fidei commendat qui antea dis immortalibus com-
mendavit, ut eiusdem hominis voce et declaratus consul
20 et defensus beneficium populi Romani cum vestra atque
omnium civium salute tueatur.

Et quoniam in hoc officio studium meae defensionis ab

1 quae precatus *Naugerius*: quae deprecatus *codd.* *(cf. Quintil.* ix.
4.107, *Creticus et initiis optimus,* Quod precatus a dis immortalibus
sum): quod precatus *Halm* (2) *cum Quintil.*   a Σ¹χψ: ab Σ²BAπ
3 fidei *Lambinus*: fides ΣAπ, *om.* Bχψ   5 eadem] idem *Boot*
16 tralata Σπ   17 consulem *Boot*: consul ei (eum ω) *codd.*

accusatoribus atque etiam ipsa susceptio causae reprensa
est, ante quam pro L. Murena dicere instituo, pro me ipso
pauca dicam, non quo mihi potior hoc quidem tempore
sit offici mei quam huiusce salutis defensio, sed ut meo
facto vobis probato maiore auctoritate ab huius honore 5
fama fortunisque omnibus inimicorum impetus propulsare
possim.

2
  Et primum M. Catoni vitam ad certam rationis normam
3 derigenti et diligentissime perpendenti momenta officiorum
omnium de officio meo respondebo.   Negat fuisse rectum 10
Cato me et consulem et legis ambitus latorem et tam severe
gesto consulatu causam L. Murenae attingere.   Cuius
reprehensio me vehementer movet, non solum ut vobis,
iudices, quibus maxime debeo, verum etiam ut ipsi Catoni,
gravissimo atque integerrimo viro, rationem facti mei pro- 15
bem.   A quo tandem, M. Cato, est aequius consulem
defendi quam a consule?   Quis mihi in re publica potest
aut debet esse coniunctior quam is cui res publica a me
iam traditur sustinenda magnis meis laboribus et periculis
sustentata?   Quod si in eis rebus repetendis quae mancipi 20
sunt is periculum iudici praestare debet qui se nexu
obligavit, profecto etiam rectius in iudicio consulis designati
is potissimum consul qui consulem declaravit auctor bene-
4 fici populi Romani defensorque periculi esse debebit.   Ac
si, ut non nullis in civitatibus fieri solet, patronus huic 25
causae publice constitueretur, is potissimum summo honore
adfecto defensor daretur qui eodem honore praeditus non
minus adferret ad dicendum auctoritatis quam facultatis.
Quod si e portu solventibus ei qui iam in portum ex alto

---

3 quidem *Lag.* 9: quidem in *cett.*   9 derigenti Σ*Aπφ*: dirigenti
χψω   18 a me iam *Klotz*: ame/77/a Σ (*m. 2 in lac.*): a me una
cett.: a me uno *Lambinus:* a me in manum *Müller: fort.* a me universa (universa a me *Landgraf)*   20 iis (is) *φ*[1]: his *cett.*   21
iudici *om. A*   23 consul *del. Madvig*   26 potissimum summo
Madvig: potissimo (-e *ψ*[2]) *codd.*   29 e portu *Quintil.* v. 11. 23:
portu *Bψ*: portus *cett.*   ei qui] qui *Quintil.*

invehuntur praecipere summo studio solent et tempestatum
rationem et praedonum et locorum, quod natura adfert
ut eis faveamus qui eadem pericula quibus nos perfuncti
sumus ingrediantur, quo tandem me esse animo oportet
5 prope iam ex magna iactatione terram videntem in hunc
cui video maximas rei publicae tempestates esse subeundas?
Qua re si est boni consulis non solum videre quid agatur
verum etiam providere quid futurum sit, ostendam alio
loco quantum salutis communis intersit duos consules in
10 re publica Kalendis Ianuariis esse.   Quod si ita est, non 5
tam me officium debuit ad hominis amici fortunas quam
res publica consulem ad communem salutem defendendam
vocare. Nam quod legem de ambitu tuli, certe ita tuli ut **3**
eam quam mihimet ipsi iam pridem tulerim de civium
15 periculis defendendis non abrogarem.   Etenim si largitionem factam esse confiterer idque recte factum esse
defenderem, facerem improbe, etiam si alius legem tulisset;
cum vero nihil commissum contra legem esse defendam,
quid est quod meam defensionem latio legis impediat?
20   Negat esse eiusdem severitatis Catilinam exitium rei 6
publicae intra moenia molientem verbis et paene imperio
ex urbe expulisse et nunc pro L. Murena dicere. Ego
autem has partis lenitatis et misericordiae quas me natura
ipsa docuit semper egi libenter, illam vero gravitatis seve-
25 ritatisque personam non appetivi, sed ab re publica mihi
impositam sustinui, sicut huius imperi dignitas in summo
periculo civium postulabat.   Quod si tum, cum res publica
vim et severitatem desiderabat, vici naturam et tam vehemens fui quam cogebar, non quam volebam, nunc cum

1 solent et ψ^2: solent ei $\Sigma A\pi\phi\omega$: solent eis $\chi\psi^1$ 2 adfert]
fert *Victorius (contra Quintil.)*   4 ingrediantur $\pi\phi\omega$, *Quintil.*: in-
grediuntur $\Sigma A\chi\psi$ animo esse *Quintil.*   6 rei p. *om. Quintil.*
14 tuleram *Bake*   15 abrogarim *Wesenberg*   20 negat]
negas *Kayser* (Cato *ante* Catilinam *add. Hotoman*)   22 ex χ: et
cett   23 partis *Sylvius*: artis codd.

omnes me causae ad misericordiam atque ad humanitatem
vocet, quanto tandem studio debeo naturae meae consuetudinique servire?   Ac de officio defensionis meae ac de
ratione accusationis tuae fortasse etiam alia in parte
orationis dicendum nobis erit.   5

7   Sed me, iudices, non minus hominis sapientissimi atque
ornatissimi, Ser. Sulpici, conquestio quam Catonis accusatio
commovebat qui gravissime et acerbissime *se* ferre dixit me
familiaritatis necessitudinisque oblitum causam L. Murenae
contra se defendere.   Huic ego, iudices, satis facere cupio 10
vosque adhibere arbitros.   Nam cum grave est vere accusari
in amicitia, tum, etiam si falso accuseris, non est negle-
gendum.   Ego, Ser. Sulpici, me in petitione tua tibi omnia
studia atque officia pro nostra necessitudine et debuisse
confiteor et praestitisse arbitror.   Nihil tibi consulatum 15
petenti a me defuit quod esset aut ab amico aut a gratioso
aut a consule postulandum.   Abiit illud tempus; mutata
ratio est.   Sic existimo, sic mihi persuadeo, me tibi contra
honorem Murenae quantum tu a me postulare ausus sis,
8 tantum debuisse, contra salutem nihil debere.   Neque 20
enim, si tibi tum cum peteres *consulatum studui, nunc* cum
Murenam ipsum petas, adiutor eodem pacto esse debeo.
Atque hoc non modo non laudari sed ne concedi quidem
potest ut amicis nostris accusantibus non etiam alienissimos
4 defendamus.   Mihi autem cum Murena, iudices, et magna 25
et vetus amicitia est, quae in capitis dimicatione a Ser.
Sulpicio non idcirco obruetur quod ab eodem in honoris
contentione superata est.   Quae si causa non esset, tamen

1 atque ad] atque *Aπ*   7 accusatio commovebat] cattio acom-
movebat Σ: captio commovebat *A*   8 se ferre *Lambinus*: ferme
codd.   17 abiit *χψω*: abit *cett.*   19 L. Murenae *Lambinus*
21 consulatum studui nunc *scripsi* (*ex Quintil*. xi. 1. 68 se studuisse
petitioni Sulpicii contra honorem Murenae, non idem debere actioni
contra caput): consulatum adfui nunc *ψ²*: *om. cett.*   23 non
modo non] non modo *Müller*   27 ab eodem (eod Σ*B*) *mei*: ab eo
w, Halm

vel dignitas hominis vel honoris eius quem adeptus est
amplitudo summam mihi superbiae crudelitatisque infamiam
inussisset, si hominis et suis et populi Romani ornamentis
amplissimi causam tanti periculi repudiassem.   Neque enim
5 iam mihi licet neque est integrum ut meum laborem hominum periculis sublevandis non impertiam.   Nam cum
praemia mihi tanta pro hac industria sint data quanta antea
nemini, sic *existimo, labores quos in petitione* exceperis, eos,
cum adeptus sis, deponere, esse hominis et astuti et ingrati.
10 Quod si licet desinere, si te auctore possum, si nulla inertiae 9
infamia, nulla superbiae turpitudo, nulla inhumanitatis culpa
suscipitur, ego vero libenter desino.   Sin autem fuga laboris
desidiam, repudiatio supplicum superbiam, amicorum neglectio improbitatem coarguit, nimirum haec causa est eius
15 modi quam nec industrius quisquam nec misericors nec
officiosus deserere possit.   Atque huiusce rei coniecturam
de tuo ipsius studio, Servi, facillime ceperis.   Nam si tibi
necesse putas etiam adversariis amicorum tuorum de iure
consulentibus respondere, et si turpe existimas te advocato
20 ilum ipsum quem contra veneris causa cadere, noli tam
esse iniustus ut, cum tui fontes vel inimicis tuis pateant,
nostros etiam amicis putes clausos esse oportere.   Etenim 10
si me tua familiaritas ab hac causa removisset, et si hoc
idem Q. Hortensio, M. Crasso, clarissimis viris, si item
25 ceteris a quibus intellego tuam gratiam magni aestimari
accidisset, in ea civitate consul designatus defensorem non
haberet in qua nemini umquam infimo maiores nostri

2 summae *Bake*   infamiam *Gulielmius*: famam *codd.*   8 sic existimo, labores quos in petitione exceperis *scripsi*: si (sic πω) exiceperis
(excep. φ, excip. ω) Σπφω: sic et **si** ceperis Aχψ: sic existimo si
ceperis *Lag.* 9: sic censeo quos labores adipiscendi spe susceperis
Madvig: labores per quos ea ceperis *Angelius*   9 esse Σφω:
esse et A: esset πχψ   11 infamia *Wesenberg*: om. *codd.*   turpitudo *del. Bake*   12 desinon Σ: desinam *Bake*   14 causa Aπψ²:
arum Σ: causarum χψ¹   15 quisquam *Gulielmius*: quam *codd*
16 possit *ed. R*: posset *mei*   20 causa ψ²: causae *cett.*

patronum deesse voluerunt.   Ego vero, iudices, ipse me
existimarem nefarium si amico, crudelem si misero, superbum si consuli defuissem.   Qua re quod dandum est
amicitiae, large dabitur a me, ut tecum agam, Servi, non
secus ac si meus esset frater, qui mihi est carissimus, isto 5
in loco; quod tribuendum est officio, fidei, religioni, id ita
moderabor ut meminerim me contra amici studium pro
amici periculo dicere.

5
     Intellego, iudices, tris totius accusationis partis fuisse, et
11
earum unam in reprehensione vitae, alteram in contentione 10
dignitatis, tertiam in criminibus ambitus esse versatam.
Atque harum trium partium prima illa quae gravissima
debebat esse ita fuit infirma et levis ut illos lex magis
quaedam accusatoria quam vera male dicendi facultas de
vita L. Murenae dicere aliquid coegerit.   Obiecta est enim 15
Asia; quae ab hoc non ad voluptatem et luxuriam expetita
est sed in militari labore peragrata.   Qui si adulescens
patre suo imperatore non meruisset, aut hostem aut patris
imperium timuisse aut a parente repudiatus videretur.   An
cum sedere in equis triumphantium praetextati potissimum 20
filii soleant, huic donis militaribus patris triumphum deco-
rare fugiendum fuit, ut rebus communiter gestis paene simul
12 cum patre triumpharet?   Hic vero, iudices, et fuit in Asia
et viro fortissimo, parenti suo, magno adiumento in periculis,
solacio in laboribus, gratulationi in victoria fuit.   Et si 25
habet Asia suspicionem luxuriae quandam, non Asiam numquam vidisse sed in Asia continenter vixisse laudandum
est.   Quam ob rem non Asiae nomen obiciendum Murenae
fuit ex qua laus familiae, memoria generi, honos et gloria
nomini constituta est, sed aliquod aut in Asia susceptum 30

     5 esset $\Sigma A\pi\phi\omega$: esses $\chi\psi$ 10 reprehensione ψ^2: reprehensio-
nem *cett.*   13 *illos om. w, del. Halm*   17 sed ψ: sed et
(etiam ϕ) *cett.*   18 hostis *w, Halm*   19 an *Naugerius* (2):
aut *mei*   22 ut] ne $B\psi^2$: ne ut $\chi\psi^1$ 23 triumphares $\Sigma A\pi^2\psi^1$
28 abiciendum $\Sigma A\psi^1$

aut ex Asia deportatum flagitium ac dedecus.   Meruisse
vero stipendia in eo bello quod tum populus Romanus non
modo maximum sed etiam solum gerebat virtutis, patre
imperatore libentissime meruisse pietatis, finem stipendiorum
5 patris victoriam ac triumphum fuisse felicitatis fuit. Male-
dicto quidem idcirco nihil in hisce rebus loci est quod
omnia laus occupavit.   **6**

   Saltatorem appellat L. Murenam Cato. Maledictum est,
si vere obicitur, vehementis accusatoris, sin falso, maledici ¹³
10 conviciatoris.   Qua re cum ista sis auctoritate, non debes,
M. Cato, adripere maledictum ex trivio aut ex scurrarum
aliquo convicio neque temere consulem populi Romani
saltatorem vocare, sed circumspicere quibus praeterea vitiis
adfectum esse necesse sit eum cui vere istud obici possit.
15 Nemo enim fere saltat sobrius, nisi forte insanit, neque in
solitudine neque in convivio moderato atque honesto.
Tempestivi convivi, amoeni loci, multarum deliciarum
comes est extrema saltatio.   Tu mihi adripis hoc quod
necesse est omnium vitiorum esse postremum, relinquis
20 illa quibus remotis hoc vitium omnino esse non potest?
Nullum turpe convivium, non amor, non comissatio, non
libido, non sumptus ostenditur, et, cum ea non reperiantur
quae voluptatis nomen habent quamquam vitiosa sunt,
in quo ipsam luxuriam reperire non potes, in eo te
25 umbram luxuriae reperturum putas? Nihil igitur in vitam 14
L. Murenae dici potest, nihil, inquam, omnino, iudices.
Sic a me consul designatus defenditur ut eius nulla fraus,
nulla avaritia, nulla perfidia, nulla crudelitas, nullum petu-
lans dictum in vita proferatur. Bene habet; iacta sunt

3 etiam *om. w, del. Halm*   8 L. $\psi^2\omega$: fl. (falso ψ^1) *cett.*   11
M. (Marce) Cato arripere $B\psi^2$: marre anni ripere ΣA: Marce, arripere *cett.*   aut ex] aut $A\pi$ 12 convicio] convivio *Lambinus*
13 circumspicere χ^2, *Gulielmius*: cumspicere $\Sigma\chi^1$: conspicere *cett.*
17 intempestivi $\chi\psi$ 18 hoc] id ψ^1 21 amors (-s *add. m.* 2)
Σ (*cf.* §26 aios, conspicios)   26 iudices *Naugerius*: iudicio *codd.*
29 in vita *del. Ernesti* (in eius vita nulla . . . dictum prof. *w*)

fundamenta defensionis.   Nondum enim nostris laudibus,
quibus utar postea, sed prope inimicorum confessione virum
bonum atque integrum hominem defendimus.   Quo consti-
tuto facilior est mihi aditus ad contentionem dignitatis, quae
pars altera fuit accusationis.   5

7   Summam video esse in te, Ser. Sulpici, dignitatem generis,
15 integritatis, industriae ceterorumque ornamentorum omnium
quibus fretum ad consulatus petitionem adgredi par est.
Paria cognosco esse ista in L. Murena, atque ita paria ut
neque ipse dignitate vinci *a te* potuerit neque te dignitate 10
superarit. Contempsisti L. Murenae genus, extulisti tuum.
Quo loco si tibi hoc sumis, nisi qui patricius sit, neminem
bono esse genere natum, facis ut rursus plebes in Aventinum
sevocanda esse videatur.   Sin autem sunt amplae et honestae
familiae plebeiae, et proavus L. Murenae et avus praetor 15
fuit, et pater, cum amplissime atque honestissime ex praetura
triumphasset, hoc faciliorem huic gradum consulatus adipiscendi reliquit quod is iam patri debitus a filio petebatur.
16 Tua vero nobilitas, Ser. Sulpici, tametsi summa est, tamen
hominibus litteratis et historicis est notior, populo vero 20
et suffragatoribus obscurior.   Pater enim fuit equestri loco,
avus nulla inlustri laude celebratus.   Itaque non ex sermone
hominum recenti sed ex annalium vetustate eruenda memoria est nobilitatis tuae. Qua re ego te semper in nostrum
numerum adgregare soleo, quod virtute industriaque per- 25
fecisti ut, cum equitis Romani esses filius, summa tamen
amplitudine dignus putarere. Nec mihi umquam minus
in Q. Pompeio, novo homine et fortissimo viro, virtutis esse
visum est quam in homine nobilissimo, M. Aemilio.   Etenim
eiusdem animi atque ingeni est posteris suis, quod Pompeius 30

---

10 vinci a te *scripsi*: vince . . . Σ: vinci *cett.*: a te vinci *Campe*
13 plebes Σχ: plebs *cett.*   16 et pater] *sequuntur in codd. vv.*
etenim mihi §17 *ad* multis profutura §19: *rectum ordinem restituit*
Naugerius

fecit, amplitudinem nominis quam non acceperit tradere et,
ut Scaurus, memoriam prope intermortuam generis sua **8**
virtute renovare. Quamquam ego iam putabam, iudices, 17
multis viris fortibus ne ignobilitas generis obiceretur meo
5 labore esse perfectum, qui non modo Curiis, Catonibus,
Pompeiis, antiquis illis fortissimis viris, novis hominibus,
sed his recentibus, Mariis et Didiis et Caeliis, commemorandis id agebam. Cum vero ego tanto intervallo claustra
ista nobilitatis refregissem, ut aditus ad consulatum posthac,
10 sicut apud maiores nostros fuit, non magis nobilitati quam
virtuti pateret, non arbitrabar, cum ex familia vetere et
inlustri consul designatus ab equitis Romani filio consule
defenderetur, de generis novitate accusatores esse dicturos.
Etenim mihi ipsi accidit ut cum duobus patriciis, altero
15 improbissimo atque audacissimo, altero modestissimo atque
optimo viro, peterem; superavi tamen dignitate Catilinam,
gratia Galbam. Quod si id crimen homini novo esse
deberet, profecto mihi neque inimici neque invidi defuissent.
Omittamus igitur de genere dicere cuius est magna in 18
20 utroque dignitas; videamus cetera.

'Quaesturam una petiit et sum ego factus prior.' Non
est respondendum ad omnia. Neque enim vestrum quemquam fugit, cum multi pares dignitate fiant, unus autem
primum solus possit obtinere, non eundem esse ordinem
25 dignitatis et renuntiationis, propterea quod renuntiatio
gradus habeat, dignitas autem sit persaepe eadem omnium.
Sed quaestura utriusque prope modum pari momento sortis
fuit. Habuit hic lege Titia provinciam tacitam et quietam,

2 sua *Halm*: sui *codd.*   6 novis hominibus *del. Boot*   8 id
agebam *Badham*: iacebant Σ: iacebam ψ²: iacebant *cett.*   15 atque audacissimo *om. Quintil.* v.11.11   17 crimini *coni. Müller*
22 vestrum quemquam Σφχ: quemquam vestrum *cett.*   23 pares
w: pare Σπχω: pari Aφψ   24 primum locum *Mommsen*   possit *ed. R*: posset *mei*   26 habet . . . est *Bake*   27 momentu
ΣAπ²

tu illam cui, cum quaestores sortiuntur, etiam adclamari
solet, Ostiensem, non tam gratiosam et inlustrem quam
negotiosam et molestam.   Consedit utriusque nomen in
quaestura.   Nullum enim vobis sors campum dedit in quo
19 excurrere virtus cognoscique posset.   Reliqui temporis spa- 5
tium in contentionem vocatur.   Ab utroque dissimillima
9 ratione tractatum est.   Servius hic nobiscum hanc urbanam militiam respondendi, scribendi, cavendi plenam sollicitudinis ac stomachi secutus est; ius civile didicit, multum
vigilavit, laboravit, praesto multis fuit, multorum stultitiam 10
perpessus est, adrogantiam pertulit, difficultatem exsorbuit;
vixit ad aliorum arbitrium, non ad suum.   Magna laus et
grata hominibus unum hominem elaborare in ea scientia
20 quae sit multis profutura.   Quid Murena interea? Fortissimo et sapientissimo viro, summo imperatori legatus, 15
L. Lucullo, fuit; qua in legatione duxit exercitum, signa
contulit, manum conseruit, magnas copias hostium fudit,
urbis partim vi, partim obsidione cepit, Asiam istam refertam et eandem delicatam sic obiit ut in ea neque avaritiae
neque luxuriae vestigium reliquerit, maximo in bello sic est 20
versatus ut hic multas res et magnas sine imperatore ges-
serit, nullam sine hoc imperator.   Atque haec quamquam
praesente L. Lucullo loquor, tamen ne ab ipso propter
periculum nostrum concessam videamur habere licentiam
fingendi, publicis litteris testata sunt omnia, quibus L. Lu- 25
cullus tantum laudis impertiit quantum neque ambitiosus
imperator neque invidus tribuere alteri in communicanda
21 gloria debuit.   Summa in utroque est honestas, summa
dignitas; quam ego, si mihi per Servium liceat, pari atque eadem in laude ponam.   Sed non licet; agitat rem 30

---

5 excurrere] excuti ψ^2 spatium quo in ψ^2 13 hominibus]
omnibus *Richter*   17 fundit $\Sigma\pi$ 18 refertam $\chi^2\psi$: repertam
(repara- ω) *cett.*   19 obiit $\chi\psi$: obit *cett.*   23 loquor *s, Ernesti:*
loquar *mei*   26 tantum huic laudis *Halm* impertiit *Lambinus:*
impertit *codd.*   29 pari] parem *Bake*   30 eadem in *Lambinus:*
in eadem *codd.*

militarem, insectatur totam hanc legationem, adsiduitatis
et operarum harum cotidianarum putat esse consulatum.
'Apud exercitum mihi fueris' inquit; 'tot annos forum non
attigeris; afueris tam diu et, cum longo intervallo veneris,
5 cum his qui in foro habitarint de dignitate contendas?'
Primum ista nostra adsiduitas, Servi, nescis quantum interdum adferat hominibus fastidi, quantum satietatis. Mihi
quidem vehementer expediit positam in oculis esse gratiam;
sed tamen ego mei satietatem magno meo labore superavi
10 et tu item fortasse; verum tamen utrique nostrum desiderium nihil obfuisset.   Sed ut hoc omisso ad studiorum atque 22
artium contentionem revertamur, qui potest dubitari quin
ad consulatum adipiscendum multo plus adferat dignitatis
rei militaris quam iuris civilis gloria?   Vigilas tu de nocte
15 ut tuis consultoribus respondeas, ille ut eo quo intendit
mature cum exercitu perveniat; te gallorum, illum bucinarum cantus exsuscitat; tu actionem instituis, ille aciem
instruit; tu caves ne tui consultores, ille ne urbes aut
castra capiantur; ille tenet et scit ut hostium copiae, tu
20 ut aquae pluviae arceantur; ille exercitatus est in propagandis finibus, tuque in regendis. Ac nimirum—dicen- **10**
dum est enim quod sentio—rei militaris virtus praestat
ceteris omnibus. Haec nomen populo Romano, haec huic
urbi aeternam gloriam peperit, haec orbem terrarum pa-
25 rere huic imperio coegit; omnes urbanae res, omnia haec
nostra praeclara studia et haec forensis laus et industria
latet in tutela ac praesidio bellicae virtutis.   Simul atque
increpuit suspicio tumultus, artes ilico nostrae conticiscunt.

---

3 tot annos, forum *Halm*: tot annis *Quintil* v. 13. 27   4 et
Quintil.: ut *codd.*   cum tam longo *Quintil.*   5 habitarint Σπψ¹ω:
habitarunt Aχψ², *Quintil.*   8 expediit *Lambinus*: expedit *codd.*
10 item *Orelli*: idem *codd.*   12 potest dubitari *Beroaldus*: potest
dubitare *codd*: potes dubitare *Zumpt*   15 ille vero ut quo *B*
contendit *Quintil.* ix. 2. 100 (*idem* intendit ix. 3. 32)   18 consultores tui *Quintil.* ix. 3. 32   20 exercitatur in *Quintil.*   21
tuque in (quin Σ) *mei*: tu in *w, ed. R cum Quintil.*   27 latet
scripsi: latent *codd.*   28 conticiscunt Σπχ: conticescunt *cett.*

₂₃   Et quoniam mihi videris istam scientiam iuris tamquam
filiolam osculari tuam, non patiar te in tanto errore versari
ut istud nescio quid quod tanto opere didicisti praeclarum
aliquid esse arbitrere.   Aliis ego te virtutibus, continentiae,
gravitatis, iustitiae, fidei, ceteris omnibus, consulatu et omni 5
honore semper dignissimum iudicavi; quod quidem ius
civile didicisti, non dicam operam perdidisti, sed illud dicam,
nullam esse in ista disciplina munitam ad consulatum viam.
Omnes enim artes, quae nobis populi Romani studia concilient, et admirabilem dignitatem et pergratam utilitatem 10

II debent habere.   Summa dignitas est in eis qui militari
²⁴ laude antecellunt; omnia enim quae sunt in imperio et in
statu civitatis ab his defendi et firmari putantur; summa
etiam utilitas, si quidem eorum consilio et periculo cum re
publica tum etiam nostris rebus perfrui possumus.   Gravis 15
etiam illa est et plena dignitatis dicendi facultas quae saepe
valuit in consule deligendo, posse consilio atque oratione
et senatus et populi et eorum qui res iudicant mentis per-
movere.   Quaeritur consul qui dicendo non numquam
comprimat tribunicios furores, qui concitatum populum 20
flectat, qui largitioni resistat. Non mirum, si ob hanc
facultatem homines saepe etiam non nobiles consulatum
consecuti sunt, praesertim cum haec eadem res plurimas
gratias, firmissimas amicitias, maxima studia pariat.   Quo-
₂₅ rum in isto vestro artificio, Sulpici, nihil est.   Primum 25
dignitas in tam tenui scientia non potest esse; res enim
sunt parvae, prope in singulis litteris atque interpunctionibus
verborum occupatae.   Deinde, etiam si quid apud maiores
nostros fuit in isto studio admirationis, id enuntiatis vestris
mysteriis totum est contemptum et abiectum.   Posset agi 30

---

3 didicisti] dilexisti *Campe*   8 ista *Halm*: illa *codd.*   9
concilient *Ernesti*: conciliant *codd.*   11 iis *ed. R*: his *mei*   21
largitioni ψ²: largitione *cett.*   29 in isto studio ψ²: in istros (iis
tres ψ¹) duo *cett.*   admirationis ψ²: admiserationis (miser- ψ¹) *cett.*
id enuntiatis] i (et χ) denuntiatis Σχ

lege necne pauci quondam sciebant; fastos enim volgo non
habebant.   Erant in magna potentia qui consulebantur;
a quibus etiam dies tamquam a Chaldaeis petebatur.   Inventus est scriba quidam, Cn. Flavius, qui cornicum oculos con-
5 fixerit et singulis diebus ediscendis fastos populo proposuerit
et ab ipsis *his* cautis iuris consultis eorum sapientiam com-
pilarit.   Itaque irati illi, quod sunt veriti ne dierum ratione
pervolgata et cognita sine sua opera lege *agi* posset, verba
quaedam composuerunt ut omnibus in rebus ipsi inter- **12**
10 essent.   Cum hoc fieri bellissime posset: 'Fundus Sabinus 26
meus est.' 'Immo meus,' deinde iudicium, noluerunt.
'FVNDVS' inquit 'QVI EST IN AGRO QVI SABINVS VOCATVR.'
Satis verbose; cedo quid postea?   'EVM EGO EX IVRE QVIRI-
TIVM MEVM ESSE AIO.'   Quid tum?   'INDE IBI EGO TE EX
15 IVRE MANVM CONSERTVM VOCO.'   Quid huic tam loquaciter
litigioso responderet ille unde petebatur non habebat.
Transit idem iuris consultus tibicinis Latini modo.   'VNDE
TV ME' inquit 'EX IVRE MANVM CONSERTVM VOCASTI,
INDE IBI EGO TE REVOCO.'   Praetor interea ne pulchrum
20 se ac beatum putaret atque aliquid ipse sua sponte loque-
retur, ei quoque carmen compositum est cum ceteris rebus
absurdum tum vero in illo: 'SVIS VTRISQVE SVPERSTITIBVS
PRAESENTIBVS ISTAM VIAM DICO; ITE VIAM.'   Praesto aderat
sapiens ille qui inire viam doceret.   'REDITE VIAM.'   Eo-
25 dem duce redibant.   Haec iam tum apud illos barbatos

3 petebantur ψ: petebant ω   5 ediscendis w: discendis ω:
eliscendis (eli- π² *in ras.*) *cett.*   6 his *scripsi; om. codd.*   cautis
Beroaldus: causis *mei*: capsis *cod. Sambuci, Madvig,* catis *Manutius*
consultis eorum] consultorum *Madvig*   8 promulgata φw   lege
agi *ed. Guar.*: lege *codd.*   posset *edd. VR*: possit *mei*   verba
quaedam *Niebuhr*: vero (vere χ¹) acaedam (attedam ψ²) *codd.*   13
quid] . . . quid Σ: *fort.* ecquid   iure Quiritium *Lambinus (cf.
Gaium* iv.16): iureque *codd.*   14 aios ΣA   ibi *om.* Aπ   15
manum *Gellius* xx.10: manu *codd.*   19 praetor πψ²: praeter *cett.*
22 in illo suis] nullo usui ψ²   23 ite *Arusianus (s.v.* it illam
viam): inite *codd.*   25 barbatos ψ² : barbaros *cett.*

ridicula, credo, videbantur, homines, cum recte atque in
loco constitissent, iuberi abire ut, unde abissent, eodem
statim redirent.   Isdem ineptiis fucata sunt illa omnia:
'QVANDO TE IN IVRE CONSPICIO' et haec: 'ANNE TV DICAS
QVA EX CAVSA VINDICAVERIS?'   Quae dum erant occulta, 5
necessario ab eis qui ea tenebant petebantur; postea vero
pervolgata atque in manibus iactata et excussa, inanissima
prudentiae reperta sunt, fraudis autem et stultitiae plenis-
27 sima.   Nam, cum permulta praeclare legibus essent constituta, ea iure consultorum ingeniis pleraque corrupta 10
ac depravata sunt.   Mulieres omnis propter infirmitatem
consili maiores in tutorum potestate esse voluerunt; hi
invenerunt genera tutorum quae potestate mulierum contine-
rentur.   Sacra interire illi noluerunt; horum ingenio senes
ad coemptiones faciendas interimendorum sacrorum causa 15
reperti sunt.   In omni denique iure civili aequitatem reli-
querunt, verba ipsa tenuerunt, ut, quia in alicuius libris
exempli causa id nomen invenerant, putarunt omnis mulieres
quae coemptionem facerent 'Gaias' vocari.   Iam illud mihi
quidem mirum videri solet, tot homines, tam ingeniosos, 20
post tot annos etiam nunc statuere non potuisse utrum
'diem tertium' an 'perendinum,' 'iudicem' an 'arbitrum,'
13 'rem' an 'litem' dici oporteret.   Itaque, ut dixi, dignitas
28 in ista scientia consularis numquam fuit, quae tota ex rebus
fictis commenticiisque constaret, gratiae vero multo etiam 25
minus.   Quod enim omnibus patet et aeque promptum est
mihi et adversario meo, id esse gratum nullo pacto potest.
Itaque non modo benefici conlocandi spem sed etiam illud
quod aliquamdiu fuit 'LICET CONSVLERE?' iam perdidistis.

1 videbantur] rudebantur Σ: ridebantur *A*   3 fucata *ed. R:*
fugata *codd.*   4 conspicios Σ*A*   et haec *Nangerius* (2): et haec
sed *codd.*   tu dicas *Halm:* tudiciis Σπ: tu dicus *A*φω: tu dicis χψ:
dicas *Gaius*   5 qua ex *Gaius:* qui *codd.*   17 quia π¹ψ²ω: cuia
cett.   18 putarunt *ed: R* putarent *codd.*   21 post *Pluygers:*
per *codd.*   26 minus *Angelius:* minores *codd.*: inanior est
Zumpt   28 collocandi *A*ψ²ω: collocandis *cett.*   29 aliquando χ¹

Sapiens existimari nemo potest in ea prudentia quae neque
extra Romam usquam neque Romae rebus prolatis quicquam
valet. Peritus ideo haberi nemo potest quod in eo quod
sciunt omnes nullo modo possunt inter se discrepare. Diffi-
5 cilis autem res ideo non putatur quod et perpaucis et
minime obscuris litteris continetur. Itaque si mihi, homini
vehementer occupato, stomachum moveritis, triduo me
iuris consultum esse profitebor. Etenim quae de scripto
aguntur, scripta sunt omnia, neque tamen quicquam tam
10 anguste scriptum est quo ego non possim 'QVA DE RE
AGITVR' addere; quae consuluntur autem, minimo periculo
respondentur. Si id quod oportet responderis, idem videare
respondisse quod Servius; sin aliter, etiam controversum
ius nosse et tractare videare. Quapropter non solum illa 29
15 gloria militaris vestris formulis atque actionibus anteponenda
est verum etiam dicendi consuetudo longe et multum isti
vestrae exercitationi ad honorem antecellit. Itaque mihi
videntur plerique initio multo hoc maluisse, post, cum id
adsequi non potuissent, istuc potissimum sunt delapsi.
20 Vt aiunt in Graecis artificibus eos auloedos esse qui citharoedi fieri non potuerint, sic nos videmus, qui oratores
evadere non potuerint, eos ad iuris studium devenire.
Magnus dicendi labor, magna res, magna dignitas, summa
autem gratia. Etenim a vobis salubritas quaedam, ab eis
25 qui dicunt salus ipsa petitur. Deinde vestra responsa atque
decreta et evertuntur saepe dicendo et sine defensione
orationis firma esse non possunt. In qua si satis profecissem, parcius de eius laude dicerem; nunc nihil de me dico,
sed de eis qui in dicendo magni sunt aut fuerunt.

4 omnes *Naugerius*: homines *codd.* 7 me esse iuris cons. *w*,
Halm 8 esse *del. Ernesti* (*cf. Tusc.* ii. 12) 9 tamen *om. w*
12 videare] iudicare A$\psi^1\omega$ 13 controversum $\chi\psi$: contraversum
cett. 17 antecellit B, *Lambinus*: antecellet *cett.* 21–22 potuerunt . . . potuerunt $\chi\psi$ (*variant codd. Quintil.* viii. 3. 79) 21 nos
Quintil.: nonnullos *codd.* 27 orationis *scripsi*: oratoris *codd.*
qua] qua re *Naugerius*: quo *Zumpt*

14
30   Duae sint artes *igitur* quae possint locare homines in amplissimo gradu dignitatis, una imperatoris, altera oratoris boni. Ab hoc enim pacis ornamenta retinentur, ab illo belli pericula repelluntur. Ceterae tamen virtutes ipsae per se multum valent, iustitia, fides, pudor, temperantia; 5 quibus te, Servi, excellere omnes intellegunt. Sed nunc de studiis ad honorem appositis, non de insita cuiusque virtute disputo. Omnia ista nobis studia de manibus excutiuntur, simul atque aliqui motus novus bellicum canere coepit. Etenim, ut ait ingeniosus poeta et auctor valde bonus, 10 'proeliis promulgatis pellitur e medio' non solum ista vestra verbosa simulatio prudentiae sed etiam ipsa illa domina rerum, 'sapientia; vi geritur res, spernitur orator' non solum odiosus in dicendo ac loquax verum etiam 'bonus; horridus miles amatur,' vestrum vero studium totum iacet. 15 'Non ex iure manum consertum, sed mage ferro' inquit 'rem repetunt.' Quod si ita est, cedat, opinor, Sulpici, forum castris, otium militiae, stilus gladio, umbra soli; sit denique in civitate ea prima res propter quam ipsa est civitas omnium princeps.   20

31   Verum haec Cato nimium nos nostris verbis magna facere demonstrat et oblitos esse bellum illud omne Mithridaticum cum mulierculis esse gestum. Quod ego longe secus existimo, iudices; deque eo pauca disseram; neque enim causa in hoc continetur. Nam si omnia bella quae 25 cum Graecis gessimus contemnenda sunt, derideatur de

1 sint artes igitur *scripsi*: sint artes (*ante lac.* 4 *litt.* Σ) ΣA: sunt artes *cett.*   possint ΣAπ: possunt *cett.*   6 nunc] non nunc Σ: non ψ² 7 ad honorem χ: ab honorem Σ: ab honore *cett.*   appositis *Lambinus*: depositis (deposs. Σ) *codd.*: potissimis *Kayser*   9 novus ψ²: novos *cett.*   11 pellitur ψ², *Gellius* xx.10: bellitur Σ: tollitur *cett.*   13 vi geritur res, spernitur *Gellius*: videtur (videre ω) respernitur ΣAπψ¹ω: videtur et spernitur φ: videtur resperni χ: videtur respui spernitur ψ²   16 manum Σπφ: manu *cett.*   mage *Ascens.* (3) *ex Gellio: om. codd.*   17 Sulpici *om.* ω, *del. Halm* 21   nos ψ²: vos *cett.*

rege Pyrrho triumphus M'. Curi, de Philippo T. Flaminini,
de Aetolis M. Fulvi, de rege Perse L. Pauli, de Pseudophilippo Q. Metelli, de Corinthiis L. Mummi. Sin haec
bella gravissima victoriaeque eorum bellorum gratissimae
5 fuerunt, cur Asiaticae nationes atque ille a te hostis contemnitur? Atqui ex veterum rerum monumentis vel maximum bellum populum Romanum cum Antiocho gessisse
video; cuius belli victor L. Scipio aequa parta cum P.
fratre gloria, quam laudem ille Africa oppressa cognomine
10 ipso prae se ferebat, eandem hic sibi ex Asiae nomine
adsumpsit. Quo quidem in bello virtus enituit egregia 32
M. Catonis, proavi tui; quo ille, cum esset, ut ego mihi
statuo, talis qualem te esse video, numquam cum Scipione
esset profectus, si cum mulierculis bellandum arbitraretur.
15 Neque vero cum P. Africano senatus egisset ut legatus
fratri proficisceretur, cum ipse paulo ante Hannibale ex
Italia expulso, ex Africa eiecto, Carthagine oppressa maxi
mis periculis rem publicam liberasset, nisi illud grave bellum
et vehemens putaretur. Atqui si diligenter quid Mithri- **15**
20 dates potuerit et quid effecerit et qui vir fuerit consideraris,
omnibus quibuscum populus Romanus bellum gessit hunc
regem nimirum antepones. Quem L. Sulla maximo et fortissimo exercitu, pugnax et acer et non rudis imperator, ut
aliud nihil dicam, cum bello invectum totam in Asiam cum
25 pace dimisit; quem L. Murena, pater huiusce, vehementissime vigilantissimeque vexatum repressum magna ex parte,

1 Flaminini *Manutius*: Flamini *codd.*   3 sin *s*: si *mei*   4
gratissimae *Lag.* 13: gravissimae *mei*   7 cum rege Antiocho
Priscian. (K. iii. p. 74)   8 aequa parta *Kayser*: si qua parta
(partha Σ) *codd.*: aequiparata *Madvig*   12 ego mihi] *fort.* egomet
13 statuo *s, Angelius*: statuam *mei*   cum Scipione] cum Gla-
brione *Klotz* (cf. *Liv.* xxxvii.57): del. *Ernesti*   21 omnibus quibuscum *scripsi*: omnibus quibus regibus cum Σ: omnibus quibuscum
regibus Aχψ: omnibus regibus quibuscum πφω   22 regem *om. w*
23 pugnax et acer et *Niebuhr*: pugna exetaceret (exaceraret χψ²)
Σχψ²: pugna excitaret *cett* (*om.* ω)   24 bello *Naugerius* (2):
bellum *mei*

non oppressum reliquit; qui rex sibi aliquot annis sumptis
ad confirmandas rationes et copias belli tantum spe cona-
tuque valuit ut se Oceanum cum Ponto, Sertori copias cum
33 suis coniuncturum putaret.   Ad quod bellum duobus con-
sulibus ita missis ut alter Mithridatem persequeretur, alter 5
Bithyniam tueretur, alterius res et terra et mari calamitosae
vehementer et opes regis et nomen auxerunt; L. Luculli
vero res tantae exstiterunt ut neque maius bellum comme-
morari possit neque maiore consilio et virtute gestum.
Nam cum totius impetus belli ad Cyzicenorum moenia 10
constitisset eamque urbem sibi Mithridates Asiae ianuam
fore putasset qua effracta et revolsa tota pateret provincia,
perfecta a Lucullo haec sunt omnia ut urbs fidelissimorum
sociorum defenderetur et omnes copiae regis diuturnitate
obsessionis consumerentur.   Quid? illam pugnam navalem
ad Tenedum, cum contento cursu acerrimis ducibus hostium 15
classis Italiam spe atque animis inflata peteret, mediocri
certamine et parva dimicatione commissam arbitraris?
Mitto proelia, praetereo oppugnationes oppidorum; expul-
sus regno tandem aliquando tantum tamen consilio atque au- 20
ctoritate valuit ut se rege Armeniorum adiuncto novis opibus
16 copiisque renovarit.   Ac si mihi nunc de rebus gestis esset
nostri exercitus imperatorisque dicendum, plurima et maxima proelia commemorare possem; sed non id agimus.
34 Hoc dico: Si bellum hoc, si hic hostis, si ille rex conte- 25
mnendus fuisset, neque tanta cura senatus et populus Romanus suscipiendum putasset neque tot annos gessisset neque
tanta gloria L. *Lucullus*, neque vero eius belli conficiendum
exitum tanto studio populus Romanus ad Cn. Pompeium

1 qui *s, ed. R*: quid *mei*   2 spe *Klotz*: ipse *codd.*   5
Mithridatem *s, Ascens.* (1): Mithrydate non Σ: Mithridatem non
cett.   11 constitisset *Angelius*: exstitisset *codd.*   13 ut et *Halm*
14 et *cod. Graevii*: ut *mei*   16 ad Tenedum *ed. R*: attenedum πχω:
attened. ΣAφ: attenedo ψ   22 renovaret *cod. Graevii*   27
gessisset *ed. R*: cessisset *codd.*   28 L. Lucullus *Angelius*: Luculli
ψ²: L. (*ante lac.* χ) *cett.*   conficiendum exitum *mei*: conficiendi
exitum *s*: conficiendi negotium *Boot*

detulisset. Cuius ex omnibus pugnis, quae sunt innumera-
biles, vel acerrima mihi videtur illa quae cum rege commissa
est et summa contentione pugnata. Qua ex pugna cum se
ille eripuisset et Bosphorum confugisset quo exercitus adire
5 non posset, etiam in extrema fortuna et fuga nomen tamen
retinuit regium. Itaque ipse Pompeius regno possesso ex
omnibus oris ac notis sedibus hoste pulso tamen tantum in
unius anima posuit ut, cum ipse omnia quae tenuerat, adie-
rat, sperarat, victoria possideret, tamen non ante quam illum
10 vita expulit bellum confectum iudicarit. Hunc tu hostem,
Cato, contemnis quocum per tot annos tot proeliis tot imperatores bella gesserunt, cuius expulsi et eiecti vita tanti aestimata est ut morte eius nuntiata denique bellum confectum
arbitrarentur? Hoc igitur in bello L. Murenam legatum
15 fortissimi animi, summi consili, maximi laboris cognitum
esse defendimus, et hanc eius operam non minus ad consulatum adipiscendum quam hanc nostram forensem industriam
dignitatis habuisse.

17

At enim in praeturae petitione prior renuntiatus est 35
20 Servius. Pergitisne vos tamquam ex syngrapha agere cum
populo ut, quem locum semel honoris cuipiam dederit,
eundem *in* reliquis honoribus debeat? Quod enim fretum,
quem Euripum tot motus, tantas, tam varias habere putatis
agitationes commutationesque fluctuum, quantas perturba-
25 tiones et quantos aestus habet ratio comitiorum? Dies
intermissus aut nox interposita saepe perturbat omnia, et

2 vel] valde Σ   6 ipse *m, Angelius*: ipso *cett.*   8 ipse
scripsi: ille *codd.*: illa *Zumpt* (omnia quae ille *Manutius*)   10
expulisset *Ernesti*   12 aestimata *Ascens.* (1): existimata *codd.*
14 arbitrarentur *Zumpt*: arbitraretur *codd.*: arbitraremur *Manutius*
22 in reliquis *Ernesti*: reliquis *codd.*: reliquis in *ed.* V   23 quem
Quintil. viii. 6. 49: quod. *codd.*   putatis] creditis *Quintil.*   24
agitationes commutationesque fluctuum *Kayser*: agitationes commuta-
tiones fluctus *Quintil.*: agitationes quos fluctus ψ^2: agitationesque
(*om.* que πφω) fluctuum *cett.*   26 aut] unus aut *Quintil.*   saepe
et *Quintil.*

totam opinionem parva non numquam commutat aura
rumoris.   Saepe etiam sine ulla aperta causa fit aliud atque
existimaris, ut non numquam ita factum esse etiam populus
36 admiretur, quasi vero non ipse fecerit.   Nihil est incertius
volgo, nihil obscurius voluntate hominum, nihil fallacius 5
ratione tota comitiorum.   Quis L. Philippum summo
ingenio, opera, gratia, nobilitate a M. Herennio superari
posse arbitratus est? quis Q. Catulum humanitate, sapientia,
integritate antecellentem a Cn. Mallio? quis M. Scaurum,
hominem gravissimum, civem egregium, fortissimum sena- 10
torem, a Q. Maximo?   Non modo horum nihil ita fore
putatum est sed, ne cum esset factum quidem, qua re ita
factum esset intellegi potuit.   Nam, ut tempestates saepe
certo aliquo caeli signo commoventur, saepe improviso
nulla ex certa ratione obscura aliqua ex causa concitantur, 15
sic in hac comitiorum tempestate populari saepe intellegas
quo signo commota sit, saepe ita obscura causa est ut casu
18 excitata esse videatur.   Sed tamen si est reddenda ratio,
37 duae res vehementer in praetura desideratae sunt quae
ambae in consulatu multum Murenae profuerunt, una ex- 20
spectatio muneris quae et rumore non nullo et studiis sermonibusque competitorum creverat, *altera* quod ei quos in
provincia ac legatione omni et liberalitatis et virtutis suae
testis habuerat nondum decesserant.   Horum utrumque ei
fortuna ad consulatus petitionem reservavit.   Nam et L. 25
Luculli exercitus qui ad triumphum convenerat idem
comitiis L. Murenae praesto fuit, et munus amplissimum

1 commutat aura rumoris *Quintil.*: commutata aura rumores (comm.
vestrarum mores Σ) *codd.*   2 fit ψ: sit *cett.*   4 quasi . . . fecerit
del. ψ²   7 opera] opibus *Hotoman*   15 excitantur χψ¹ 17
causa est *scripsi (fort.* vis est): est Σ: est *cett.*: est causa
Lambinus   casu] sine causa *Quintil.* viii. 3. 80   18 esse *om.*
Quintil.   20 consulatu multum *Orelli*: consulatum ut tum Σ: consulatu tum *cett.*   21 quae et] quae ex Aφω   22 alterata ψ: *om.*
cett.   23 omni Σ: omnis *cett.*   24 decesserant] exercitum
Luculli significat *add. codd.* (ψ¹): *del.* ψ²   27 comitiis *Hotoman*:
comes *codd.*

quod petitio praeturae desiderarat praetura restituit.   Num ₃₈
tibi haec parva videntur adiumenta et subsidia consulatus,
voluntas militum, quae*que* cum per se valet multitudine,
cum apud suos gratia, tum vero in consule declarando
5 multum etiam apud universum populum Romanum auctoritatis habet, suffragatio militaris?   Imperatores enim comitiis
consularibus, non verborum interpretes deliguntur.   Qua re
gravis est illa oratio: 'Me saucium recreavit, me praeda
donavit; hoc duce castra cepimus, signa contulimus; num-
10 quam iste plus militi laboris imposuit quam sibi sumpsit,
ipse cum fortis tum etiam felix.' Hoc quanti putas esse ad
famam hominum ac voluntatem?   Etenim, si tanta illis
comitiis religio est ut adhuc semper omen valuerit praerogativum, quid mirum est in hoc felicitatis famam sermo-
15 nemque valuisse?

   Sed si haec leviora ducis quae sunt gravissima et hanc **19**
urbanam suffragationem militari anteponis, noli ludorum
huius elegantiam et scaenae magnificentiam tam valde
contemnere; quae huic admodum profuerunt.   Nam
20 quid ego dicam populum ac volgus imperitorum ludis
magno opere delectari?   Minus est mirandum.   Quamquam
huic causae id satis est; sunt enim populi ac multitudinis
comitia.   Qua re, si populo ludorum magnificentia voluptati
est, non est mirandum eam L. Murenae apud populum
25 profuisse.   Sed si nosmet ipsi qui et ab delectatione com- ₃₉
muni negotiis impedimur et in ipsa occupatione delectationes
alias multas habere possumus, ludis tamen oblectamur et
ducimur, quid tu admirere de multitudine indocta?   L. Otho, ₄₀
vir fortis, meus necessarius, equestri ordini restituit non

---

1 desiderarat *Ernesti*: desiderabat *codd.*   3 quaeque *scripsi*:
quae *codd.*: et illa quae *Reid*   7 deliguntur χψ: diliguntur *cett.*
10 sumpsit ipse, cum *Gulielmius*   11 fortis est *Nohl*   13 praerogativae *Zumpt*   18 magnificentiam tam *Wrampelmeyer*: magnificentiam a Σ: magnificentiam *cett.*   20 imperitum *Ernesti*   25
oblectatione *A*   communi *Benecke*: omni *codd.*   28 admirere
Aψ: admirare *cett.*   Otho χψ: Otito *cett.*

solum dignitatem sed etiam voluptatem.   Itaque lex haec
quae ad ludos pertinet est omnium gratissima, quod honestissimo ordini cum splendore fructus quoque iucunditatis est
restitutus.   Qua re delectant homines, mihi crede, ludi,
etiam illos qui dissimulant, non solum eos qui fatentur; 5
quod ego in mea petitione sensi.   Nam nos quoque habuimus scaenam competitricem.   Quod si ego qui trinos ludos
aedilis feceram tamen Antoni ludis commovebar, tibi qui
casu nullos feceras nihil huius istam ipsam quam inrides
argenteam scaenam adversatam putas?   10

41   Sed haec sane sint paria omnia, sit par forensis opera
militari, militaris suffragatio urbanae, sit idem magnificentissimos et nullos umquam fecisse ludos; quid? in ipsa
praetura nihilne existimas inter tuam et huius sortem
20 interfuisse?   Huius sors ea fuit quam omnes tui necessarii 15
tibi optabamus, iuris dicundi; in qua gloriam conciliat
magnitudo negoti, gratiam aequitatis largitio; qua in sorte
sapiens praetor qualis hic fuit offensionem vitat aequabilitate decernendi, benivolentiam adiungit lenitate audiendi.
Egregia et ad consulatum apta provincia in qua laus aequi- 20
tatis, integritatis, facilitatis ad extremum ludorum voluptate
42 concluditur.   Quid tua sors?   Tristis, atrox, quaestio
peculatus ex altera parte lacrimarum et squaloris, ex altera
plena accusatorum atque indicum; cogendi iudices inviti,
retinendi contra voluntatem; scriba damnatus, ordo totus 25
alienus; Sullana gratificatio reprehensa, multi viri fortes
et prope pars civitatis offensa est; lites severe aestimatae;
cui placet obliviscitur, cui dolet meminit.   Postremo tu in
provinciam ire noluisti.   Non possum id in te reprehendere

---

     12 militari *Halm: om. codd.*   urbanae Σ: urbana *cett.*   16
conciliat *ed. R:* conciliatam *codd.*   18 offensionem vitat aequab.
Naugerius: offensionem vitata equab. Σ: offensione vitata aequab.
cett.   24 accusatorum *Novák (coni. eandem ipse feci):* catenarum
codd.: calumniarum *Richter (cf.* § 7 cattio, captio = accusatio *et* § 43)
26 alienatus *Halm*   27 est *del. Lambinus*   29 voluisti Σψ¹

quod in me ipso et praetore et consule probavi.   Sed tamen
L. Murenae provincia multas bonas gratias cum optima
existimatione attulit.   Habuit proficiscens dilectum in
Vmbria; dedit ei facultatem res publica liberalitatis, qua
5 usus multas sibi tribus quae municipiis Vmbriae conficiuntur
adiunxit.   Ipse autem in Gallia ut nostri homines desperatas
iam pecunias exigerent aequitate diligentiaque perfecit.   Tu
interea Romae scilicet amicis praesto fuisti; fateor; sed
tamen illud cogita non nullorum amicorum studia minui
10 solere in eos a quibus provincias contemni intellegunt.

21

Et quoniam ostendi, iudices, parem dignitatem ad consulatus petitionem, disparem fortunam provincialium negoti- 43
orum in Murena atque in Sulpicio fuisse, dicam iam apertius
in quo meus necessarius fuerit inferior, Servius, et ea dicam
15 vobis audientibus amisso iam tempore quae ipsi soli re
integra saepe dixi.   Petere consulatum nescire te, Servi,
persaepe tibi dixi; et in eis rebus ipsis quas te magno et
forti animo et agere et dicere videbam tibi solitus sum
dicere magis te fortem accusatorem mihi videri quam
20 sapientem candidatum.   Primum accusandi terrores et
minae quibus tu cotidie uti solebas sunt fortis viri, sed et
populi opinionem a spe adipiscendi avertunt et amicorum
studia debilitant.   Nescio quo pacto semper hoc fit—neque
in uno aut altero animadversum est sed iam in pluribus—
25 simul atque candidatus accusationem meditari visus est,
ut honorem desperasse videatur.   Quid ergo? acceptam 44
iniuriam persequi non placet?   Immo vehementer placet;
sed aliud tempus est petendi, aliud persequendi.   Petitorem
ego, praesertim consulatus, magna spe, magno animo,
30 magnis copiis et in forum et in campum deduci volo.   Non

1 et praetore et consule *Gruter*: et p̄s et consule χ: et praes. (*om.*
et praes. ω) consule (consulto ψ²) *cett*.   3 delectum ψ ²   6 ipsa
Ernesti   8 Romae scilicet *del. Halm* (2)   10 intellegant
ψ¹   19 accusatorem *Campe*: senatorem *codd.* (*cf.* §§ 7, 42)   22
a spe] aspem. Σ: *fort.* a spe mag[istratum]

placet mihi inquisitio candidati, praenuntia repulsae, non
testium potius quam suffragatorum comparatio, non minae
magis quam blanditiae, non denuntiatio potius quam persalutatio, praesertim cum iam hoc novo more omnes fere
domos omnium concursent et ex voltu candidatorum con- 5
iecturam faciant quantum quisque animi et facultatis habere
45 videatur. 'Videsne tu illum tristem, demissum? iacet,
diffidit, abiecit hastas.' Serpit hie rumor. 'Scis tu illum
accusationem cogitare, inquirere in competitores, testis
quaerere? Alium fac iam, quoniam sibi hic ipse desperat.' 10
Eius modi *rumoribus* candidatorum amici intimi debilitantur,
studia deponunt; aut certam rem abiciunt aut suam operam
22 et gratiam iudicio et accusationi reservant. Accedit eodem
ut etiam ipse candidatus totum animum atque omnem
curam operam diligentiamque suam in petitione non possit 15
ponere. Adiungitur enim accusationis cogitatio, non parva
res sed nimirum omnium maxima. Magnum est enim te
comparare ea quibus possis hominem e civitate, praesertim
non inopem neque infirmum, exturbare, qui et per se et per
suos et vero etiam per alienos defendatur. Omnes enim 20
ad pericula propulsanda concurrimus et qui non aperte
inimici sumus etiam alienissimis in capitis periculis amicissi-
46 morum officia et studia praestamus. Qua re ego expertus
et petendi et defendendi et accusandi molestiam sic intellexi
in petendo studium esse acerrimum, in defendendo officium, 25
in accusando laborem. Itaque sic statuo fieri nullo modo
posse ut idem accusationem et petitionem consulatus diligenter adornet atque instruat. Vnum sustinere pauci

1 praenuntia *ed. R*: pronuntia (provincia Σ *mg.) mei*   3 denuntiatio *Bake*: declamatio *codd.*   5 et ex] ut ex ψ¹   8 diffidet
Σπ   10 fac iam ω (*ut ipse conieceram*): faci iam *cett.*: faciam
edd. VR   11 rumoribus *supplevi*: *om. codd.*   candidatorum]
de candidato rumore *Jeep*   12 studium ψ²   certam ψ², *ed.
R*: testam (textam χ) *cett.*: statim *Müller*: totam *Lambinus*: desertam *coni. Halm*

possunt, utrumque nemo.   Tu cum te de curriculo petitionis deflexisses animumque ad accusandum transtulisses,
existimasti te utrique negotio satis facere posse. Vehementer errasti.   Quis enim dies fuit, postea quam in istam
5 accusandi denuntiationem ingressus es, quem tu non totum
in ista ratione consumpseris?   Legem ambitus flagitasti, **23**
quae tibi non deerat; erat enim severissime scripta Calpurnia.
Gestus est mos et voluntati et dignitati tuae.   Sed tota illa
lex accusationem tuam, si haberes nocentem reum, fortasse
10 armasset; petitioni vero refragata est.   Poena gravior in 47
plebem tua voce efflagitata est; commoti animi tenuiorum.
Exsilium in nostrum ordinem; concessit senatus postulationi
tuae, sed non libenter duriorem fortunae communi condicionem te auctore constituit.   Morbi excusationi poena
15 addita est; voluntas offensa multorum quibus aut contra
valetudinis commodum laborandum est aut incommodo
morbi etiam ceteri vitae fructus relinquendi.   Quid ergo?
haec quis tulit?   Is qui auctoritati senatus, voluntati tuae
paruit, denique is tulit cui minime proderant.   Illa *quidem*
20 quae mea summa voluntate senatus frequens repudiavit
mediocriter adversata tibi esse existimas?   Confusionem
suffragiorum flagitasti, †praerogationum legis Maniliaet†,
aequationem gratiae, dignitatis, suffragiorum.   Graviter
homines honesti atque in suis vicinitatibus et municipiis
25 gratiosi tulerunt a tali viro esse pugnatum ut omnes et
dignitatis et gratiae gradus tollerentur.   Idem editicios
iudices esse voluisti, ut odia occulta civium quae tacitis

3 si existimasti *Wunder*   posse sed *Boot*   18 haec *om.*
w, *del. Halm*   19 cui Aψ^2: cum *cett.*   quidem quae *scripsi*:
quae *codd.*: autem quae *Nohl* (*Quid?* illa quae *v. l. apud Lambinum*)
22 praerogationum *codd.* (ψ^1): prorogationem ψ^2, *edd.* VR: perrogationem *Mommsen* (*Locus videtur a Scholiasta nescio quo corruptus
Maniliae legis mentionem inferciente: in corruptela* praerogativae
nomen subesse puto.   Ad sententiam similis est locus Ps. Sall. ii.   7 ut ex
confusis quinque classibus sorte centuriae vocarentur. Ita coaequatur
dignitate pecunia *etc.*)   24 vicinitatibus Σ: civitatibus *cett.* (*cf. Pet.
Cons.* 24)   27 occulta *om.* w, *del. Bake*

nunc discordiis continentur in fortunas optimi cuiusque
48 erumperent.　Haec omnia tibi accusandi viam muniebant,
adipiscendi obsaepiebant.

　　Atque ex omnibus illa plaga est iniecta petitioni tuae non
tacente me maxima, de qua ab homine ingeniosissimo et 5
copiosissimo, Q. Hortensio, multa gravissime dicta sunt.
Quo etiam mihi durior locus est dicendi datus ut, cum ante
me et ille dixisset et vir summa dignitate et diligentia et
facultate dicendi, M. Crassus, ego in extremo non partem
aliquam agerem causae sed de tota re dicerem quod mihi 10
videretur.　Itaque in isdem rebus fere versor et quoad
24 possum, iudices, occurro vestrae satietati.　Sed tamen,
Servi, quam te securim putas iniecisse petitioni tuae, cum
populum Romanum in eum metum adduxisti ut pertimesceret
ne consul Catilina fieret, dum tu accusationem compares 15
49 deposita atque abiecta petitione?　Etenim te inquirere
videbant, tristem ipsum, maestos amicos; observationes,
testificationes, seductiones testium, secessiones subscri-
ptorum animadvertebant, quibus rebus certe ipsi candidatorum *voltus* obscuriores videri solent; Catilinam interea 20
alacrem atque laetum, stipatum choro iuventutis, vallatum
indicibus atque sicariis, inflatum cum spe militum *tum*
conlegae mei, quem ad modum dicebat ipse, promissis,
circumfluentem colonorum Arretinorum et Faesulanorum
exercitu; quam turbam dissimillimo ex genere distinguebant 25
homines perculsi Sullani temporis calamitate.　Voltus erat
ipsius plenus furoris, oculi sceleris, sermo adrogantiae, sic ut
ei iam exploratus et domi conditus consulatus videretur.

---

　　1 cuiusque Σχψ: cuius π: civis Aφ　　　　6 Q. *Klotz: om. codd.*
11 quoad ψ²: quod *cett.*　　　12 satietati *w, Hotoman:* sapietati Σ:
sapientiae *cett.*　　　18 secessiones *Campe:* secessionem *codd.*　　　19
certe ipsi] certe spes *Boot:* cretae ipsae *Madvig*　　　20 voltus *ed. V:*
om. codd. (cf. infra l. 26)　　　obscuriores πφψ²ω: obscurior ei ΣAχψ¹
solet χψ　　　22 militum tum ψ²: militum *cett.* 26　　　perculsi
Lambinus, pauci dett.: percuṣsi Σ: percussi *cett.*　　　ipsius erat χ,
ed. V

Murenam contemnebat, Sulpicium accusatorem suum nu-
merabat non competitorem; ei vim denuntiabat, rei publicae
minabatur.　Quibus rebus qui timor bonis omnibus iniectus: **25**
sit quantaque desperatio rei publicae, si ille factus esset, **50**
5 nolite a me commoneri velle; vosmet ipsi vobiscum recorda-
mini.　Meministis enim, cum illius nefarii gladiatoris voces
percrebruissent quas habuisse in contione domestica dicebatur, cum miserorum fidelem defensorem negasset inveniri
posse nisi eum qui ipse miser esset; integrorum et fortuna-
10 torum promissis saucios et miseros credere non oportere;
qua re qui consumpta replere, erepta reciperare vellent,
spectarent quid ipse deberet, quid possideret, quid auderet;
minime timidum et valde calamitosum esse oportere eum
qui esset futurus dux et signifer calamitosorum.　Tum igitur, 51
15 his rebus auditis, meministis fieri senatus consultum referente
me ne postero die comitia haberentur, ut de his rebus in
senatu agere possemus.　Itaque postridie frequenti senatu
Catilinam excitavi atque eum de his rebus iussi, si quid
vellet, quae ad me adlatae essent dicere.　Atque ille, ut
20 semper fuit apertissimus, non se purgavit sed indicavit
atque induit.　Tum enim dixit duo corpora esse rei publicae,
unum debile infirmo capite, alterum firmum sine capite;
huic, si ita de se meritum esset, caput se vivo non defuturum.
Congemuit senatus frequens neque tamen satis severe pro
25 rei indignitate decrevit; nam partim ideo fortes in decer-
nendo non erant, quia nihil timebant, partim, quia *omnia*.
Erupit e senatu triumphans gaudio quem omnino vivum
illinc exire non oportuerat, praesertim cum idem ille in
eodem ordine paucis diebus ante Catoni, fortissimo viro,

7 percrebruissent Σ: percrebuissent *cett.*　21 esse duo corpora
A　23 si] cum ψ^2　26 omnia *scripsi*: timebant *codd.*: time-
bant nimium *Müller*　27 *ante* erupit *add.* cue $\Sigma\chi^1$ (*al.* que *vel* cur Σ
mg.), cum A$\pi\phi\omega$, qui χ^2, cur ψ^1, tum ψ^2: atque *Mommsen* (*in archetypo
videtur fuisse* que (= quaere) *aliquid amissum esse significans*)

iudicium minitanti ac denuntianti respondisset, si quod
esset in suas fortunas incendium excitatum, id se non aqua
26 sed ruina restincturum. His tum rebus commotus et quod
52 homines iam tum coniuratos cum gladiis in campum deduci
a Catilina sciebam, descendi in campum cum firmissimo 5
praesidio fortissimorum virorum et cum illa lata insignique
lorica, non quae me tegeret—etenim sciebam Catilinam non
latus aut ventrem sed caput et collum solere petere—verum
ut omnes boni animadverterent et, cum in metu et periculo
consulem viderent, id quod est factum, ad opem prae- 10
sidiumque concurrerent. Itaque cum te, Servi, remissiorem
in petendo putarent, Catilinam et spe et cupiditate inflammatum viderent, omnes qui illam ab re publica pestem
depellere cupiebant ad Murenam se statim contulerunt.
53 Magna est autem comitiis consularibus repentina voluntatum 15
inclinatio, praesertim cum incubuit ad virum bonum et
multis aliis adiumentis petitionis ornatum. Qui cum
honestissimo patre atque maioribus, modestissima adulescentia, clarissima legatione, praetura probata in iure, grata
in munere, ornata in provincia petisset diligenter, et ita 20
petisset ut neque minanti cederet neque cuiquam minaretur,
huic mirandum est magno adiumento Catilinae subitam
spem consulatus adipiscendi fuisse?
54   Nunc mihi tertius ille locus est relictus orationis, de
ambitus criminibus, perpurgatus ab eis qui ante me dixerunt, 25
a me, quoniam ita Murena voluit, retractandus; quo in loco
C. Postumo, familiari meo, ornatissimo viro, de divisorum
indiciis et de deprehensis pecuniis, adulescenti ingenioso et
bono, Ser. Sulpicio, de equitum centuriis, M. Catoni, homini
in omni virtute excellenti, de ipsius accusatione, de senatus 30

1 si ψ: etsi *cett.*   2 esset] esse $\Sigma A\phi$ 3 extincturum *A*
10 factum est *w, Halm*   24 locus est relictus ẹṣṭ Σ: locus reli-
quus est *Halm*   25 eis] his ϕ, *codd. Halmii*   27 C. *Zumpt*:
P. *Halm*: om. *Codd.*   28 et de] et $\Sigma^1 A\phi$

consulto, de re publica respondebo. Sed pauca quae meum [27]
animum repente moverunt prius de L. Murenae fortuna [55]
conquerar. Nam cum saepe antea, iudices, et ex aliorum
miseriis et ex meis curis laboribusque cotidianis fortunatos
5 eos homines iudicarem qui remoti a studiis ambitionis
otium ac tranquillitatem vitae secuti sunt, tum vero in his
L. Murenae tantis tamque improvisis periculis ita sum
animo adfectus ut non queam satis neque communem
omnium nostrum condicionem neque huius eventum fortu-
10 namque miserari. Qui primum, dum ex honoribus continuis
familiae maiorumque suorum unum ascendere gradum dignitatis conatus est, venit in periculum ne et ea quae *ei* relicta,
et haec quae ab ipso parta sunt amittat, deinde propter
studium novae laudis etiam in veteris fortunae discrimen
15 adducitur. Quae cum sunt gravia, iudices, tum illud [56]
acerbissimum est quod habet eos accusatores, non qui
odio inimicitiarum ad accusandum, sed qui studio accusandi
ad inimicitias descenderint. Nam ut omittam Servium
Sulpicium quem intellego non iniuria L. Murenae sed
20 honoris contentione permotum, accusat paternus amicus,
C. Postumus, vetus, ut ait ipse, vicinus ac necessarius, qui
necessitudinis causas compluris protulit, simultatis nullam
commemorare potuit. Accusat Ser. Sulpicius, sodalis
filius, cuius ingenio paterni omnes necessarii munitiores
25 esse debebant. Accusat M. Cato qui cum a Murena nulla
re umquam alienus fuit, tum ea condicione nobis erat in
hac civitate natus ut eius opes, ut ingenium praesidio multis

3 et cx] ex $\Sigma^1 A\phi$ 11 unum] in hunc *Müller*: summum
Pluygers 12 ei *Halm*: om. *codd.*: *fort.* ab eis   13 parta *Naugerius*
(2): parata *codd.*   15 sint ϕ, *Ernesti*   18 descenderint
Lambinus: descenderent *codd.*   21 C. *Zumpt*: tum *codd.* (T. *et
hic et* § 54 *coni. Nohl*)   24 filius *Zumpt*: fil. χ, om. Σ, filii *cett.*
25-26 cum . . . tum *Kayser*: quamquam . . . tamen *codd.*   26 nobis
ed. V, Ox. Canon. 304 m. 2: nobilis *cett.*, *del. Mommsen*   27 ut ingen.]
et ingen. *ed. Guar.*: atque ingen. *ed.* V

etiam alienis, exitio vix cuiquam inimico esse deberet.
57 Respondebo igitur Postumo primum qui nescio quo pacto
mihi videtur praetorius candidatus in consularem quasi
desultorius in quadrigarum curriculum incurrere.　Cuius
competitores si nihil deliquerunt, dignitati eorum concessit, 5
cum petere destitit; sin autem eorum aliquis largitus est,
expetendus amicus est qui alienam potius iniuriam quam
suam persequatur.

28　DE POSTVMI CRIMINIBVS, DE SERVI ADVLESCENTIS.

58　　Venio nunc ad M. Catonem, quod est fundamentum ac 10
robur totius accusationis; qui tamen ita gravis est accusator
et vehemens ut multo magis eius auctoritatem quam crimi-
nationem pertimescam.　In quo ego accusatore, iudices,
primum illud deprecabor ne quid L. Murenae dignitas illius,
ne quid exspectatio tribunatus, ne quid totius vitae splendor 15
et gravitas noceat, denique ne ea soli huic obsint bona
M. Catonis quae ille adeptus est ut multis prodesse possit.
Bis consul fuerat P. Africanus et duos terrores huius imperi,
Carthaginem Numantiamque, deleverat cum accusavit L.
Cottam.　Erat in *eo* summa eloquentia, summa fides, summa 20
integritas, auctoritas tanta quanta in imperio populi Romani
quod illius opera tenebatur.　Saepe hoc maiores natu dicere
audivi, hanc accusatoris eximiam vim *et* dignitatem plurimum
L. Cottae profuisse.　Noluerunt sapientissimi homines qui
tum rem illam iudicabant ita quemquam cadere in iudicio 25
59 ut nimiis adversarii viribus abiectus videretur.　Quid?

1 alienis exitio ψ^1, *Lambinus*: alienis ex7770 Σ: alienissimis ψ:
alienissimo *cett.*　　　inimico ψ^2: inimico ‖ Σ (*cf.* §§ 13, 26): inimico
ψ^1: inimicus *cett.*　deberent Σψ^1　　7 est] ei est *Heine*　9
DE . . . ADVLESCENTIS *om.* A$\chi^1\psi$ (*in lac.* χ^1): *in mg.* π est *ʰic non est
textus'*　10 fundamentum Σ: firmamentum *cett.*　　ac] et
Aχ　　14 illud *om. w, del. Halm* deprecor ϕ　　17 prodesse
possit] prodesset $\chi\psi$: prodesse posset *ed. R*　　20 in eo $\chi\psi$: in
cett.: fort. ei　　23 vim *et pauci dett.*: vim *mei: om. ed. R*　plurimum $\chi\psi$: plurimam *cett.*　　26 nimiis *edd.* VR: nimis *codd.*
(unius ψ^2)

Ser. Galbam—nam traditum memoriae *est*—nonne proavo
tuo, fortissimo atque florentissimo viro, M. Catoni, incumbenti
ad eius perniciem populus   Romanus eripuit?   Semper
in hac civitate nimis magnis accusatorum opibus et populus
5 universus et sapientes ac multum in posterum prospicientes
iudices restiterunt.   Nolo accusator in iudicium potentiam
adferat, non vim maiorem aliquam, non auctoritatem
excellentem, non nimiam gratiam.   Valeant haec omnia ad
salutem innocentium, ad opem impotentium, ad auxilium
10 calamitosorum, in periculo vero et in pernicie civium repu-
dientur.   Nam si quis hoc forte dicet, Catonem descensurum 60
ad accusandum non fuisse, nisi prius de causa iudicasset,
iniquam legem, iudices, et miseram condicionem instituet
periculis hominum, si existimabit iudicium accusatoris in
15 reum pro aliquo praeiudicio valere oportere.

Ego tuum consilium, Cato, propter singulare animi mei **29**
de tua virtute iudicium vituperare *non possum*; non nulla
forsitan conformare et leviter emendare possim. 'Non
multa peccas,' inquit ille fortissimo viro senior magister,
20 'sed peccas; te regere possum.'   At ego non te; verissime
dixerim peccare te nihil neque ulla in re te esse huius modi
ut corrigendus potius quam leviter inflectendus esse videare.
Finxit enim te ipsa natura ad honestatem, gravitatem,
temperantiam, magnitudinem animi, iustitiam, ad omnis
25 denique virtutes magnum hominem et excelsum.   Accessit
istuc doctrina non moderata nec mitis sed, ut mihi videtur,
paulo asperior et durior quam aut veritas aut natura patitur.
Et quoniam non est nobis haec oratio habenda aut in 61
imperita multitudine aut in aliquo conventu agrestium,

1 memoriae χψ: iniuriae *cett.*   est ψ: *om. cett.*   17 non
possum ψ²: non audeo *Lag.* 24: *om. cett.*: nolo *Boot*   18 forsitan
in re ψ²   20 sed] sed si ψ, *ed. R* non te *del. Halm*   21 te
esse] esse *w, Halm*   25 accessit istuc *Ernesti*: accessitis tot Σ:
accessit his (iis πχ) tot *cett.*: accessit his dotibus *coni. Ernesti*   27
patiatur φψ

audacius paulo de studiis humanitatis quae et mihi et vobis
nota et iucunda sunt disputabo.   In M. Catone, iudices,
haec bona quae videmus divina et egregia ipsius scitote
esse propria; quae non numquam requirimus, ea sunt
omnia non a natura verum a magistro.   Fuit enim quidam 5
summo ingenio vir, Zeno, cuius inventorum aemuli Stoici
nominantur.   Huius sententiae sunt et praecepta eius modi.
Sapientem gratia numquam moveri, numquam cuiusquam
delicto ignoscere; neminem misericordem esse nisi stultum
et levem; viri non esse neque exorari neque placari; 10
solos sapientes esse, si distortissimi sint, formosos, si
mendicissimi, divites, si servitutem serviant, reges; nos
autem qui sapientes non sumus fugitivos, exsules,
hostis, insanos denique esse dicunt; omnia peccata esse
paria; omne delictum scelus esse nefarium, nec minus 15
delinquere eum qui gallum gallinaceum, cum opus non
fuerit, quam eum qui patrem suffocaverit; sapientem nihil
opinari, nullius rei paenitere, nulla in re falli, sententiam
30 mutare numquam.   Hoc homo ingeniosissimus, M. Cato,
⁶² auctoribus eruditissimis inductus adripuit, neque disputandi 20
causa, ut magna pars, sed ita vivendi.   Petunt aliquid
publicani; cave *ne* quicquam habeat momenti gratia.
Supplices aliqui veniunt miseri et calamitosi;   sceleratus
et nefarius fueris, si quicquam misericordia adductus feceris.
Fatetur aliquis se peccasse et sui delicti veniam petit; 25
'nefarium est facinus ignoscere.'   At leve delictum est.
'Omnia peccata sunt paria.'   Dixisti quippiam: 'fixum et
statutum est.'   Non re ductus es sed opinione;   'sapiens
nihil opinatur.'   Errasti aliqua in re; male dici putat.   Hac
ex disciplina nobis illa sunt: 'Dixi in senatu me nomen 30

2 iucunda *ed. V, Lambinus*: iudicanda *codd. (etiam B)*   5
verum] sed ψ¹   7 huiusmodi *w, Halm*   13 simus *Wesenberg*
19 hoc] haec φw, *ed. V*   20 inductus] iter (inter ψ) inductus χψ
22 cave ne *scripsi*: cave. Σ: cave *cett.*   25 sui *Halm*: cui Σ:
eius (eiusdem φ) *cett.*   27 quippiam *Manutius*: quippe iam *codd.*

consularis candidati delaturum.' Iratus dixisti. 'Numquam'
inquit 'sapiens irascitur.' At temporis causa. 'Improbi'
inquit 'hominis *est* mendacio fallere; mutare sententiam
turpe est, exorari scelus, misereri flagitium.' Nostri autem 63
5 illi—fatebor enim, Cato, me quoque in adulescentia diffisum
ingenio meo quaesisse adiumenta doctrinae—nostri, inquam,
illi a Platone et Aristotele, moderati homines et temperati,
aiunt apud sapientem valere aliquando gratiam; viri boni
esse misereri; distincta genera esse delictorum et disparis
10 poenas; esse apud hominem constantem ignoscendi locum;
ipsum sapientem saepe aliquid opinari quod nesciat, irasci
non numquam, exorari eundem et placari, quod dixerit
interdum, si ita rectius sit, mutare, de sententia decedere
aliquando; omnis virtutes mediocritate quadam esse mode- 31
15 ratas. Hos ad magistros si qua te fortuna, Cato, cum ista 64
natura detulisset, non tu quidem vir melior esses nec fortior
nec temperantior nec iustior—neque enim esse potes—sed
paulo ad lenitatem propensior. Non accusares nullis
adductus inimicitiis, nulla lacessitus iniuria, pudentissimum
20 hominem summa dignitate atque honestate praeditum;
putares, cum in eiusdem anni custodia te atque L. Murenam
fortuna posuisset, aliquo te cum hoc rei publicae vinculo
esse coniunctum; quod atrociter in senatu dixisti, aut non
dixisses aut, si potuisses, mitiorem in partem interpretarere.
25 Ac te ipsum, quantum ego opinione auguror, nunc et animi 65
quodam impetu concitatum et vi naturae atque ingeni
elatum et recentibus praeceptorum studiis flagrantem iam
usus flectet, dies leniet, aetas mitigabit. Etenim isti ipsi
mihi videntur vestri praeceptores et virtutis magistri finis

3 est ψ, *ed. R: om. cett.* 4 autem illi, fatebor enim *ed.* V: enim
illi fatebor (fatebor illi Σ) enim *codd.* 9 esse genera *w, Halm*
11 quod] quid ΣA 14 moderandas *ed.* V 17 temperatior ψ
21 in *om.* Σπ¹ custodia] custodiam Σ: custodem ψ² 24 aut si
potuisses *Hotoman:* aut seposuisses (se pos. Σ) aut *codd.:* aut si
posuisses *Halm* (2): aut si dixisses *Campe* 28 mihi isti ipsi χ

officiorum paulo longius quam natura vellet protulisse ut,
cum ad ultimum animo contendissemus,   ibi tamen ubi
oporteret consisteremus.   'Nihil ignoveris.'   Immo aliquid,
non omnia.   'Nihil gratiae causa feceris.'   Immo resistito
gratiae, cum officium et fides postulabit.   'Misericordia 5
commotus ne sis.'   Etiam, in dissolvenda severitate; sed
tamen est laus aliqua humanitatis.   'In sententia permaneto.'
66 Vero, nisi sententiam sententia alia vicerit melior.   Huiusce
modi Scipio ille fuit quem non paenitebat facere idem quod
tu, habere eruditissimum hominem Panaetium domi; cuius 10
oratione et praeceptis, quamquam erant eadem ista quae te
delectant, tamen asperior non est factus sed, ut accepi
a senibus, lenissimus.   Quis vero C. Laelio comior *fuit*,
quis iucundior eodem ex studio isto, quis illo gravior,
sapientior?   Possum de L. Philo, de C. Gallo dicere haec 15
eadem, sed te domum iam deducam tuam.   Quemquamne
existimas Catone, proavo tuo, commodiorem, communiorem,
moderatiorem fuisse ad omnem rationem humanitatis?   De
cuius praestanti virtute cum vere graviterque diceres,
domesticum te habere dixisti exemplum ad imitandum. 20
Est illud quidem exemplum tibi propositum domi, sed
tamen naturae similitudo illius ad te magis qui ab illo ortus
es quam ad unum quemque nostrum pervenire potuit, ad
imitandum vero tam mihi propositum exemplar illud est
quam tibi.   Sed si illius comitatem et facilitatem tuae 25
gravitati severitatique asperseris, non ista quidem erunt
32 meliora, quae nunc sunt optima, sed certe condita iucundius.
  67   Qua re, ut ad id quod institui revertar, tolle mihi e causa

3 non consisteremus *Lambinus*   4 nihil *Angelius*: nihil
omnino *Lag.* 9: immo *mei*   causa feceris *Naugerius*: confeceris
mei: concesseris *Lag.* 9   6 sed tamen est *ante* etiam *transp.*
Hotoman   8 vero] enimvero *ed. Mediol.*: Permaneto vero *ed.* V
aliqua χψ   10 Panaetium *Lag.* 9: et pane Σ: et pene (pae- *A*)
cett.   13 fuit *supplevi: om.* Σ *in lac., sine lac. cett.*   15 Philo
Manutius: Philippo *codd.*   Galo *Müller* (*e Fast. Capitol. a.* 511,588)
22 qui] quam *w*: quoniam *Halm*   23 es ψχω: est *cett.*

nomen Catonis, remove vim, praetermitte auctoritatem quae
in iudiciis aut nihil valere aut ad salutem debet valere, con-
gredere mecum criminibus ipsis.   Quid accusas, Cato, quid
adfers ad iudicium, quid arguis?   Ambitum accusas; non
5 defendo.   Me reprehendis, quod idem defendam quod
lege punierim.   Punivi ambitum, non innocentiam; ambitum vero ipsum vel tecum accusabo, si voles.   Dixisti
senatus consultum me referente esse factum, si mercede
obviam candidatis issent, si conducti sectarentur, si gladia-
10 toribus volgo locus tributim et item prandia si volgo essent
data, contra legem Calpurniam factum videri.   Ergo ita
senatus iudicat, contra legem facta haec videri, si facta sint;
decernit quod nihil opus est, dum candidatis morem gerit.
Nam factum sit necne vehementer quaeritur; sin factum
15 sit, quin contra legem sit dubitare nemo potest.   Est igitur 68
ridiculum, quod est dubium, id relinquere incertum, quod
nemini dubium potest esse, id iudicare.   Atque id de
cernitur omnibus postulantibus candidatis, ut ex senatus
consulto neque cuius intersit, neque contra quem sit
20 intellegi possit.   Qua re doce ab L. Murena illa esse
commissa; tum egomet tibi contra legem commissa esse
concedam.

'Multi obviam prodierunt de provincia decedenti.'   Con- **33**
sulatum petenti solet fieri; eccui autem non proditur rever-
25 tenti?   'Quae fuit ista multitudo?'   Primum, si tibi istam
rationem non possim reddere, quid habet admirationis tali

---

1 vim *scripsi* (*cf*. §§ 58, 59): in Σ: ac *s*: *om. cett.*   praetermitte
ambitum
del. Halm (2)   6 poenierim Σ   poenivi Σ non ambitum vero Σ
8 mercede] conducti *add.* Σχψ: corrupti *add. cett.*: *del. Garatoni* 12
senatus χψ: senatum Σ: senatus si *cett. met*: senatus nisi *Lag.* 9
13 candidato *A*   14 sin ω: in Σ: nam π: si *cett.*   17 indicare
Boot   20 doce ab *Halm:* doceat Σ: doce a *cett.*   24 petenti.
Solet *edd. ante Müller* eccui *Ascens.* (1): et cui *codd.*   26
possum φχ

viro advenienti, candidato consulari, obviam prodisse multos? quod nisi esset factum, magis mirandum videretur.
69 Quid? si etiam illud addam quod a consuetudine non ab-
horret, rogatos esse multos, num aut criminosum sit aut
mirandum, qua in civitate rogati infimorum hominum filios 5
prope de nocte ex ultima saepe urbe deductum venire sole-
amus, in ea non esse gravatos homines prodire hora tertia
in campum Martium, praesertim talis viri nomine rogatos?
Quid? si omnes societates venerunt quarum ex numero
multi sedent iudices; quid? si multi homines nostri ordinis 10
honestissimi; quid? si illa officiosissima quae neminem
patitur non honeste in urbem introire tota natio candidatorum, si denique ipse accusator noster Postumus obviam
cum bene magna caterva sua venit, quid habet ista multitudo admirationis? Omitto clientis, vicinos, tribulis, exerci- 15
tum totum Luculli qui ad triumphum per eos dies venerat;
hoc dico, frequentiam in isto officio gratuitam non modo
dignitati nullius umquam sed ne voluntati quidem defuisse.
70 At sectabantur multi. Doce mercede; concedam esse
34 crimen. Hoc quidem remoto quid reprendis? 'Quid 20
opus est' inquit 'sectatoribus?' A me tu id quaeris, quid
opus sit eo quo semper usi sumus? Homines tenues unum
habent in nostrum ordinem aut promerendi aut referendi
benefici locum, hanc in nostris petitionibus operam atque
adsectationem. Neque enim fieri potest neque postulan- 25
dum est a nobis aut ab equitibus Romanis ut suos necessarios candidatos adsectentur totos dies; a quibus si domus
nostra celebratur, si interdum ad forum deducimur, si uno
basilicae spatio honestamur, diligenter observari videmur

---

2 videretur χψω: videtur *cett.*   4 sit] est *Halm*   5 rogati
ψ²: roganti *cett.*   10 sedent] hic sedent *ed.* V, *Halm*   12
pon] nisi *A*   16 totum χψ: motum *cett.*   18 nullius *Zumpt*:
ullius *codd.*   19 sectabuntur ΣA   contendam *A*   23
referendi *ed.* V, *Lambinus*: proferendi *codd.*   27 adsectentur
Klotz: aut (non ψ²) sectentur *codd.*

et coli; tenuiorum amicorum et non occupatorum est ista
adsiduitas, quorum copia bonis viris et beneficis deesse non
solet.	Noli igitur eripere hunc inferiori generi hominum
fructum offici, Cato; sine eos qui omnia a nobis sperant [71]
5 habere ipsos quoque aliquid quod nobis tribuere possint.
Si nihil erit praeter ipsorum suffragium, tenues, etsi suffra-
gantur, nil valent gratia.	Ipsi denique, ut solent loqui, non
dicere pro nobis, non spondere, non vocare domum suam
possunt.	Atque haec a nobis petunt omnia neque ulla
10 re alia quae a nobis consequuntur nisi opera sua compen-
sari putant posse.	Itaque et legi Fabiae quae est de numero
sectatorum, et senatus consulto quod est L. Caesare consule
factum restiterunt.	Nulla est enim poena quae possit
observantiam tenuiorum ab hoc vetere instituto officiorum
15 excludere.	At spectacula sunt tributim data et ad pran- [72]
dium volgo vocati.	Etsi hoc factum a Murena omnino,
iudices, non est, ab eius amicis autem more et modo factum
est, tamen admonitus re ipsa recordor quantum hae con-
questiones in senatu habitae punctorum nobis, Servi, detra-
20 xerint.	Quod enim tempus fuit aut nostra aut patrum
nostrorum memoria quo haec sive ambitio est sive libera-
litas non fuerit ut locus et in circo et in foro daretur
amicis et tribulibus?	Haec homines tenuiores praemia
commodaque a suis tribulibus vetere instituto adseque-
25 bantur***

[*Deest non nihil.*]

Praefectum fabrum semel locum tribulibus suis dedisse, 	**35**
73

6 ipsorum] eorum *w, Halm*	tenues, etsi *scripsi:* tenuẹ est si ut
Σ: tenue est si (sed ω) ut *cett.:*	*fort.* tenues, si cui (leve est, ut
suffragentur *Reid*)	9 possunt *Angelius:*	possint (-it Σ) *coda.*
12 est a L. *Lag.* 9	21 nostrum Σπ	23	praemia commodaque
Halm: primum nondum qui *codd.* (*om.* Σ *in* 15 *litt. lac.*)	24 a
suis *Halm:* ea suis *codd.* adsequebantur] adsequi . . . Σ: *sequitur
lac. in codd.* (1 *vers. in* Σ, 1 *vers. et* 14 *litt. in* A, *variant cett.*)	27
praefectum] fectum Σ

quid statuent in viros primarios qui in circo totas tabernas
tribulium causa compararunt?   Haec omnia sectatorum,
spectaculorum, prandiorum item crimina a multitudine in
tuam nimiam diligentiam, Servi, coniecta sunt, in quibus
tamen Murena ab senatus auctoritate defenditur.   Quid 5
enim? senatus num obviam prodire crimen putat?   Non,
sed mercede.   Convince.   Num sectari multos? Non, sed
conductos. Doce.   Num locum ad spectandum dare aut
ad prandium invitare?   Minime, sed volgo, passim.   Quid
est volgo?   Vniversos.   Non igitur, si L. Natta, summo 10
loco adulescens, qui et quo animo iam sit et qualis vir
futurus sit videmus, in equitum centuriis voluit esse et ad
hoc officium necessitudinis et ad reliquum tempus gratiosus,
id erit eius vitrico fraudi aut crimini, nec, si virgo Vestalis,
huius propinqua et necessaria, locum suum gladiatorium 15
concessit huic, non et illa pie fecit et hic a culpa est remo-
tus.   Omnia haec sunt officia necessariorum, commoda
tenuiorum, munia candidatorum.

74   At enim agit mecum austere et Stoice Cato, negat verum
esse adlici benivolentiam cibo, negat iudicium hominum in 20
magistratibus mandandis corrumpi voluptatibus oportere.
Ergo, ad cenam petitionis causa si quis vocat, condemnetur?
'Quippe' inquit 'tu mihi summum imperium, tu summam auctoritatem, tu gubernacula rei publicae petas foven-
dis hominum sensibus et deleniendis animis et adhibendis 25
voluptatibus?   Vtrum lenocinium' inquit 'a grege delicatae iuventutis, an orbis terrarum imperium a populo

3 crimina multitudine invita tua nimia diligentia, Servi, collecta
Madvig   5 ab (a φ) *codd.*, *del. Ernesti*   7 convince] mercede
convince *Hotoman*   sectari *ed. Guar.*: sectare *codd.*   8 doce]
conductos doce *Hotoman*   aut ad χψ: aut *cett.*   9 passim *om.*
Lag. 9, *del. Beck* (sed *cf. Pet. Cons.* 44 in conviviis . . . et passim et
tributim)   11 iam *om. w*, *del. Halm*   14 vitricos ΣA   15
suum] sane Aχ   gladiatoribus *Lambinus*   20 in *om.* Aπ
23 tu summam *Lambinus*: summam *codd.*   25 deleniendis Σπω:
deliniendis Aφχψ

Romano petebas?' Horribilis oratio; sed eam usus, vita,
mores, civitas ipsa respuit. Neque tamen Lacedaemonii,
auctores istius vitae atque orationis, qui cotidianis epulis in
robore accumbunt, neque vero Cretes quorum nemo gu-
5 stavit umquam cubans, melius quam Romani homines qui
tempora voluptatis laborisque dispertiunt res publicas suas
retinuerunt; quorum alteri uno adventu nostri exercitus
deleti sunt, alteri nostri imperi praesidio disciplinam suam
legesque conservant. Qua re noli, Cato, maiorum instituta **36**
10 quae res ipsa, quae diuturnitas imperi comprobat nimium 75
severa oratione reprehendere. Fuit eodem ex studio vir
eruditus apud patres nostros et honestus homo et nobilis,
Q. Tubero. Is, cum epulum Q. Maximus P. Africani,
patrui sui, nomine populo Romano daret, rogatus est a
15 Maximo ut triclinium sterneret, cum esset Tubero eiusdem
Africani sororis filius. Atque ille, homo eruditissimus ac
Stoicus, stravit pelliculis haedinis lectulos Punicanos et
exposuit vasa Samia, quasi vero esset Diogenes Cynicus
mortuus et non divini hominis Africani mors honestaretur;
20 quem cum supremo eius die Maximus laudaret, gratias egit
dis immortalibus quod ille vir in hac re publica potissimum natus esset; necesse enim fuisse ibi esse terrarum
imperium ubi ille esset. Huius in morte celebranda graviter tulit populus Romanus hanc perversam sapientiam
25 Tuberonis, itaque homo integerrimus, civis optimus, cum 76
esset L. Pauli nepos, P. Africani, ut dixi, sororis filius, his
haedinis pelliculis praetura deiectus est. Odit populus
Romanus privatam luxuriam, publicam magnificentiam dili-
git; non amat profusas epulas, sordis et inhumanitatem
30 multo minus; distinguit rationem officiorum ac temporum,
vicissitudinem laboris ac voluptatis. Nam quod ais nulla
re adlici hominum mentis oportere ad magistratum man-

30 ratione *Klotz*

dandum nisi dignitate, hoc tu ipse in quo summa est dignitas non servas.   Cur enim quemquam ut studeat tibi, ut te
adiuvet rogas?   Rogas tu me ut mihi praesis, ut commit-
tam ego me tibi. Quid tandem?   istuc me rogari oportet
abs te, an te potius a me ut pro mea salute laborem pericu- 5
77 lumque suscipias?   Quid quod habes nomenclatorem? in
eo quidem fallis et decipis.   Nam, si nomine appellari abs
te civis tuos honestum est, turpe est eos notiores esse servo
tuo quam tibi. Sin iam noris, tamen*ne* per monitorem
appellandi sunt cum petis, quasi incertus sis?   Quid quod, 10
cum admoneris, tamen, quasi tute noris, ita salutas?   Quid,
postea quam es designatus, multo salutas neglegentius?   Haec
omnia ad rationem civitatis si derigas, recta sunt; sin perpendere ad disciplinae praecepta velis, reperiantur pravissima.
Qua re nec plebi Romanae eripiendi fructus isti sunt ludorum, 15
gladiatorum, conviviorum, quae omnia maiores nostri com-
paraverunt, nec candidatis ista benignitas adimenda est
quae liberalitatem magis significat quam largitionem.
37   At enim te ad accusandum res publica adduxit.   Credo,
78 Cato, te isto animo atque ea opinione venisse; sed tu im- 20
prudentia laberis.   Ego quod facio, iudices, cum amicitiae
dignitatisque L. Murenae gratia facio, tum me pacis, oti,
concordiae, libertatis, salutis, vitae denique omnium nostrum
causa facere clamo atque testor.   Audite, audite consulem,
iudices, nihil dicam adrogantius, tantum dicam totos dies 25
atque noctes de re publica cogitantem!   Non usque eo
L. Catilina rem publicam despexit atque contempsit ut ea

---

4 istuc *ed. Mediol.*: istunc (ais an ψ^2) *Mei*   9 iam *scripsi*: etiam
codd.: etiam si *Lambinus* tamenne *scripsi*: tamen *codd.*   10
cum *scripsi*: curam (cur ante ψ^2, *Naugerius*) *codd.*   quasi *Zumpt*:
quam *codd.*   incertus sis *scripsi*: incertum sit *Lag.* 9: inceravit
(narravit ψ^2) *mei*: insusurravit *Naugerius*   quid quod cum *Priscian* (*K.* ii. 592): aquid quod Σ: a (ad ψ^2) quid cum $\chi\psi^2$: quid
quom $A\pi$: a quid quom ψ: quid quomodo ω 11 quid] quidem (quid
enim ψ^2) $\chi\psi$: quod *Lag.* 9   20 ea *om.* $A\pi\Phi$ opinioni $\Sigma A\chi$
26 non Σ, *Lambinus*: *om. cett.*

copia quam secum eduxit se hanc civitatem oppressurum
arbitraretur. Latius patet illius sceleris contagio quam quisquam putat, ad pluris pertinet.   Intus, intus, inquam, est
equus Troianus; a quo numquam me consule dormientes
5 opprimemini. Quaeris a me ecquid ego Catilinam metuam. 79
Nihil, et curavi ne quis metueret, sed copias illius quas hic
video dico esse metuendas; nec tam timendus est nunc
exercitus L. Catilinae quam isti qui illum exercitum dese-
ruisse dicuntur. Non enim deseruerunt sed ab illo in
10 speculis atque insidiis relicti in capite atque in cervicibus
nostris restiterunt. Hi et integrum consulem et bonum
imperatorem et natura et fortuna cum rei publicae salute
coniunctum deici de urbis praesidio et de custodia civitatis
vestris sententiis deturbari volunt. Quorum ego ferrum
15 et audaciam reieci in campo, debilitavi in foro, compressi
etiam domi meae saepe, iudices, his vos si alterum consulem tradideritis, plus multo erunt vestris sententiis quam
suis gladiis consecuti. Magni interest, iudices, id quod ego
multis repugnantibus egi atque perfeci, esse Kalendis
20 Ianuariis in re publica duo consules. Nolite arbitrari, 80
mediocribus consiliis aut usitatis viis *eos* uti. Non lex
improba, non perniciosa largitio, non auditum aliquando
aliquod malum rei publicae quaeritur. Inita sunt in hac
civitate consilia, iudices, urbis delendae, civium trucidan-
25 dorum, nominis Romani exstinguendi. Atque haec cives,
cives, inquam, si eos hoc nomine appellari fas est, de patria
sua et cogitant et cogitaverunt. Horum ego cotidie con-

---

2 patet ... Σ: *fort.* patet iam   3 pertinet ... Σ: *fort.* pertinet.
Iam   5 a me ecquid *Bake*: a me (auiae Σ *mg.*) quid *codd.*   10
speculis] seculis Σ: speluncis $\chi^2\psi^2$ in insidiis *Halm*   20 duo
Σ: duos *cett.*   21 viis *ed. Guar.*: vitis Σ*A*χ: vitiis *cett.*   eos uti
scripsi: aut *codd.*: *lacunam statuit Ernesti* 22 largitio non *w*: largi-
tionum *mei*   25 cives, cives ψ^2, *ed. R*: quae siue (*in mg.* quae-
sciue) Σ: quae cives *A*$\pi\omega$: quae si cives $\chi\psi^1$: cives ϕ, *Quintil.* ix.
2, 18

siliis occurro, audaciam debilito, sceleri resisto. Sed moneo,
iudices. In exitu iam est meus consulatus; nolite mihi
subtrahere vicarium meae diligentiae, nolite adimere eum cui
rem publicam cupio tradere incolumem ab his tantis periculis defendendam.   5

38   Atque ad haec mala, iudices, quid accedat aliud non
⁸¹ videtis? Te, te appello, Cato; nonne prospicis tempestatem anni tui? Iam enim *in* hesterna contione intonuit
vox perniciosa designati tribuni, conlegae tui; contra quem
multum tua mens, multum omnes boni providerunt qui te 10
ad tribunatus petitionem vocaverunt. Omnia quae per hoc
triennium agitata sunt, iam ab eo tempore quo a L. Catilina et Cn. Pisone initum consilium senatus interficiendi
scitis esse, in hos dies, in hos mensis, in hoc tempus erum-
⁸² punt. Qui locus est, iudices, quod tempus, qui dies, quae 15
nox cum ego non ex istorum insidiis ac mucronibus non
solum meo sed multo etiam magis divino consilio eripiar
atque evolem? Neque isti me meo nomine interfici sed
vigilantem consulem de rei publicae praesidio demoveri
volunt. Nęc minus vellent, Cato, te quoque aliqua ratione, 20
si possent, tollere; id quod, mihi crede, et agunt et moli-
untur. Vident quantum in te sit animi, quantum ingeni,
quantum auctoritatis, quantum rei publicae praesidi; sed,
cum consulari auctoritate et auxilio spoliatam vim tribu-
niciam viderint, tum se facilius inermem et debilitatum te 25
oppressuros arbitrantur. Nam ne sufficiatur consul non
timent. Vident in tuorum potestate conlegarum fore; sperant sibi *D.* Silanum, clarum virum, sine conlega, te sine
⁸³ consule, rem publicam sine praesidio obici posse. His
tantis in rebus tantisque in periculis est tuum, M. Cato, qui 30

---

6 quid] quod *Kayser*   8 in *Halm: om. codd.*   18 interficere *Richter*   19 demoveri *Lambinus:* demovere (remov. χ)
mei: dimoveri *Lag.* 9   26 ñam ne Σ   28 D. *Hirschfelder: om.*
codd.

mihi non tibi, sed patriae natus esse *videris*, videre quid
agatur, retinere adiutorem, defensorem, socium in re publica, consulem non cupidum, consulem, quod maxime
tempus hoc postulat, fortuna constitutum ad amplexandum
5 otium, scientia ad bellum gerendum, animo et usu ad quod
velis negotium *sustinendum*.

Quamquam huiusce rei potestas omnis in vobis sita est, 39
iudices; totam rem publicam vos in hac causa tenetis, vos
gubernatis.   Si L. Catilina cum suo consilio nefariorum
10 hominum quos secum eduxit hac de re posset iudicare,
condemnaret L. Murenam, si interficere posset, occideret.
Petunt enim rationes illius ut orbetur auxilio res publica,
ut minuatur contra suum furorem imperatorum copia, ut
maior facultas tribunis plebis detur depulso adversario
15 seditionis ac discordiae concitandae.   Idemne igitur
delecti ex amplissimis ordinibus honestissimi atque
sapientissimi viri iudicabunt quod ille importunissimus
gladiator, hostis rei publicae iudicaret?   Mihi credite, 84
iudices, in hac causa non solum de L. Murenae verum
20 etiam de vestra salute sententiam feretis.   In discrimen
extremum venimus; nihil est iam unde nos reficiamus aut
ubi lapsi resistamus.   Non solum minuenda non sunt
auxilia quae habemus sed etiam nova, si fieri possit, com-
paranda.   Hostis est enim non apud Anienem, quod bello
25 Punico gravissimum visum est, sed in urbe, in foro—di
immortales! sine gemitu hoc dici non potest—non nemo
etiam in illo sacrario rei publicae, in ipsa, inquam, curia
non nemo hostis est.   Di faxint ut meus conlega, vir fortissi-
mus, hoc Catilinae nefarium latrocinium armatus opprimat!
30 ego togatus vobis bonisque omnibus adiutoribus hoc quod
conceptum res publica periculum parturit consilio discutiam

1 mihi] non mihi ψ^2 esse] esset Σ: es π   videris *Klotz: om.
codd.*   6 sustinendum *Völkel: om. codd. (cf. Zielinski p.* **204**)
13 suum] summum *w, Halm*   18 iudicaret ψ^2, *ed. R:* iudicarit
cett.   31 periculum] peric. Σ (*cf. Rosc. Am.* 9)

85 et comprimam.   Sed quid tandem fiet, si haec elapsa de
manibus nostris in eum annum qui consequitur redundarint?
Vnus erit consul, et is non in administrando bello sed in
sufficiendo conlega occupatus.   Hunc iam qui impedituri
sint*** illa pestis immanis importuna Catilinae prorumpet, 5
qua po*** minatur; in agros suburbanos repente advolabit;
versabitur *in urbe* furor, in curia timor, in foro coniuratio,
in campo exercitus, in agris vastitas; omni autem in sede
ac loco ferrum flammamque metuemus.   Quae iam diu
comparantur, eadem ista omnia, si ornata suis praesidiis 10
erit res publica, facile et magistratuum consiliis et privatorum
40 diligentia comprimentur.

86   Quae cum ita sint, iudices, primum rei publicae causa,
qua nulla res cuiquam potior debet esse, vos pro mea
summa et vobis cognita in re publica diligentia moneo, 15
pro auctoritate consulari hortor, pro magnitudine periculi
obtestor, ut otio, ut paci, ut saluti, ut vitae vestrae et
ceterorum civium consulatis; deinde ego idem et defensoris
et amici officio adductus oro atque obsecro, iudices, ut ne
hominis miseri et cum corporis morbo tum animi dolore 20
confecti, L. Murenae, recentem gratulationem nova lamentatione obruatis.   Modo maximo beneficio populi Romani
ornatus fortunatus videbatur, quod primus in familiam
veterem, primus in municipium antiquissimum consulatum
attulisset; nunc idem *in* squalore et sordibus, confectus 25

---

5 sint] *sequitur lacuna in codd.* (2 *vers. et* 5 *litt. in* Σ, 2 *vers in* A,
variant cett.)   pestis immanis (immanis et A) Aπφψω: om. Σχ
prorumpet AΦω: perrumpet Σπψ: perrumperet χ   6 qua po . . .
Σχ: qua p. r. Aπψ¹: qua populo Romano Φ: qua poterit et iam ψ²
advolabit *edd.* VR: advolavit *mei*   7 in urbe *Halm*: . . . . . .
Σχ: L. Catilinae A: in castris (*om.* versabitur ψ¹) πΦψω: in rostris
Lag. 24   12 comprimentur *Lag.* 24, *Lambinus*: confirmentur
(-matur Φ) *mei*   17 ut vitae] vitae Σ: *om.* A   18 idem et
scripsi: fidem vel Σχ: fide in vos (fidem vestram ψ²) *cett.*: idem vos
Madvig   22 obruatis χ²ψ: observatis Σπχ¹: obstruatis *cett.*   25
in *supplevi*: *om. codd.* sordibus Aχψ²: sordidus *cett.*

morbo, lacrimis ac maerore perditus vester est supplex,
iudices, vestram fidem obtestatur, *vestram* misericordiam
implorat, vestram potestatem ac vestras opes intuetur.
Nolite, per deos immortalis! iudices, hac eum cum re qua 87
5 se honestiorem fore putavit etiam ceteris ante partis
honestatibus atque omni dignitate fortunaque privare.
Atque ita vos L. Murena, iudices, orat atque obsecrat, si iniuste neminem laesit, si nullius auris volun-
tatemve violavit, si nemini, ut levissime dicam, odio
10 nec domi nec militiae fuit, sit apud vos modestiae
locus, sit demissis hominibus perfugium, sit auxilium
pudori. Misericordiam spoliatio consulatus magnam habere debet, iudices; una enim eripiuntur cum consulatu omnia; invidiam vero his temporibus habere
15 consulatus ipse nullam potest; obicitur enim contionibus
seditiosorum, insidiis coniuratorum, telis Catilinae, ad
omne denique periculum atque ad omnem iniuriam solus
opponitur. Qua re quid invidendum Murenae aut cuiquam 88
nostrum sit in hoc praeclaro consulatu non video, iudices;
20 quae vero miseranda sunt, ea et mihi ante oculos versantur
et vos videre et perspicere potestis. Si, quod Iuppiter omen **41**
avertat! hunc vestris sententiis adflixeritis, quo se miser
vertet? domumne? ut eam imaginem clarissimi viri,
parentis sui, quam paucis ante diebus laureatam in sua
25 gratulatione conspexit, eandem deformatam ignominia
lugentemque videat? An ad matrem quae misera modo
consulem osculata filium suum nunc cruciatur et sollicita
est ne eundem paulo post spoliatum omni dignitate

1 morbo *AπΦω*: idem ψ^2: om. *ΣχΨ*^{1} (*Σ lac. hab. inter vv.* confectus
et perditus, *et in mg.* lacrimis ac memore perditus)   2 vestram
Halm: om. *codd.*   3 intuetur *χψ*: i̯n̯t̯u̯e̯t̯u̯r̯ *Σ*: tuetur *cett.* (*etiam B*)
4 eum cum *Garatoni*: cum *B*: eum *cett.*   7 L. *Lag.*   24: si
(sic *χψ*) *mei*   8 iniuste *ατ. Σ in lac.*   11 demisso animo
Bake   17 iniuriam *Halbertsma*: invidiam *codd.*   18 quid
w: qui *cett.*

89 conspiciat?   Sed quid eius matrem aut domum appello
quem nova poena legis et domo et parente et omnium
suorum consuetudine conspectuque privat?   Ibit igitur in
exsilium miser?   Quo?   ad Orientisne partis in quibus
annos multos legatus fuit, exercitus duxit, res maximas 5
gessit?   At habet magnum dolorem, unde cum honore
decesseris, eodem cum ignominia reverti.   An se in con-
trariam partem terrarum abdet, ut Gallia Transalpina, quem
nuper summo cum imperio libentissime viderit, eundem
lugentem, maerentem, exsulem videat?   In ea porro 10
provincia quo animo C. Murenam fratrem suum aspiciet?
Qui huius dolor, qui illius maeror erit, quae utriusque
lamentatio, quanta autem perturbatio fortunae atque
sermonis, cum, quibus in locis paucis ante diebus factum
esse consulem Murenam nuntii litteraeque celebrassent et 15
unde hospites atque amici gratulatum Romam concurre-
90 rent, repente exstiterit ipse nuntius suae calamitatis !
Quae si acerba, si misera, si luctuosa sunt, si alienissima   *a*   mansuetudine et misericordia vestra, iudices,
conservate populi Romani beneficium, reddite rei publicae 20
consulem, date hoc ipsius pudori, date patri mortuo,
date generi et familiae, date etiam Lanuvio, municipio
honestissimo, quod in hac tota *causa* frequens maestumque vidistis.   Nolite a sacris patriis Iunonis Sospitae,
cui omnis consules facere necesse est, domesticum et 25
suum consulem potissimum avellere.   Quem ego vobis,
si quid habet aut momenti commendatio aut auctoritatis
confirmatio mea, consul consulem, iudices, ita commendo

---

1 eius matrem *Zumpt*: ego matrem *codd.*:   ego matrem eius
Halm   5 exercitus *Lag.* 9: et exercitus *τei*   14 cum
Richter: quod *codd.*   15 celebrassent] celebrarint *Richter*: cele-
brarant *Boot*   16 concurrerent χ^2: concurrerint *cett.*: concur-
rerant *Lag.* 9, *Boot*   17 exstiterit *scripsi*: exciderit ψ^2: excidet
cett.: existet *Gulielmius*   19 a Bχ: *om. cett.*   22 Lanuvino
ψ, *ed. R*   23 causa A$\psi^2\omega$: *om. cett.* (*etiam B*)   26 potissimum *om.* A

ut cupidissimum oti, studiosissimum bonorum, acerrimum contra seditionem, fortissimum in bello, inimicissimum huic coniurationi quae nunc rem publicam labefactat futurum esse promittam et spondeam.

1 ut cupidissimum otii ψ^2, *ed. R*: cupidissimum osci Σ: cupidissimum hosti $\pi\psi^1\omega$: ut cupidissimi hostes ϕ: cupidissimum $B\chi$: cupidissime A

Commentary

Roman speeches often opened with an elaborate periodic sentence, like the imposing gateway of a castle or palace. The structure of this first sentence frames two of the highest and most revered concepts that could be invoked by a Roman speaker: the Roman People itself and the immortal gods, whom Cicero invokes far more frequently in addressing a public assembly (*contio*) or the mixed official and unofficial audience of a public trial than he does in senatorial speeches. This opening combines religious dignity and an appeal to ancestral values with a symmetry and solemnity of phrasing that will have kept the audience in suspense until the second limb and main clause (*eadem precor . . . ob eiusdem hominis consulatum . . . obtinendum et ut vestrae mentes etc*) unfolded to its end.

1. QVAE precatus a dis immortalibus sum. . . . ut ea res mihi fidei magistratuique meo populo plebique Romanae bene atque feliciter eveniret: "What I prayed for from the immortal gods, that this action should turn out well and fortunately for me, my good faith as magistrate and the Roman people." Latin *precor* can take as direct object either a noun/pronoun or an indirect command (noun clause object) expressed by *ut* and the subjunctive. In this opening but subordinate clause, the (aorist) perfect *precatus sum* leads to a secondary imperfect subjunctive (*eveniret*), but the corresponding present *eadem precor* governs the two primary present subjunctives *ut vestrae mentes consentiant* and *eaque res . . . pacem . . . adferat.*

iudices: "Gentlemen of the jury." After the jury law of the praetor L. Aurelius Cotta (RE 102) in 70 BCE, the panel of jurors judging cases of *ambitus* in the bribery court, as in other standing courts (*quaestiones perpetuae*), consisted of three equal groups selected from the album of 450 posted annually by the praetor. Normally 50 or 75 persons, the jury consisted of one-third senators and two-thirds *equites* (wealthy citizens with a census of 400,000 HS [sesterces]) and *tribuni aerarii*, the next social class, who are generally assumed to have a census of 300–400,000 HS. Jurors were selected for any given case and voted without deliberation on the defendant's innocence or guilt. The sentence was determined not by the presiding magistrate but by the relevant legislation. See Riggsby 2010: 195–202.

ut ea res . . . eveniret: every word and phrase in this opening sentence counts. The main formula is a variation on the more general prayer uttered on official occasions, secular and religious. Compare this to the similar prayer formula *quodque melius siet populo Romano* at the *Ludi Saeculares* in 17 BCE (*ILS* 5050 §105, also restored at 117, 121, 136). It is varied here because Cicero spoke as the presiding magistrate announcing the result (*renuntiatio*) of the consular elections, and as bound by his oath of office (*fidei*, see below) to make an honest report of the decision reached by the voting units.

populo plebique Romanae: why both? The *populus*, i.e. the body of Roman citizens, already included both patricians and plebeians, but the separate mention of *plebi* seems to have been part of a religious formula. Adamietz 1989 ad loc. compares Scipio's prayer at Liv. 29.27.2 *vos precor quaesoque ut quae in meo imperio gesta sunt geruntur, postque gerentur ea mihi populo plebique Romanae sociis . . . bene verruncent*. Cicero himself uses the doublet in the context of the public games over which he will preside as aedile, *Verr.* 5.35–36 *mihi Floram matrem populo plebique Romanae . . . placandam* and in his speech to the people in 63, *Leg. agr.* 2.27 *quia videbat potestatem neminem iniussu populi aut plebis posse habere*. (This bill was proposed for ratification by the *concilium plebis*.) Attempts to offer a political explanation of the doublet conflict with each other. On the *concilium plebis*, see Taylor 1966 and Lintott 1999: 53–55, 121–22.

auspicato: "with due taking of the auspices," a religious essential for the absolute value of the election. The neuter perfect participle passive is one of the rare ablative absolutes in Latin limited to ritual actions or their fulfillment. Compare this to Liv. 1.36.6, which reports that after the Tarquins, so much honor was given to augurs and augury that *nihil belli domique postea nisi auspicato gereretur, concilia populi, exercitus vocati, summa rerum, ubi aves non admisissent dirimerentur*. For similar adverbs compare Liv. 1.18.3 *Romulus augurato urbe condenda regnum adeptus est*; 5.38, where the tribunes wrongly draw up their battle array *nec auspicato nec litato*; and 5.52.3 when Camillus affirms the sacred nature of Rome's site *urbem auspicato inauguratoque conditam*. By contrast *inauspicato* (Liv. 21. 63.5; Val. Max. 6.6.1) denoted public acts taken without or in violation of the auspices.

eadem precor ab isdem dis immortalibus ob eiusdem: the polyptoton (juxtaposition of case endings) of *idem* stresses the identity of this utterance with the previous official act; the man praying, his prayer, and the object of his prayer are the same on this occasion as when this consul's election was so recently declared.

consulatum una cum salute obtinendum: *obtinere* is not to obtain but to retain what is already held. Murena's *salus* (also referred to as *caput*) is his citizen status that would be lost by his condemnation in this trial.

Vt vestrae mentes atque sententiae . . . consentiant: "that your attitudes and votes agree." The *sententia* is the formal vote of a senator or judge. There is moral pressure in Cicero's formulation that the judges ought to agree with the will and votes of the Roman people, but he has made it axiomatic (here and throughout his plea) that the vote, which his adversaries claimed was distorted by Murena's bribery, was in fact the expression of popular will.

eaque res . . . otium concordiamque adferat: Murena's acquittal is seen as the guarantee of peace and internal harmony, something in the power of this panel of judges. Cicero is anticipating his most urgent argument in the speech, that Murena's conviction will leave the *res publica* with only one consul as it enters a perilous period (see esp. §78–83). The four synonyms are more than a sonorous clausula: they hint at the civil unrest that Cicero had himself outlined in his first two "Catilinarian" speeches earlier in November but avoid ill omen by focusing on positive *tranquillitas* and *concordia*, which Cicero himself had made into a catchword for the desirable cooperation of Senate and *equites*.

EXCURSUS: THE QUESTION OF TRANSLATION, PARTICULAR AND GENERAL

There is always a choice to be made in translating from another language, especially from another period and society, between an alienating translation that preserves the strangeness of this other world and an assimilating translation that aims to use our own language and thought patterns. Where Cicero's sentences are complex, this commentary will at times offer both modes of translation. For example, below is the opening sentence of the *Pro Murena* separated into individual cola.

> Quae precatus a dis immortalibus sum, iudices,
> more institutoque maiorum
> illo die quo auspicato comitiis centuriatis
> L. Murenam consulem renuntiavi
> ut ea res . . . feliciter eveniret . . .
> eadem precor . . .

A literal translation keeping Latin syntax and word order might be "what things I prayed for from the immortal gods . . . on that day when after the auspices had been taken I announced to the centuriate assembly . . . that this event should turn out successfully . . ., these same prayers I now utter." This simply adds to modern notions that the Romans were stiff-necked old fellows. The reordering of clauses and modern diction of Zetzel's translation (2009) are more easily understood, but his version has the disadvantage of making Cicero stress his role in the auspication whereas the Latin affirms religious and political correctness:

On the day I took the auspices and reported to the voting
assembly the selection of Lucius Murena as consul, I made
a prayer to the immortal gods according to the traditional
custom of our ancestors that this result should be successful
for me in the faithful conduct of my office . . . I now make
the same prayer to these same immortal gods that this same
man should enter the office of consul. . . .

Where English prefers adverbial correlatives, "as I prayed to the
immortal gods . . . so I utter the same prayers," Latin typically put
significant relative clauses (*quae precatus sum*) before the principal
clause carrying their antecedent (*eadem . . . precor*). In this case,
Cicero expands his prayer into three units: (1) *ob consulatum . . .*
obtinendum (a gerundive of purpose; see below), (2) *ut vestrae*
mentes atque sententiae . . . consentiant (word play on *sententiae* =
votes, and *consentire* = to vote or agree with, (3) *eaque res . . .*
adferat.

Quod si . . . consecrata: compare the language of Liv. 39.15.1
solemne carmen precationis, quod praefari solent priusquam quam
adloquantur magistratus. Demosthenes actually began his famous
speech *On the Crown* defending his political follower Ctesiphon
with a prayer, "First, Athenians, I pray to all the gods and god-
desses to grant me as much goodwill from you for this trial as I
continue to have goodwill to the city and to you all." (Cf. Leeman
1982: 202.) We have examined the prayer and its elements, to
which we should add *fidei magistratuique meo*, where the paired
nouns are a sort of hendiadys for Cicero's observance of his magistrate's oath of office when conducting the election for the consuls
of 62 BCE. Throughout this speech Cicero will focus only on Murena's consulship, ignoring until just before the *peroratio* (§83) the
election of Silanus as his colleague, which he must have announced
at the same time.

2. Et quoniam . . . pro me ipso pauca dicam: as if he himself
were a defendant against the charge of impropriety. Unlike Athe-
nian speech-writers, who composed a speech to be acted in person

by their clients, Roman orators spoke in their own person on behalf of their clients. See Kennedy 1968, May 1988.

studium meae defensionis . . . atque etiam ipsa susceptio causae: while orators as *patroni* in court often included in their speeches their own motivation for supporting their clients, Cicero uses the prosecution's criticisms to introduce what Leeman 1982 called *oratio pro se*, §3–10. In denying it was right for the consul Cicero to speak, Cato has not apparently argued that Cicero's influence as consul would prejudice the jurors, but suggested that Cicero should not be defending his client while consul in office, implying that he should be concentrating on more urgent political issues like the potential coup of Catiline. Cato's other grounds for criticism, viz. that Cicero had passed a law against *ambitus*, particularly since he had conducted his consulship so strictly, are dealt with below.

non quo mihi potior . . . sit offici mei quam huiusce salutis defensio sed ut . . . maiore auctoritate . . . inimicorum impetus propulsare possim: *potior* shows that Cicero is not using a purpose clause, with *quo* introducing a comparative (A&G §414), but giving the rejected motive for his action—not from preference for his own obligation over his client's survival, but so that (now comes the purpose clause) *meo facto uobis probato* (abl. absolute), "I can thrust away the assaults of our enemies."

3. Et primum . . . momenta officiorum omnium: just as it is a good rhetorical tactic to imply that one is responding to attack, so Cicero wins goodwill by attributing the attack not to the wronged Servius, but to the moral watchdog Cato (§3–6). When the speech was delivered, Cato (see Introduction) had only made his mark by rigorous investigations in the quaestor's office in 65 BCE: he may have been elected tribune but had not yet delivered his famous denunciation of Catiline's fellow conspirators.

norma: Cicero borrows the vocabulary of weights and measures, implying something mechanical without nuances. The word *norma* is derived from Greek *gnomon*, through Etruscan, and denotes a right angle (cf. *regula*, Gk. *canon*). Compare this to *de Orat.* 2.178,

Leg. 2.62. Thus in *Laelius* 18 Cicero distinguishes the pragmatic patriotism of *sapientes* like Coruncanius from Stoic inflexibility *ad istam normam*. Cato is not only steering (*derigenti*) his life along this rigid course; he is weighing (*perpendenti*) the niceties of every dutiful act. Cicero will first answer the charge about his own duty. For *perpendere* cf. the same context in *Laelius* 97.

Negat fuisse rectum . . . me et consulem: Cicero had defended a number of clients (C. Calpurnius Piso [RE 63] cos. 67 BCE, and Rabirius charged with *perduellio*) during his year of office, as had other consuls before him.

et . . . latorem: Cicero's *lex Tullia* of this very year, forced upon him as consul presiding over the Senate by Sulpicius's moral pressure (see §46–47), increased the penalties for guilty candidates and their agents set by the *lex Calpurnia* of 67 BCE (see commentary below, §46). The earlier law banned those found guilty of bribery from a political career; the *lex Tullia* changed this to a sentence of ten years' exile. The *lex Calpurnia* had already been enhanced by additional clauses in recent *senatus consulta*, passed in desperation at the escalating bribery of Catiline and Antonius, but at the time of Cicero's own candidacy in 64, new *senatus consulta* had been vetoed by the tribune Mucius Orestinus.

tam severe gesto: chiefly an allusion to Cicero's recent harangue expelling Catiline, perhaps also to his rejection of a proposal to restore the civil rights of the children of those proscribed by Sulla.

rationem facti mei probem: Cicero does not need to say what his audience knew, viz. that the refusal of Rome's leading advocate to defend a consular on trial could only be read as an act of malice or condemnation of the man's behavior. Roman values put a high premium on defending even the guilty if they belonged to the right social background. Instead, Cicero argues from the claims of peers that a consul should be defended by a consul and from the special circumstances of Murena because Cicero had announced his election as his successor. In Roman thinking, a benefaction to a junior (such as that of a consul or praetor to his quaestor) created a bond of obligation. But note that Cicero will repeat his antithesis of rigorous Stoic *ratio* opposed to flexible moral *officia* below (§6 *de officio defensionis et. . . . ratione accusationis*).

cui res publica a me iam traditur sustinenda . . . periculis sustentata: the dative *cui* is *apo koinou*, serving as both indirect obj. of the finite verb *traditur* and dative of agent in the normal construction of a gerundive (A&G §374; W 207.2a). The *res publica* is a burden, which Cicero has supported at great risk and cost and is now handing on for Murena to take on and sustain; cf. *Dom.* 1.142, *rem publicam quam vestries cervicibus sustinetis*; *Sest.* 138, *qui autem praecipue suis cervicibus tanta munia atque rem publicam sustinent*; *Rep.* 2.46. *Res publica* denotes the stable operation of the magistrates, Senate, and people in Rome's (unwritten) constitution.

Here Cicero introduces three "parallels" to support his claim of obligation to support Murena. They are not equally cogent, but move from the sphere of private law (a), in which Ser. Sulpicius is most at home, to a superficial consideration (b) of public defense in political trials in other communities, to a comparison (c) with maritime trade and the responsibility of ship's captains to advise those who are following them on the same trade route. The last of these is most fruitful for Cicero's argument because the by now well-established metaphor of the ship of state would automatically assimilate successors in office to a sequence of ship's captains.

Quod si in eis rebus repetendis quae mancipi sunt: Cicero compares a civil lawsuit for real property. (*Res mancipi* were items requiring the full formal sale or *mancipium* as in *manu capere*, the more valuable possessions, trained slaves, large cattle, plots of land). *Mancipia* is actually a common term for slaves. He suggests that the presiding magistrate who announces his successor(s) is like the seller of a *res mancipi, qui se nexu obligavit*, who has bound himself by a bond (*nexus—ūs* from *nectere* to bind). The seller participated silently in the transaction by displaying scales for a notional weighing or payment when the purchaser in return offers his *aes* ("bronze, cash," see *OCD*, s.v. *mancipatio per aes et libram*). Just as the seller holds himself responsible for guaranteeing the new purchaser's lawful ownership if a third party challenges him, so the presiding consul who reports the election of the new consul(s) about to enter office (*designatus* = marked for office) is obliged to be both source of the office (*auctor benefici populi Romani*, the last three words—"the Roman people's benefaction"—being the euphemism regularly used to denote elective office) and defender against his condemnation (*defensorque periculi*, where *defendere* is used in the sense of averting or warding off harm.)

4. ut non nullis in civitatibus fieri solet: *ut* is used here simply as a comparative conjunction "as" and so with the indicative (not subjunctive) mood (A&G §323a; W 215–16). The protasis (*ac si . . . constitueretur*) of this present contrary to fact condition (A&G §517; W 193, 199) is separated from its apodosis (*is potissimus . . . daretur*) by *ut* + indicative *solet*, an adverbial clause of manner (A&G §323g; W 253 n.iii) and followed by a qualifying relative clause (A&G §535; W 155), *is, qui eodem honore praeditus non minus adferret . . . quam facultatis*. Cicero treats this as a political charge for which other, unidentified, states would appoint a public defender (*patronus*) of equal rank with the accused; the right defender would contribute both his authority and his expertise. Cicero does not name any state, but he will have drawn on his knowledge of the compilation of 158 Greek *politeiae* made by Aristotle and his students (see Lloyd 1967: 16–17, 244–46). The lack of specificity makes the statement weak in comparison with what precedes and follows. *Is potissi<mum summo> honore* is Madvig's expansion of the Mss *potissimo*. *Potissimo honore adfecto* cannot stand, even if we construe it as "for the office sought in preference."

quod si e portu solventibus . . . ex alto invehuntur: on *quod si* see §1 above. This comparison is singled out and quoted in full (but omitting *ei*) by Quint. 5.11.23, discussing *parabolae*. Its chief merit is perhaps not in the closeness of the analogy between holding office and captaining a voyage, but in the typical evocation of political life as exposure to storms (*tempestates*). Cicero adapts the traditional nautical imagery to compare novice consuls with mariners starting a new journey. We should probably imagine a shuttle or relay trade route like the grain fleet travelling between Alexandria and Puteoli (Pozzuoli). The reference to pirates is highly topical, since the trial came only three years after Pompey took up his major command and wiped the Cilician pirates off the Mediterranean. Cicero's minor premise is human goodwill to those who are embarking on the same hazards others have just survived. Combining metaphor and circumstance, Cicero represents himself as coming in sight of land after being buffeted by a great tempest and so bound to give all practical and moral support to the man now forced to undergo the greatest political storms.

si est boni consulis: the possessive genitive (A&G §343 1c) as a predicate is characterizing "it is the mark of a good consul." Disregarding Cato's claim that a scrupulous consul would not defend one accused under the terms of the consul's own legislation, Cicero turns to his strongest argument: if the consul's duty is not just to see but to *foresee* events (*prouidere quid futurum sit*), he has already taken thought and will subsequently show (*ostendam alio loco*, see §79) how important it is for public welfare to have both consuls in place on 1 January.

quantum salutis communis intersit: for *interesse* (A&G §355; W 213) with the genitive of the person affected, compare *quorum modo interfuerit aliquid*, *Part Or.* 114; but the ablative of the possessive adjective in *interest mea, tua* etc. is more common. Cicero drives home the theme of *salus communis* in the very next sentence.

5. Quod si ita est: *quod* here is not the conjunction but subject of *ita est*. Cicero considers himself first in terms of his sense of obligation (*officium*) as a friend to the fortune of his friend (*hominis amici fortunas*) then in terms of the needs of the state, and the common welfare this calls him as consul to defend. Note the interweaving of *non tam me officium* with *quam res publica consulem ad communem salutem defendendam*.

ita tuli . . . ut eam (sc. *legem*) . . . **non abrogarem:** "in such a way that I did not/would not repeal." *Ita* restricts and defines; *ut . . . non* is a result clause. Cicero is substituting a higher "natural" law for the precise clauses of the *lex Tullia*, which he proposed (cf. *latio legis*) as consul earlier in 63 BCE. There is no logical or moral problem in supporting this plea of not guilty.

mihimet: dative of reference with the enclitic particle—*met* adding emphasis (A&G §146d)—qualifies Cicero's personal stake in the action (A&G §376–77; W64).

largitionem . . . idque recte factum esse: since *largitionem* is feminine, it cannot be the antecedent of *id*, which must refer to the whole acc. and infinitive phrase.

quid est quod impediat?: a characterizing relative clause taking the subjunctive after questions and negative statements implying a negative answer.

6. esse eiusdem severitatis: as with *est boni consulis* (cf. §4 above), the predicative genitive denotes what is characteristic, in this case not of a *severus* but of the abstract *severitas*.

Catilinam exitium . . . expulisse: compare *Cat.* 2.1, *L. Catilinam . . . pestem patriae nefarie molientem . . . ex urbe uel eiecimus vel emisimus*. As consul Cicero no doubt had the authority to expel Catiline from a meeting of the Senate, but it is not clear how he could expel Catiline from the whole city without some formal decree, such as the formal decree of the consul A. Gabinius expelling Lucius Lamia from Rome in 58 BCE. Hence *paene imperio* "virtually by command."

has partis . . . illam vero gravitatis severitatisque personam . . . : Cicero uses the image of a theatrical role to imply that his severe actions were imposed on his normally mild nature by his magistracy. He actually uses the notion of nature three times in this paragraph to mark the discrepancy between his innate temperament and actions forced on him by present circumstance: *quas me natura ipsa docuit . . . vici naturam . . . naturae meae consuetudinique servire* to introduce the ideology of the *patronus*, with its positive *misericordia* and *lenitas* (*humanitas*). Compare the same principle of balance between *misericordia* and *severitas* at *Off.*

1.88 *et tamen ita probanda est mansuetudo atque clementia ut adhibeatur rei publicae causa severitas*.

ad humanitatem: the Latin noun *humanitas*, here aligned with *lenitas*, *mansuetudo*, and *misericordia* and opposed to Cato's *severitas*, was developed by Cicero and his contemporary Varro to cover not only humane-ness (*philanthropia*), but social grace and refinement (as, e.g., *de Orat.* 1.27) and culture, even learning (*paideia*). Compare the later judgment of Gell. 13.17, claiming that Cicero and Varro extended the concept to include *eruditionem institutionemque in bonas artes*. In *Mur.* 9 Cicero will rely on his previous contrasts to expose Cato's ostensibly moral *severitas* as actual *inhumanitas*, hard heartedness, cruelty. (See also §76 below for a different sense of *inhumanitas*.) Of the many (mostly German) scholarly discussions, see Haffter 1967.

7. (Ser. Sulpici) conquestio: *conquestio* could be used to denote advocates' laments over their clients' potential victimization or the inflammatory protests with which prosecutors normally ended their accusation. Here Sulpicius has supposedly accused Cicero of neglecting their friendship in defending Murena's case against him. He has talked of *familiaritas* and *necessitudo*, two levels of friendship and commitment, of which the first speaks to intimate companionship and the second to obligations. Inviting the jury to act as umpires, Cicero now distinguishes between **(a)** his obligation to Sulpicius as a friend during the campaign *contra honorem Murenae*, and **(b)** acting *contra salutem Murenae*, as he would do by failing to defend Murena, let alone prosecuting him. The risk of losing citizen status (*salus* or *caput*) incurred by condemnation in a political trial was commonly referred to simply as *periculum* (§10), or more dramatically as *capitis dimicatio* (§8).

The ideology of defense rhetoric was intimately associated with the ideology of social solidarity among men of the governing class: just as rhetoric was valuable because it could defend the interest of the state and one's family, so the obligation to support one's friends (even if they were guilty) was one of the first principles taught to students of rhetoric. Compare this to *Inv.* 1.5: *hinc amicis quoque eorum certissimum et tutissimum praesidium comparatur.* The art of the politician and defense counsel gave him power, and he was obliged in return to use both the power of office and the gift of eloquence to protect members of his class and preserve their political survival (*salus*). Hence Cicero's claim (*de Orat.* 1.34) *perfecti oratoris moderatione et sapientia non solum ipsius dignitatem sed et privatorum plurimorum et universae rei publicae salutem maxume contineri.* This pride and sense of obligation, already assumed in *Inv.* and *Rhet. Her.*, is reiterated throughout *de Orat.* (55 BCE) from Cicero's personal introduction acknowledging his commitment as a senior statesman to *causae amicorum* (1.3; cf. 2.192, 201 *amicorum periculis*, 3.134 *in causis amicorum*). In fact, Crassus's opening encomium of rhetoric (Book 1, 32) stresses this power above others: "What is so lordly, so gentlemanly, so generous, as to bring aid to suppliants (i.e., men accused), to rouse up those struck down, to confer survival, to free from threats, and to preserve citizens in society?" (*quid tam porro regium, tam liberale, tam munificum, quam opem ferre supplicibus, excitare adflictos, dare salutem, liberare periculis, retinere homines in civitate?*) This general obligation felt by the elite to exercise their authority in support of the defense explains the recent increase in the number of defense advocates appearing in a single case, which Cicero criticizes at *Brut.* 207: *hoc quod nunc fit, ut causae singulae defenderentur a pluribus, quo nihil est vitiosius.* In the present case, Crassus and Hortensius would have had no special expertise in the details of Murena's trial, but served more as character witnesses to guarantee that the defendant was socially approved. Cicero, however, labors from the difficulty that he has bonds of goodwill with both accusers: that he is going against them needs special palliatives; cf. below (§8) his claiming that even when friends are the accusers (*amicis nostris accusantibus*) the obligation to defend should compel giving support. See for further information Craig 1981.

dixit me . . . oblitum . . . contra se defendere: here the reflexive pronoun *se* refers back to Sulpicius, the subject of the main clause (A&G §300,1; W 36).

satis facere cupio . . . vosque adhibere arbitros: *arbitri* were private individuals chosen by agreement of both parties in a civil dispute to propose a settlement that they would accept. Here the issue is one of obligation toward a friend.

me in petitione . . .: Cicero acknowledges (*et debuisse*) and claims to have fulfilled (*et praestitisse*) all the obligations of his *necessitudo* (bond, commitment) to Sulpicius.

So do we know whom Cicero supported during the election? He could have declared his support for two candidates, and he tells us here that Ser. Sulpicius was one of them. Who would the other be? NOT Murena, as Cicero makes clear by his omissions.

The elephant in the room here and throughout the speech is the rival candidate Decimus Silanus (RE 163), who is only mentioned once, in §83. Since he was asked to speak first in the Catilinarian debate, we can infer he was elected ahead of Murena, and he would have been the natural conservative candidate for Cicero to back. But apart from the advantage of suppressing the fact that there was available a perfectly conventional optimate colleague to share Murena's fight against Catiline, Silanus may have been a source of embarrassment because Cato had declared he would prosecute any candidate guilty of *ambitus* except Silanus, his own brother-in-law, if he should be liable to the charges (Plut. *Cato min.* 21.2). Throughout the speech, then, we are supposed to dismiss the thought of Silanus as a competitor and potential colleague with Sulpicius and/or Murena.

Nihil . . . quod esset: the imperfect subjunctive is both characteristic and contrary-to-fact, as in *quid est quod impediat* (§5), but it is more common in Latin to retain the indicative (as in *fugiendum fuit*, §11) when counterfactuals state a possibility or obligation. The possibility/obligation was a fact, even if it was not enacted (A&G §517b, c).

ab amico . . . postulandum. Abiit illud tempus: *ab* is the normal preposition with *postulare* to refer to the person from whom something is requested (A&G §396a). Cicero changes pace from the expansive tricolon *aut ab amico aut a gratioso aut a* *consule*, to the brusque cola *abiit illud tempus* and *ratio mutata est*. Objective circumstance needs a new policy, and this is backed up by the staccato anaphoras of *sic existimo, sic mihi persuadeo*, and the antithesis in §8 between *contra honorem/contra salutem*. Cicero returns to *honor* in §8.

quantum tu a me postulare ausus sis: here and throughout Cicero uses *postulare* "demand" of Servius's claims; cf. §46–47, where it is replaced by the more demanding (*ef*)*flagitare* and *postulatio*.

8. si tibi tum cum peteres consulatum studui, nunc: *studui* (Clark), *adfui* (Adamietz). The text is reconstructed on the basis of Quint. 11.1.68 *se studuisse petitioni Sulpicii*.

nunc cum Murenam ipsum petas: puns on the sense of legal and physical assault, opposing *petere* (aspire to) *consulatum* and *petere* (assail, attack) *ipsum*.

Atque hoc non modo non . . . potest: Cicero moves from declaring that he should not help his friend Sulpicius when he is attacking his other friend Murena, to the more extreme position that it is not only not praiseworthy but not even admissible to fail to defend even *alienissimos* (those who have no connection with us) just because our friend is prosecuting.

Mihi . . . amicitia est: the dative of possession with *esse* (A&G §373; W 63) places stress on the person claiming ownership.

Quae si causa non esset: imperfect subjunctive in a contrary-to-fact condition.

Neque enim iam mihi licet neque est integrum: Cicero reinforces his denial of obligation with a renewed stress on changed times; *iam* and *integrum* both declare it is too late. The word *integrum* refers to an uncompromised situation, when a man has a moral choice; to deny it is to reject the issue as already decided.

ut meum laborem hominum periculis sublevandis non impertiam: *impertire* (from *in* + *pars*, "giving a share") governs the dative: hence the dative gerundive *periculis sublevandis* (for the relief of men's risk in court) to convey his purpose, as it were *ut . . . pericula sublevarem*.

labores quos in petitione exceperis: again the text is reconstructed. A masculine antecedent is needed for *eos* (the text has only the neuter *praemia . . . tanta . . . sint data*). Hence various scholarly conjectures providing an appropriate verb to govern *labores*.

esse hominis et astuti et ingrati: once again the predicative use of the characterizing genitive (cf. §4, 6 above).

9. Quod si licet desinere, si te auctore: *te auctore* is abl. absolute (cf §1: *me rogante*). Cicero now involves Sulpicius himself (*si te auctore possum*) but implies that abstention from defending Murena would be a crime of indifference, arrogance, and cruelty, repeated in the forms *desidia*, *superbia*, and *improbitas*.

si nulla inertiae *infamia*: without Wesenberg's supplement the genitive *inertiae* would need to be governed by an abstract noun parallel to *turpitudo* and *culpa*.

amicorum neglectio: the noun ("act of neglect") occurs here for the first time, instead of the generic *negligentia*, and avoids confusion between objective (neglecting friends) and possessive genitive (neglect by friends).

causa est eius modi quam . . . possit: *eius modi* is a genitive phrase of quality equivalent to *talis* (A&G §345a) and so able to introduce a consecutive clause (A&G §537.2).

industrius . . . misericors . . . officiosus: these counter the three vicious attitudes (*desidiam*, *superbiam*, *improbitatem*) listed above.

te advocato illum ipsum . . . causa cadere: Cicero turns his argument into a form most flattering for Servius, viz. that his professionalism would make him feel shame if even his client's antagonist should botch his case on formal grounds. For *causa cadere* "to fail in his plea," see *de Orat.* 1.166 *cum Hypsaeus . . . a M. Crasso praetore contenderet ut ei quem defendebat causa cadere* *liceret, Cn. autem Octauius . . . recusaret ne aduersarius causa caderet ac ne is pro quo ipse diceret turpi tutelae iudicio . . . stultitia aduersarii liberaretur* (also 167).

quem contra veneris: *contra* was originally adverbial; as a preposition it usually precedes the noun, but Latin permits the reverse order (called *anastrophe*) with bisyllablic adverbial prepositions like *supra, infra, circum.*

10. Ego uero . . . ipse me existimarem nefarium . . . crudelem . . . superbum: Cicero returns to the three vices of the previous section, allocating each to one aspect of Murena as a friend in misfortune, and Rome's consul.

tuam gratiam magni aestimari: *magni,* the genitive of value with *aestimari* (A&G §352 n.; W 72 (7)) "to hold in great respect" goes beyond *familiaritas.* Cicero flatters Servius with the notion that most public men would set a high value on his goodwill.

non secus ac si: "not otherwise than if/just as if." For this use of *atque/ac,* see A&G §407d, 524; W 251. Cicero's point is not the actual position of Cicero's brother Quintus, newly elected praetor for 62 BCE, but the devotion to be expected between brothers.

crudelem si misero: *miser* may trigger expectations of the formal *miseratio* (§85–90), which will end Cicero's impassioned plea.

11. Intellego, iudices, tris . . . partis fuisse: *tris* and *partis* are I-stem accusative plurals (A&G §67). At this point Cicero moves to material which will have been partly treated by Hortensius, but 2–10 have only dealt with his personal involvement. The three categories treated in the accusation, *reprehensio vitae, contentio dignitatis,* and *crimina ambitus,* receive progressively expanding treatment. Again Quintilian singles out this speech for the excellence of its *partitio* (4.5.12), holding it up to his pupils as a model of lucidity and conciseness. Roman tradition expected defense speeches to include a survey of the defendant's past life, and juries took it as much into account as the actual rebuttal of the technical charges. When the defendant was young, wealthy, and reasonably attractive, he was a natural target for accusations of being a playboy or spendthrift, and allegations of, for example, sexual hanky-panky would serve to rouse a possibly indifferent jury. On the role of "character" in forming Roman opinion, see Edwards 1993, and on Cicero's use of it in his defenses and in *Pro Murena*, May 1988.

§11–14 REPREHENSIO VITAE

lex . . . quaedam accusatoria: Cicero belittles the charges against Murena as an automatic practice of accusers. The supreme example of this response is his *Pro Caelio*, defending Caelius Rufus in 56 BCE. Compare his rejection of the prosecution's allegations in *Cael.* 6 *aliud est male dicere, aliud accusare* developed in 7–8. But in defending Murena, Cicero is only the last of three advocates, and he mentions only the charges he can easily dismiss, Murena's dancing at parties and more generally his time in Asia, which could include luxury on leave from the battlefield but belongs to his service against Mithridates. In fact, these brief paragraphs seem to cover Murena's first service in Asia as a young man on his father's staff 20 years earlier, the potential follies of a young man between 17 and 20. Given Murena's present age, his behavior as a young man is barely relevant.

Obiecta est enim Asia . . . quam ob rem non Asiae nomen obiciendum: in fact the adversaries must have specifically reproached Murena with the *voluptas* and *luxuria* they go on to criticize, cf. §12. *Et si habet Asia suspicionem*, as Adamietz notes, Asia was already suspect as a source of indulgence and luxurious pleasure when Romans first engaged with Antiochus (Liv. 34.4.3). From the time that Attalus of Pergamum bequeathed his empire to Rome around 130 BCE, Romans were in this new province of Asia not just on military expeditions but as peaceful and profiteering residents and businessmen. Polybius 31.25 quotes as marks of moral decline the elder Cato's claim that a shift of values had made a pretty boy-slave cost more than a ploughman and a fancy fish more than local meat. Romans repeatedly associated luxury and extravagance with the contact of their armies with the cities of Asia. Thus Sallust *Cat.* 13, repeating what was already a cliché:

> huc accedebat quod L Sulla exercitum quem in Asia ductaverat quo sibi fidum faceret contra morem maiorum luxuriose nimisque liberaliter habuerat, loca amoena, voluptaria facile in otio ferocis militum animos molliverant. Ibi primum insuevit exercitus populi Romani amare potare.

> Add to this that Sulla had treated the army he led into Asia, in order to make it loyal to himself, so luxuriously and generously in violation of ancestral custom; these agreeable and pleasant places had easily softened the soldiers' fierce spirits with leisure. This was the first time the Roman army formed the habit of whoring and drinking. . . .

Instead Murena should be praised for living with restraint, unless the antagonists can mention some scandal incurred in Asia or brought back home from there.

Qui si . . . non meruisset . . . videretur: a mixed conditional (past and present contrary-to-fact).

An cum: "Or is it that." *An*, usually introducing an alternative question (*utrum . . . an*), is often used to express irony or suggest a preferred explanation.

sedere in equis: Roman custom placed younger sons in their father's triumphal chariot, and teenage *praetextati* on the chariot horses (cf. Augustus, who according to Suet. *Tib.* 6, set Marcellus on the right-hand trace horse of his chariot, relegating Tiberius to the less prestigious left-hand trace horse). Here Cicero is arguing that if even boys below military age took part in their fathers' triumphs, Murena, being of military age, should surely not have shunned (*fugiendum fuit*) campaigning in Asia with the chance to win military decorations and almost share in his father's triumph. The point of *paene* here is that his father was awarded a triumph but seems not to have lived to celebrate it.

12. magno adiumento . . . solacio . . . gratulationi: another tricolon, this time of predicative datives or the dative of purpose/ end (A&G §382; W 67–68), but unlike the first two datives, the predicative use of *gratulationi* is exceptional and striking. Compare the three increasing cola (often called tricolon crescendo) with the predicative use of the genitive: *meruisse . . . virtutis /, patre imper- atore libentissime meruisse pietatis, / finem stipendiorum . . . victo- riam ac triumphum fuisse felicitatis fuit*, and the third cluster: *laus familiae, memoria generi, honos et gloria nomini*, which prepares the audience for Cicero's exaltation of Murena's family.

quod tum populus . . . solum gerebat: in fact Appian's *Mithri- datic Wars* (and the corresponding chapter of Magie 1950, esp. 242–45) suggest that his father's campaigns in the second Mithri- datic war were both unprovoked and unsuccessful. In 81 BCE, Sulla ordered him back to Rome, but allowed him a triumph. Magie comments: "Eighteen years later, Cicero had the hardihood to refer to this outrageous war as a victory which brought glory and honor to Murena's house." Cicero has suppressed the fact that father Murena renewed hostilities in 84 BCE contrary to the Peace of Dardanus and against the express orders of the Senate. The theme here is *laus*, linking the praise Murena deserves for living soberly in Asia with the next topic, Murena's *familia* and *genus*. Murena's qualities as a warrior mark his valor, his willingness to serve under his father, his piety, and most important, the culmina- tion of Murena's years of campaigning in his father's triumph was a mark of divine blessing. *Felicitas* is the most significant of the four excellences that Cicero requires of a great general in his earlier speech *De imperio Gnaei Pompei* 27.

nihil . . . loci est, quod omnia laus occupavit: *loci* is a partitive genitive (A&G §346; W 77); the spatial metaphor is unusual.

13. Saltatorem: it is most unlikely that Servius and his *subscrip- tores* had produced the charge of being a "dancer" out of the blue. Did it spring from allegations (not acknowledged by Cicero) of bad behavior or debauchery committed by Licinius Murena after returning from military service? Did his antagonists depict him as a party animal like Verres and his associates or Catiline's cronies, who danced *nudi* (not naked but clad only in a tunic or *subligaculum*); cf. *Verr.* 2.3.23; *Cat.* 2.23; *Pis.* 22? Our *locus classicus* for dancing as ill-becoming a consul is Gabinius, against whom Cicero's chief sources of mockery were his carefully curled hairstyle and his dancing (*saltatrix calamistrata, Red. Sen.* 13), and Nepos, who introduced his *Lives of Foreign Generals* with an expression of surprise that Greek biographers praised Epaminondas of Thebes for his skillful dancing and flute-playing. Roman gentlemen did not dance: hence Demea's mockery of Micio dancing with a skipping rope between his daughter-in-law and a sex-slave (Ter. *Ad.* 752) and Cicero's report that the orator Titius pranced so much as he spoke that his name was given to a kind of dance (*Brut.* 225). However, we need to distinguish such solo performance from dancing in a religious rite and note the changing associations of *saltare* with the coming of pantomime under Augustus. Cicero maintains that no one dances unless drunk, *nemo fere saltat sobrius*. But such behavior may have been pretty common in the parties of the younger generation. And what form did this dancing take? We are not talking about dancing with a sexual partner or as part of a male group. Perhaps the best evidence is the Ionic solo number performed by Plautus's Pseudolus (*Ps.* 1274), a staggering display of teetering pyrotechnics. For ladies dancing, cf. Sempronia in Sall. *Cat.* 25 *saltare elegantius quam necesse est probae* and Horace *Od.* 2.12.19 on Licymnia dancing (*ludere*) ceremonially with other women.

ista sis auctoritate: a noun with adjective in the ablative case (ablative of quality) can qualify another noun or pronoun (A&G §415; W 43.5, and 83).

consulem populi Romani: the full phrase puts an unusual stress on the direct relation of magistrate and electoral body, implying that to abuse Murena is to abuse "the people's consul," an insult to the body that elected him. This recalls the stress of *populus Romanus*, named three times in §1–2.

14. Bene habet: using the idiom of the umpire in arena combat, Cicero claims his case can rest (Quint. 9.2.26). The defense of

Murena's lifestyle was simply a foundation on which Cicero will set out the second element of the charge, the *contentio dignitatis* or contest in merit.

§15–53 CONTENTIO DIGNITATIS

§15–18: a defense of Murena's *genus* and contrast with the recent lack of distinction of Sulpicius's ancient family, bolstered by examples from the last century and a modest (?) allusion to his record as both consul and son of a knight (*equitis filius*). Like the *reprehensio uitae*, this section, occupying two-fifths of the whole speech, has nothing to do with the specific charges (which Cicero does not reach until well after §54), but Roman juries trying the sort of offences committed by their peers looked beyond the evidence for the individual charges and the specific type of offence to the man's whole record and career and inclined toward indulgence. Modern juries too can give verdicts contrary to the apparent facts but reflecting their bias, as in the acquittals of Morgenthaler (on charges of running illegal abortion clinics) in Canada and O. J. Simpson in the United States. On this see Riggsby 1997.

§18: comparison of their quaestorships.

§19–21: Servius's urbana militia, contrasted with Murena's position as legatus to the great Lucullus (present in court; his previous dispatches attest to Murena's service).

§22–31 studiorum atque artium contentio: parallel and antithetical contrast of warfare and jurisprudence.

(23) Separation of Sulpicius's personal virtues from his profession leads to substitution of dicendi facultas (24) as a factor in electing a consul able to control the mob and resist bribery.

(25–26) Lack of dignity in jurisprudence, parodic history, and mock illustration of procedure in civil law and ingenuity of jurisconsults in getting round ancestral law

(28) Resumes from 25 the weaknesses of jurisprudence: lack of dignity and limitation of material, now available to all, and useless except during civil processes, equally adaptable to both parties in a dispute.

(30) A return to eloquence; new pairing of *ars imperatoris* and *ars oratoris boni*. Superiority of military skill eclipses the civilian arts.

§32–34: Cato's belittling of the war with Mithridates (see §31 below: "Retrospective of the Newly Ended Mithridatic War"), including (§33) Lucullus's achievements and the seriousness of the war for which Roman people conferred an overarching command on Pompey. This enemy and this war proved Murena's courage, good judgment, and energy, and his service had no less dignity to earn him the consulship than our forensis industria.

§35–40: resumes chronological sequence through the rivals' *cursus honorum*, with praetorships of 65 BCE. Servius's relative success and unreliability of electorate.

(37) Murena was handicapped by the lack of public games and the fact that Lucullus had not yet been granted his triumph and his forces could not return to Rome.

(37–38) on the support of veteran soldiers and

(39–40) on the popularity of games.

§41–42: Cicero returns to parity of *forensis opera* with military service to consider the advantages of Murena's praetorship, his choice of a province and success in governing it, as opposed to (§42) Sulpicius's grim assignment of investigating embezzlement.

§43: their equal *dignitas* offset by unequal fortune in provincial assignments.

§44–49: at this point Cicero turns to the actual electoral campaign and Sulpicius's big mistake: the threat of prosecution that showed his expectation of defeat and distracted him from conducting his candidacy. The unwelcome demands for a new bribery law (48–49) and growing popular fear at Catiline's increased confidence.

§50–53: a blow-by-blow account of events since mid-October.

§53: the power of sudden shifts of support; given Murena's merits it is not surprising that Catiline's sudden hope of a consulship resulted in increased support for Murena.

15. dignitatem generis . . . par est: Cicero starts from *dignitas* (status), shifting the notion of *par est* (i.e., it is right and fair) to the literal parity of *ista* (i.e., *cetera ornamenta*) and insisting that Servius and Murena are so well matched that Murena could not be outdone in prestige (Clark's edition inserts *a te*) nor outdo (*superarit = superauerit*, the contracted perfect subjunctive in a consecutive clause). This turns hostile with the accusation that Servius has expressed contempt for Murena's family. No doubt Servius had pointed to the fact that Murena's family came from outside Rome and his father had not held the consulship, but Cicero turns this into the contempt of a patrician for any non-patrician. Given that only 14 patrician families survived in this generation (Augustus would add to their number) the assumptions attributed by Cicero to Sulpicius would alienate a large majority of even his elite audience.

dignitate vinci . . . dignitate superarit: two different ablative uses of *dignitas*, instrumental and ablative of specification respectively (A&G §409–11, 418; W 43, 1 and 55) support the superiority of Murena. See also *superavi dignitate*, §17 below.

facis ut rursus plebes in Aventinum . . .: in the first generation of the republic, Rome's fighting force (equivalent to the plebs) was summoned by its informal leaders to the Aventine hill beyond the city walls in a form of a strike (Liv. 2. 28 and 32–33) until the dispute was resolved by the election of tribunes to act as patrons and magistrates of the *plebs*.

amplae et honestae: well-chosen words suggesting respectability through wealth. The positive degree applies to the ancestors of Murena who achieved the praetorship, but Cicero rises to the superlative of these same epithets for his father's earning of a triumph; the prestige of that military success made his son's access to the consulship easier, since he was seeking an office to which his father had been entitled but (we are to understand) was forestalled by death from achieving.

hoc faciliorem . . . quod: "the following fact . . . namely that." The pronoun *hoc* anticipates the following substantive clause, which *quod* introduces (A&G §584; W 266).

16. nobilitas: variously defined by modern scholars (e.g., Brunt 1982, Shackleton Bailey 1986), *nobilitas* in its least questioned form means having a consular father, and its opposite *novitas* is predicated of men whose fathers have not been consul, but such men may have been more remotely descended from consuls, like Sulpicius, whose consular ancestors went back to the fifth century, or Caesar, whose family produced two consuls and a praetor between 95 and 90 BCE, and another consul in 64 BCE (a family could not often afford the cost of two sons as career statesmen). A large number of senators will have fallen between the two extremes as children of praetors (like Murena) or members of families which had missed out on the consulship for a generation.

Pater . . . equestri loco, avus . . . celebratus: it is a mistake to calibrate nobility on the basis of Cicero's usage, which will be governed by rhetorical considerations. If he wants to upgrade the standing of Murena's ancestors, he will argue differently and even inconsistently with his arguments for downgrading Sulpicius's immediate family. And the status of patricians was not automatically noble or new since only 14 patrician families survived by the 60s BCE.

litteratis et historicis: men of education and (a far smaller category) writers of history, who used material drawn from ancient records. Cicero balances these two smaller categories against the all-inclusive *populo* and the politically prominent *suffragatoribus*.

suffragatoribus: not voters as such but electoral supporters who helped to bring out the vote of individuals in their voting unit.

ex annalium vetustate: *annalium* could denote either priestly records (e.g., Ov. *Fast.* 1.7 *sacra . . . annalibus edita priscis*), prose histories organized year-by-year, or historical poems like Ennius's eighteen books of *Annales*. When and how the term gained currency is a matter of some dispute: see Gildenhard 2003.

in nostrum numerum adgregare: with ironic modesty Cicero assimilates Servius to his own case, that of a man from an equestrian not a senatorial family, turning it into a compliment to Servius's own personal efforts, which had made him seem worthy of the highest distinction (*amplus* again).

quod virtute industriaque perfecisti: Cicero's generation saw an ideological opposition develop between those newcomers whose success was credited to merit and effort and men born to the nobility. Compare to §17 below *ut aditus ad consulatum posthac . . . non magis nobilitati quam virtuti pateret*, and the new consul Marius speaking in Sallust *Jug.* 85: *vetus nobilitas, maiorum fortia facta . . . omnia haec praesidio adsunt; mihi spes omnes in memet sitae quas necesse est virtute et innocentia tutari.*

Q. Pompeio . . . M. Aemilio: this is the first substantial exemplum of many political role models: Q. Pompeius (RE 2, cos. 141 BCE and unrelated to Cicero's contemporary, the general Pompey) is singled out in Cicero *Brutus* 96 as *non contemptus orator temporibus illis . . . qui summos honores homo per se cognitus . . . est adeptus*; M. Aemilius Scaurus (RE 140, cos. 115 BCE), *homo nobilis impiger factiosus avidus potentiae honoris divitiarum ceterum vitia sua callide occultans* (Sallust *Jug.* 15), reached the consulship later, but lived to wield power and influence for a further 20–25 years through his position as *princeps senatus*. He would die in 89 BCE as father-in-law of Sulla, the consul of 88 BCE and future dictator. Scaurus's immediate ancestors had not held office (Ascon. Intro. Cic. *Scaur.: ita fuit patricius ut tribus supra eum aetatibus iacuerit domus eius fortuna, nam neque pater neque auus neque etiam proavus ut puto propter tenues opes et nullam vitae industriam honores adepti sunt*). Shackleton Bailey 1979 argues against the manuscript reading *minus in Q. Pompeio*, proposing *plus*. Cicero is arguing that it was if anything more of an achievement to rise to high office, like Aemilius Scaurus or, we hope, Sulpicius himself, when one's noble ancestors had fallen away than to create the nobility of one's family from scratch. The argument is thus an oblique compliment to Sulpicius.

prope intermortuam: *prope* serves to soften the rather bold *intermortuam*; cf. *Pis.* 16 *intermortuis Catilinae reliquiis.*

17. ignobilitas: compare *Tusc.* 5.103 *ignobilitas aut humilitas.* Cicero must have known that many in his elite audience saw him as an intruder: cf. Sallust *Cat.* 23 *antea pleraque nobilitas invidia aestuabat et quasi pollui consultatum credebant si eum quamvis egregius homo novus adeptus foret.* This is very strong language; cf. for *aestuare Har. Resp.* 2 *ille exsanguis et aestuans repente ex curia se proripuit.* Sallust notes that the danger from Catiline made the nobility forget both jealousy and snobbishness (*superbia*). Sallust was himself a *homo novus*, coming from Amiternum in central Italy. On *homines novi*, see Wiseman 1971.

Curiis, Catonibus, Pompeiis: Cicero starts from the heroes of the middle republic: Manius Curius Dentatus (cos. I 290), who helped to defeat Pyrrhus in the early third century, the elder Cato (cos. 195), and Q. Pompeius (see above). The gloss *novis hominibus* clashes literally with *antiquis . . . viris* and was rightly deleted by Boot.

his recentibus: along with Marius (cos. 107, 104–100, 87, see Wiseman 1971 §248) Cicero names the consuls of 98 BCE (T. Didius [RE 5], Wiseman 1971 §156) and 94 BCE (C. Coelius Caldus, RE Coelius 127), men distinguished both in warfare (Didius triumphed twice and Coelius won ten major battles) and in politics: Coelius as tribune carried the last of the ballot laws, extending the secret ballot to trials for *perduellio.*

id agebam: *iacebant* (Σ), *id agebam* (Clark); does this pick up *multis viris fortibus . . . commemorandis*, i.e., men who should have been recorded? The alternative first person *iacebam* does not give sense. But *putabam* supports Badham's *id agebam* and ties in with *meo labore*, "I whose purpose it was by mentioning these ancient and recent men, to ensure that ignobility of birth was not made a

reproach to good men." The center of gravity of this sentence is
the main clause.

cum duobus patriciis: there were two patrician candidates in 64
BCE, the wicked (*improbissimo*) Catiline and the respectable
(*modestissimo atque optimo*) P. Sulpicius Galba. Cicero's
explanation—that he excelled Catiline in status and Galba in popularity and influence—makes indirectly his unvoiced argument
why Murena defeated Sulpicius Rufus.

non arbitrabar . . . accusatores esse dicturos. The future infinitive is used to express the future tense in *oratio obliqua* (A&G
§584; W 266).

18. The issue of birth is resolved (as with Murena's *familia vetus et
inlustris*) by assimilating the Licinii Murenae upward: each of the
rival candidates is treated as having high status.

Omittamus igitur . . . videamus cetera: Roman practice con-
trolling the age at which a man could seek office and the intervals
that had to occur between offices meant that men of the same age
would be repeatedly pitted against each other, providing these material comparisons. In his citation of Sulpicius's complaint, Cicero
fosters the impression that his antagonist is acting petulantly.

sum ego factus prior: masks a complexity in the presentation of
Roman electoral results. While voting in elections for praetors and
consuls began with the highest social classes and might not proceed
beyond the second class if candidates had already got the necessary
majority of voting units, all 35 voting units voted simultaneously in
the *comitia tributa* for the 20 quaestors. Each tribal unit recorded
its list of candidates, but the order in which the units reported
their choice was determined by lot. Once a candidate had a majority, the choices of the remaining units were not reported but
went on record. Sulpicius scored his electoral majority *prior*, i.e.,
before Murena, but each man's support could be identified. See
Taylor 1966: 82–85. To be *factus prior* then was a matter of timing
(*ordinem renuntiationis*), not popularity (*ordinem dignitatis*). The
announcement entailed sequence (*gradus*) and determined

ranking. Given that there were 20 places for the quaestorship, *prior* could mask a rather large gap in popular success.

neque . . . vestrum quemquam fugit: so always the alternative genitive plural ending *um* serves as the partitive of *nos* and *vos* "any (one) of you."

Sed . . . pari momento sortis fuit: "met the same factor of the lot," i.e., "had more or less equal fortune" (Zetzel 2009). We do not know anything about the *lex Titia* (presumably a law passed by Titius as tribune in 98 BCE) which gave Murena (*hic* = my client) his easy area of responsibility, but Sulpicius would have been held responsible for all the conflicts and dissatisfactions of Ostia and the fluctuating grain supply, which Cicero claims provoked cries of sympathy (*adclamari*) for the man appointed.

Consedit: each man's reputation was inert during his quaestorship, since the lot gave candidates no scope or battleground on which their excellence might charge forward and be recognized.

campum . . . excurrere: develops a metaphor of equestrian prowess, with which compare *Phil.* 14.17 *magnus est in re p. campus . . . multis apertus cursus ad laudem.*

19. Reliqui temporis spatium: that is, the ten years from the men's quaestorships of 75 to the praetorships of 65 BCE, which had been used by the rivals in different ways (*dissimillima ratione tractatum*).

hanc urbanam militiam: measures Servius's activities by the standards of warfare, itemizing them with three low-key verbs: *respondendi*, giving his formal advice to the client; *scribendi*, putting the legal issue in words, phrasing it; and *cavendi*, taking precautions against risk (so also, e.g., *de Orat.*1.212 *et ad respondendum et ad agendum et ad cavendum peritus*). The negative sounding *cavere* was particularly characteristic of jurisconsults.

sollicitudinis ac stomachi: the alliteration stresses the combination of psychological and physical discomfort. On *stomachus, stomachari* see now Hoffer 2007.

didicit . . . exsorbuit: a series of seven verbs moves through Servius's training and toil to his essential submission to clients.

praesto multis fuit: *praesto esse*, like *adesse* but subordinating the jurisconsult, puts him at a disadvantage, just as his being subject to another's *arbitrium* suggests the unfreedom of a slave. To some extent this depreciation, which may well have offended Sulpicius, is canceled by the last comment on the *magna laus* of toiling on an expertise that will benefit so many.

exsorbuit: we too talk of swallowing insults or discomfort. The intensive prefix continues the intensification of the preceeding *perpeti* and *per-ferre* and is itself echoed by the intensive *e-laborare* in the next sentence.

20. Fortissimo et sapientissimo: the epithets seem chosen to combine military and civilian virtues; Cicero's praise for Lucullus (present in the audience of supporters) indirectly praises Murena, his *legatus*. But Murena is also better served than Servius was in §19 by the active verbs of military initiative and **duxit . . . contulit . . . conseruit . . . fudit . . . cepit.** After his quaestorship Murena would be eligible for a junior command and is represented as directing his own military force in victorious battle and siege warfare—we know he besieged Amisus and took it by storm (Plut. *Luc.* 15, *Imp. Pomp.* 21).

Asiam istam . . . delicatam . . . sic obiit: *obire* is used of meeting or being exposed to bad things, like danger or death, as in *mortem obire* "to die." Asia is treated as a moral hazard (*istam* = the place mentioned and made a reproach by Servius or Cato. Compare this to Cicero's account of the Syracusan Lido as a *litus delicatissimum* in *Verr.* 2.5.104).

neque avaritiae . . . maximo in bello: Cicero denies any greed or self-indulgence in Murena's record. He insists on the greatness of this war (see Cato's belittling of it in §31) and Murena's independence in what certainly was a far-ranging series of campaigns confirmed by Cicero's allusion to Lucullus's condoning possible misrepresentation *licentia fingendi*, in face of the civic danger to which Murena was exposed.

publicis litteris: these claims are openly available and must come from an official letter sent by Lucullus to the Senate, which would have been read out in a *frequens senatus* mustered to consider his claim to a triumph. See Ryan 1998. In any case, Cicero has his cake and eats it, turning Lucullus's testimonial into a proof of his generosity (*neque ambitiosus . . . neque inuidus*).

in communicanda gloria: for the gerund *in communicando* with direct object *gloriam*. When a gerund would govern a direct object, the gerundive (as an adjective agreeing with the noun in gender and number) is generally used, but with the noun undergoing a case change to match it.

21. Summa . . . honestas . . . dignitas: Cicero feigns willingness to give equal honor to the civil and military careers, but blames Servius for making it necessary for Cicero to reaffirm the value of warfare.

agitat rem militarem, insectatur . . . legationem: Servius's denunciation of Murena's military service is made more absurd by the corollary that he supposedly thinks the consulship should be won by constant attendance. For the combination of *agitare* and *insectare*, cf. *Leg.* 1.40 and, e.g., *Cael.* 16 *insectare innocentiam*.

adsiduitatis . . . cotidianarum: given the recent and continuing political crisis of Catiline's threatened coup, Cicero does not need to point the irony of this image.

'Apud exercitum mihi fueris': *mihi* is a sophisticated use of the ethical dative (A&G §380;W 66), which does not function like a literal indirect object, or even a dative of disadvantage, but always implies that the person in the dative is affected or concerned by the action of the subject.

qui in foro habitarint: for *habitare* "frequenting," cf. *de Orat.* 1.264 *qui habitant in subselliis* (the supporters' benches in a court), *Brut.* 305 *in rostris*.

ista nostra adsiduitas: the phrase makes an equally smart use of personal pronouns as Cicero identifies his own civilian career with Servius's *adsiduitas*.

quantum . . . fastidi . . . satietatis: these are partitive genitives (A&G §346; W 77). Cicero revives the image of indigestion evoked by *stomachus* in §19.

Mihi quidem vehementer . . . superavi: Cicero offsets his boast of the *gratia* of political exposure with a competing claim of avoiding surfeit with great effort.

et tu item fortasse: the malice is further softened by being shared.

utrique nostrum desiderium nihil obfuisset: "it would have done us no harm to be missed," nicely understated.

22. ad studiorum . . . revertamur: here Cicero launches into his celebrated mock comparison of the heroics of jurisprudence and campaigning. Cicero himself studied jurisprudence with both Q. Mucius Scaevola Augur (cos. 117) and his cousin the more famous Scaevola Pontifex. In fact, once removed from the demands of this brief, he offers an encomium of the importance of jurisprudence and its potential to be systematized as an art in *de Orat.* beginning at 1.170 and reaching a climactic conclusion at 1.200 with the honor and dignity of the retired jurist whose home is *quasi oraculum civitatis* (see esp. §189–91, and Fantham 2004: ch.4). Cicero leads into what became a well-known rhetorical exercise. Here he talks of *studiorum atque artium contentio* because he wants to subdivide the distinction in civil life between oratory and jurisprudence, but when Quintilian illustrates this thesis, he gives as examples of the exercise in comparison *rusticane vita an urbana potior*, then *iuris periti an militaris viri laus maior*, a clear allusion to this passage in *Mur*.

qui potest dubitari: "how can it be doubted," note the passive infinitive. The adverb *quī* (A&G §150b; W 185–87) is particularly common in the form *qui potest* and similar idioms with *posse*.

multo plus adferat dignitatis: this concept articulates the following argument, which is also complicated by inserting the third art, eloquence, as a plainly superior rival to jurisprudence in civilian life. Compare the articulating sentences: (§24) *summa dignitas est in iis qui militari laude antecellunt . . . Gravis etiam illa est et plena dignitatis dicendi facultas . . .* and (§25) *primum dignitas in tam tenui scientia non potest esse.*

gloria: naturally won by success in *res militaris*, there is some irony in its application here to the succesful practice of *ius civile*.

Vigilas tu . . . cantus exsuscitat: traditionally these private consultations began at cockcrow, before dawn and well before the working day. Compare Hor. *Ep.* 2.1.104–5 *Romae dulce diu fuit et sollemne /reclusa mane domo vigilare, clienti promere iura* and *Sat.* 1.1.10 *sub galli cantum consultor ubi ostia pulsat.* Cicero follows a set of four antitheses between the jurist's routine and the soldier's deeds with an inversion of order in two antitheses starting at *ille tenet.* This passage was probably the inspiration for Ovid's antithetical comparisons of soldier and lover in *Am.* 1.9, and is much loved by Quintilian, who quotes it at 9.2.100 (reading *contendit* as an example of "Comparison") and 9.3.32 (reading *intendit*, and *consultores tui*) under "Repetition." This whole sequence combines both verbal wit (*dicacitas*) and the more conceptual *facetiae*, continuous humorous characterization. On these contrasted types of wit, see Cicero's discussion in *de Orat.* 2.216–89, esp. 218.

bucinarum: for the bugle (so also *Verr.* 2.4.96) calling reveille, cf. *classicum* in the topos envying those who are not roused by the call to battle at Virg. *Georg.* 2.539, Hor. *Epod.* 2.5, Tibullus 1.1.4, Lucan 4.394.

actionem instituis . . . aciem instruit: the wording combines a play on sense, "drawing up" an action and a battle line and on sound.

caves . . . ne urbes . . . capiantur: another play on legal *cavere*, adding *capere* in the double sense of being deceived or tricked at law, and of a camp or city being taken by storm.

ille tenet et scit: another defensive parallel, between fending off an enemy force and excluding drainwater (*aquae pluviae*). This is an instance of the category of suits on *stillicidium*, *Orator* 72. Roman property law included injunctions to a neighbor against draining water onto property and regulations for defining a property line (*regendis finibus*) as contrasted with the ultimate Roman goal of extending empire (*propagandis finibus*).

nimirum: (= *ni* + *mirum*) "obviously," "unsurprisingly," favored by Cicero (72 instances) over the more conventional *non mirum* of §24 below. Praise of military achievement must have been the most common and ready theme on which young orators trained.

quod sentio: the antecedent of *quod* has been omitted, as is often the case when the antecedent is indefinite or obvious (A&G §307c).

Haec nomen ... haec ... aeternam gloriam ... haec orbem terrarum parere huic imperio peperit: a tricolon crescendo with anaphora, building up from *populus* to *urbs* to *imperium*, is followed by a second anaphora *omnes urbanae res, omnia haec nostra praeclara studia*, which sneaks in oratory through the allusion to civic life *forensis laus et industria*.

in tutela ac praesidio bellicae virtutis: for *bellicus*, cf. *laus bellica*, *Brut.* 84; *gloria bellica*, *Off.* 1.61. But *tutela* is essentially legal and civilian.

increpuit ... ilico ... conticiscunt: Cicero is using the language of sound: *increpare* literally denoting a sharp rebuke, is also used of, e.g., the crack of a whip: it suggests rousing citizens to action, while *conticiscere*, the intensive of *con+taceo*, marks its opposite as the civilian arts are silenced: cf. *Brut.* 324 *perterritum armis hoc studium nostrum conticuit subito et obmutuit* (as the Roman proverb had it "*silent leges inter arma*," *Pro Mil.*11).

tumultus: stands for civil disturbance, either at Rome or in Italy itself, but his fear of the impending uprising of Catiline also keeps it very much in Cicero's thoughts.

23. tamquam filiolam: the gender of most abstract arts invited wordplay on a maiden or daughter inviting a father's tender affection or requiring protection; cf. *de Oratore* 1.234, where jurisprudence is an ill-groomed and undowered maiden (*incompta et indotata* treated *tanquam ancillulam pedisequamque*) and the word play at *Brut.* 324 where Cicero sees himself and Brutus as *quasi tutores*, left to protect *orba eloquentia . . . adulta virgo ab amatorum impetus quantum possumus*, and *Fam.* 3.11.3 on the *res publica* as an orphaned girl.

istud nescio quid: *nescio quid* does not introduce an indirect question, but is used as an indefinite pronoun, "something or other" (A&G §575d).

quid quod tanto opere: I support Shackleton Bailey's proposal, *tanta opera* "with such personal effort" instead of the pointless *tanto opere*, incongruous with *discere*. The two indefinites introduce a hint of contempt, which Cicero instantly thrusts away by contrasting the personal merits of self-control, dignity, justice, integrity, by which Servius has shown himself worthy of election to the consulship or any other office.

non dicam . . . sed illud dicam: again he limits his negative with a specific criticism. **munitam . . . viam:** *munire* "to construct a road" is a vivid instance of one of the strongest metaphors in Latin, making a way or path. See, e.g., *Rosc. Am.* 140; *Verr.* 2.1.64; *Leg. Agr.* 2.17.

Omnes enim artes, quae . . . concilient: the subjunctive defines the arts in question as being able to win over public support. Cicero then launches a new claim, viz. that the arts which matter must offer utility, advantage, and dignity, but he will leave aside explicit comment on utility. From §24–§26 the theme is *dignitas*, prestige or stature.

24. dicendi facultas: divided into the three audiences of the Roman orator's three functions: addressing Senate, people, and the juries of lawcourts (*eorum qui res iudicant mentes*). Politically, the good conservative had to control the riots stirred up by tribunes (*tribunicios furores*), especially in the 70s BCE after Sulla's legislation had deprived tribunes of their legislative powers and prohibited them from standing for higher office. He also was expected to oppose the squandering of public wealth (*largitio*) as Cicero had begun his consulship by opposing Rullus's agrarian legislation.

Quaeritur consul . . . resistat: this is the optimate ideal, a consul who will control popular demands, whether from tribunes or the assembly. In the 15 years after Sulla stripped the tribunate of its legislative powers, tribunes led agitations until their powers were restored in 70 BCE, but they then returned to using those legislative powers to incite the assemblies (cf. *furores . . . concitatum*). After this it comes as a surprise when Cicero adds that the consul should resist bribery, implying not electoral malpractice but bribery of the people by democratic/demagogic measures. The eloquence required to sway the people could be found (as Cicero knew) outside the elite, promoting the election of *homines saepe etiam non nobiles*, just as he, the new man, was preferred for the consulship he now holds.

25. tam tenui scientia: although *tenuis* will become a key word of praise for refinement in Callimachean aesthetics, it is never used favorably by Cicero, whose values inclined to the ample rather than the austere. For its social reference, see §47 and §70 below; its literary and social ambiguity comes out from Horace, who acknowledges coming from humble origin (*tenui re, Ep.* 1.20.20) but also declines to write heroic lyric because his genre is *tenuis*, unsuited to grand topics (*Od.* 1.6)

in singulis litteris . . . verborum: Romans did not use formal punctuation between clauses but might use dots to mark divisions between words. On the other hand, manuscripts might not even separate words, leaving it open to interpreters to redivide and offer a different reading. Compare the deprecation of the jurisconsult in *de Orat*.1.236 as *nihil nisi leguleius . . . praeco actionum, cautor formularum, auceps syllabarum*.

si quid . . . fuit . . . admirationis: "if there was any cause for admiration," implying as much bafflement as actual respect at this mystification. The indefinite pronoun *quis/quid* is normally only found after *ne, si, nisi,* and *num.* The meaning is often close to our "whoever, whatever."

enuntiatis vestris mysteriis: compare *Chaldaeis* below for a similar quasi-religious irony, comparing legal with astrological determination of good and bad days. The metaphorical use is common and usually slightly mocking; e.g., *dicendi mysteria, de Orat.* 1.206, 3.64; *Rhetorum mysteria, Tusc.* 4.25.

Posset agi lege necne: "whether there were legal grounds for an action or not." The passive infinitive, here used impersonally (A&G §208; W 208–13), stands for the lawsuit, but *agere,* besides covering every kind of business, is also applied to the pleader or *actor* who *causam agit.* Hence the standard phrase for suing under the ancient procedure of the *legis actionis* was *lege agere.*

pauci quondam sciebant: Cicero recalls the tradition that priests and legal experts concealed from the public the calendar of days, *fasti,* on which a praetor/presiding judge could rightly operate, pronouncing the decisions *do, dico, addico.* In the priestly records, days within each month were dated in relation to the phase of the moon (*Kalends, Nones,* and *Ides*), but also marked as permissible for legal business (F) or the holding of assemblies (C).

a quibus . . . a Chaldaeis: as with *postulo,* so the person who receives the request is expressed in the ablative with *a(b)* or *e(x),* but see also the idiomatic use of the adverb in §26 below, *unde petebatur.*

Inventus est scriba quidam, Cn. Flauius: compare the shorter version of the history of jurisprudence in *de Orat.* 1.186 and the detailed narrative of Liv. 9.46, where Flavius, once made aedile, *civile ius, repositum in penetralibus pontificum, evolgauit, fastosque circa forum in albos proposuit.* From these white-painted boards the people memorized (*ediscere*) the legal calendar. Flavius was able to disseminate this knowledge of the pontifical calendar because he was a *scriba pontificius.* See Rüpke 2011.

qui cornicum oculos confixerit: "so smart he could pierce crows' eyes." The subjunctive is consecutive or generic (A&G §440, 535; W 155–59).

cautis iuris consultis: once again stress on negative *cavere*, obstructing or preventing access.

Itaque irati . . . verba quaedam composuerunt: Roman law had originally excluded laymen by sticking to the wording of *legis actiones*. Now Cicero mocks the jurists by replacing these with new written statements (*formulae*) as models for the litigants.

26. cum hoc fieri bellissime posset: the tone of *bellissime* is flippant, "very nicely."

'. . . meus est.' 'Immo meus,' deinde iudicium: a very succinct phrasing.

cedo quid postea: "tell me what happens next?" The word *cĕdo* here is not first person of *cēdere*, but an ancient attention-getter (*OLD* s.v. *cedo* 2) made from the deictic particle—*ce* "this" + an old aorist imperative of *dare*. Compare *ecce*, "[look] here" and *hicce huiusce* etc., "this here," the original forms of *hic, haec, hoc*, as in *huiusce* (§32, 83).

The whole charade is beautifully translated by Zetzel 2009: 137–38:

> THE PROPERTY, he says, WHICH IS IN THE TERRI-TORY KNOWN AS SABINE. Lots of words; what comes next? I ASSERT THAT IT IS MINE ACCORDING TO THE LAW OF THE ROMAN PEOPLE. What comes next? THENCE AND THERE I SUMMON YOU FROM THE PROCEEDINGS AT LAW TO ENGAGE THE ISSUE. The person against whom the claim was being made had no idea what to say to such a wordy plaintiff. So the legal expert crosses the stage like a Latin flute-player. FOR THE REASON FOR WHICH YOU SUMMONED ME TO ENGAGE THE ISSUE IN ACCORDANCE WITH THE LAW, FOR THAT REASON IN THE SAME

PLACE I SUMMON YOU IN RETURN. Meanwhile, so as not to let the praetor think he's sitting pretty and to say something on his own, a jingle has been made up for him that is particularly ridiculous in this. IN THE PRESENCE OF WITNESSES FOR BOTH PARTIES, I POINT OUT THE PATH: FOLLOW IT. The wise man on the spot showed them how to follow the path. COME BACK ALONG THE PATH. With the same guide they came back. Even our beloved ancestors thought that absurd, I believe, for men standing just in the right place to be ordered to go away and immediately to come back to the place they had left.

manum consertum: *consertum* is the supine of *conserere*, used to convey purpose (A&C §509; W 152) and *manum* its direct object. The most familiar use of this idiom is for a military engagement on the battlefield.

Transit idem iuris consultus: the scene is compared to procedure on the comic stage where the piper (*tibicen Latinus*) may have moved from one singer to another.

SVIS . . . SVPERSTITIBVS: "let each man with his witnesses present." Cicero singles out as most absurd the phrasing in the instruction to embark on his path and make his way back (with an expert to explain it and guide them on their return). This is an exceptional use of *superstites* (those standing by); the adjective/substantive normally means survivors.

iam tum apud illos barbatos: "even then. . . ." Romans believed that they introduced shaving in the second century (Pliny *HN* 7.211, citing Varro) and the older generation went bearded (an early Scipionic epitaph celebrates Cornelius Scipio *Barbatus*.) Parenthetic *credo* underlines the irony or absurdity of the context (A&G §599c.)

cum recte atque in loco constitissent: like *bellissime* the contrast is with common sense.

ineptiis fucata: the formalities are both out of place (cf. *de Orat.* 2.14 on *ineptus, ineptiae*) and artificial. *fucare* "to disguise" or "dye."

'QVANDO TE IN IVRE CONSPICIO' . . . 'ANNE . . . ?': not an intrinsically foolish request but clearly the plaintiff would give his reasons for making the claim even unasked.

Quae dum erant occulta: once this verbiage was buffeted around in everyone's hands (*pervolgata atque in manibus iactata et excussa*) they are obviously empty of *prudentia*. **fraudis autem et stultitiae plenissima:** these phrases contrast with *iuris prudentia*, which has been reiterated throughout this mini-narrative. Cicero is moving on to a new accusation.

27. Nam, cum permulta: the new and more general accusation is that jurisprudence is used to pervert sound legal traditions (*praeclare . . . legibus constituta*). Cicero gives three examples: (a) that tradition appointed tutors to control women because of their poor judgment (*infirmitatem consili*), corresponding to Aristotle's *akuros*, so experts devised a kind of tutor that would be under the women's control (Gardner 1987: 14–22); (b) that tradition designated to heirs the maintenance of family rites at the tombs of their father and forefathers, so the experts devised a purchase of these rites by an old man whose death would void the obligation; and (c) more generally still, that experts abandoned fairness *aequitas*, corresponding to reality here, but stuck to the wording, for example believing all women undergoing *coemptio* should be called Gaia (as in Jane Doe). For *Gaia*, cf. Plut. *Quaestiones Romanae* 30.

ad coemptiones faciendas: *coemptio* for matrimonial purposes was a form of notional sale of the woman which transferred her to her husband's *manus*; cf. *de Orat.*1.237 *neque illud est mirandum, qui quibus uerbis coemptio fiat, nesciat, eundem eius mulieris quae coemptionem fecerit causam posse defendere* and Gardner 1987: 12–13.

interimendorum: *inter* + *emere* is to terminate, or bring to an end (as *interire* is to come to an end). Our ancestors wanted family cults to survive, so the legal experts found a loophole—old men to purchase the cult-places, in order to terminate the cults.

Iam illud . . . mirum uideri solet: Cicero fastens on the legal practice of including all synonyms—thus *diem tertium* (following day) = *perendinum* (day after); similarly *iudex* (judge) = *arbiter* (umpire); so too *rem* (case) = *litem* (lawsuit)—and pretends to see this as evidence that all those clever experts (*ingeniosi*) have not been able to decide on the right wording.

28. dignitas in ista scientia consularis numquam fuit: back to the main argument of §24 but now specifying the level of *dignitas* appropriate to achieving the consulship, *dignitas consularis*.

gratiae vero multo etiam minus: a candidate needs *gratia*, as Cicero was *grattosus* in §7 above; and he needs the support of *gratiosi*, men with *gratia*. Compare this to Appendix 1, *Comm. Pet.*, 4 *referendae gratiae* and 24, 29 for *gratiosi*.

scientia . . . ex rebus fictis commenticiisque: *commenticius* is from *comminiscere* "to invent" or "devise." Cicero adds to the universal reproach of artificiality against the discipline of jurisprudence that of lacking appeal, being unpleasing (*esse gratum nullo pacto potest*), and now increasingly available from other sources. That is, it lacks the *gratia* which eloquence gives to a political candidate, since legal knowledge is open to both sides in a dispute. No wonder jurists have lost their power to gratify since they have no favor to bestow or invest (*benefici conlocandi*). Roman thought was much concerned with the proper disposition of one's favors— hence Seneca's seven books *de Beneficiis*.

Licet consvlere: answered by *"consule"* was the standard request for judicial advice (Hor. *Sat.* 2.3.192–94 represents Agamemnon consulting on the justice of denying burial to Ajax; *ergo consulere et mox respondere licebit? Consule!*).

illud . . . iam perdidistis: "you have wasted your powers." The argument ends by converting the second person element in *vestro artificio* (§25), *ista scientia* (§28) into direct denunciation.

Sapiens existimari nemo potest . . . peritus ideo haberi nemo potest: this section returns from the mock technicalities of §24–28 to express in vivid colloquial language (e.g., *perpauca*, *vehementer occupatus*, *stomachum movere*), the triviality of Servius's profession.

Romae rebus prolatis: *Romae* "at Rome" is locative (A&G §427, W 51); the idiom *res prolatae* denotes the suspension of public business, here expressed in an ablative absolute (cf. *Att.* 14.52; *Q. Fr.* 3.8.4).

perpaucis . . . litteris: for the intensive, particularly common in informal speech, cf. *de Orat.* 1.190 *ut primum omne ius civile in genera digerat, quae perpauca sunt.* Forms in *per-* (*permulta, perpauca*) are common in letters and comic dialogue.

si mihi . . . stomachum moveritis: here too the language is informal (*uehementer* adverbial). I would translate *stomachum mouere* here as "provoke."

profitebor: "I shall make claim" (cf. our word "profession"), either with the accusative of a discipline or, less commonly, indirect statement.

quae de scripto aguntur: compare this to the use of *agi* in *posset agi*, §25 above. Cicero is arguing that any dispute over written law or contracts is already set out in a written text, and yet nothing is written so unambiguously that he could not insert "in the matter at issue," but the matters on which men consult a legal expert can be answered without any risk. He will make the same point in *de Orat.*, that eloquence can get round the kind of issue legal experts fret about.

Si id quod oportet . . . videare: "If you give the correct reply, you would seem to give the same reply as Servius; but if you disagree" (*sin* = "but if," adversative) "you will seem to know and handle even disputed points of law." The dilemma favors the jurisconsult, but as is true of any specialized discipline, a smart interlocutor can impose the appearance of cleverness and inside knowledge.

sin aliter: like *sin minus* (*Planc.* 62) or *sin secus* (*Timaeus* 6), this puts the less favored version second.

29. longe et multum isti vestrae exercitationi ad honorem antecellit: *exercitatio* is depreciatory, suggesting routine repetition rather than technical *ars*; cf. *exercitatus* in *Cluent.* 50 quoted at §30 below, *formulis atque actionibus*.

responsa atque decreta: the paired plurals (cf. §49 *observationes . . . testificationes, seductiones . . . secessiones*) are rhetorical, in effect as if jurists came ready equipped with tools of the trade. But the terms are distinct. Jurists operated by answering those who consulted them either by stating the existing law on that issue or by actively determining (*decreta* from *decerno*) what should be done in a given situation.

Vt aiunt in Graecis . . . sic nos: *ut* and *sic* introduce coordinate clauses of manner (A&G §323g).

eos auloedos esse qui citharoedi fieri non potuerint: the contrast is between pipers (*auloedus* = *tibicen Latinus*, 26) who of necessity cannot sing while piping but may also be poor singers, and the consummate citharode, who exercises four skills, composing the words and music of his song, playing his cithara (a seven-stringed lyre) and singing.

See Ramsey 1984: 220–25. A modern equivalent would be to see the jurisconsult as an accompanist or a choirmaster-repetiteur.

Graecis artificibus: Cicero distances himself from music as a Greek skill, which his audience no doubt saw as marginal or foreign. Compare Nepos's introduction to *The Lives of Foreign Generals*, cited for Roman attitudes to dancing in §13.

delapsi . . . devenire: of falling back, as in *a maioribus ad minora delabimur, Part. Or.* 12, cf. *devenire* of falling into difficulties at, e.g., *Fam.* 7.3.3, *Att.* 1.9.1.

Magnus . . . magna . . . magna . . . summa autem gratia: thus influence or goodwill is far out of proportion to the effort required. Note the four-part sentence going beyond the usual tricolon with anaphora.

salubritas . . . salus: contrasts health with a man's ultimate standing, even survival.

si satis profecissem, parcius . . . dicerem: the subjunctives indicate a mixed past/present contrary-to-fact condition (cf. §11), "if I had been successful enough, I would now say . . ." This is an unconvincing claim to have in mind not himself, but great speakers of the past or present. *Parcius*, more modestly, as in *uerecundus et parcus*, *Orator* 81.

30. Duae sint artes: *sint artes* (Clark), *sunt artes* (Adamietz). The tradition is divided, but the indicative seems a stronger basis for argument.

iustitia, fides, pudor, temperantia: this section is resumptive. Servius's undisputed personal merits (cf. §23, *continentia, gravitas*, etc.) are not related to his profession, and this kind of profession falls from our hands as soon as some disturbance (*motus novus*) sounds the alarm (recalled from §22, *simul atque increpuit . . . conticiscunt*).

Omnia ista nobis . . . excutiuntur: the image is of disturbed civilians leaping up to grasp their weapons and ward off the enemy. Latin normally uses a dative of reference where English prefers a possessive adjective (A&G §376–77; W 64).

ingeniosus poeta . . . auctor valde bonus: this is Enn. *Annals* 8, fr. 1, 247–49 Sk.: *<proelia promulgata> / pellitur e medio sapientia, vi geritur res, / spernitur orator bonus, horridus miles amatur*, interpreted by Cicero at the cost of jurisprudence, but in Ennius's quotation *orator* stands for an envoy or negotiator.

ingeniosus: this epithet can be genuine praise for a brilliant orator (cf. §48 below, or *Font.* 46 on Gaius Gracchus) or damning with faint praise (cf. §50 below praising the young Sulpicius or *Cluent.* 50 *P. Cannutius, homo in primis ingeniosus et in dicendo exercitatus.*)

ista vestra verbosa simulatio prudentiae: jurisprudence is contrasted with philosophy (*sapientia*). Both are useless in a violent context, but jurisprudence differs from philosophy as the *orator odiosus ac loquax* is contrasted with the good orator in the quotation describing the onset of war in Enn. *Ann.* 7 (247–49 Sk.).

'Non ex iure manum consertum, sed mage ferro' . . . **'rem repetunt':** continues *Ann*. 8.1.252 Sk. and echoes §26, *ex iure manum consertum voco*.

mage: an early form of classical *magis*.

rem repetunt: *rem* or *res repetere* is the technical language of Roman procedure against enemies. The Fetial priests authorized to declare war went to the border of the enemy raiders' territory and demanded return of the stolen property. Compare Liv. 1.22.4, 6 and 7 on the devising of this ritual by Ancus Martius, the king associated with military procedure; but note that DH *Rom. Ant.* 2.72 and Plut. *Numa* §12 attribute the practice to Numa.

cedat . . . forum castris, otium militiae, stilus gladio, umbra soli: each antithesis marginalizes the civil art of textual interpretation, as idle playing with words sheltered from the heat of battle. But Cicero would live to reverse the claim in the poem glorifying his consulship *cedant arma togae, concedat laurea laudi* (Cic. *Off.* 1.77), which so alienated Pompey.

civitas . . . omnium princeps: compare §22 *haec orbem terrarum parere huic imperio coegit*. The domination of Rome is a source of pride, but the naming of Rome as *princeps* is uncommon; cf. *Planc.* 11 *huius principis populi*.

§31–34: a new theme and a provocative version of Cato's charge: this is not real warfare, *bellum omne Mithridaticum cum muliercu- lis esse gestum*.

31. mulierculis: war was waged by Armenians and Asian forces not by confrontation in pitched battle, which suited Rome's rigid legionary formations, but by well-timed retreats and sur- prise skirmishes. But Asian Greeks and tribes from the hinter- land were mocked for their clothing of sleeves and trousers, and their submission to monarchical satraps. For *muliercula* with varying degrees of condescension or contempt, cf. *Off.* 2.57 *pueris et mulierculis et servis esse grata. Lael.* 46 contrasts the term directly with *viri.*

longe secus existimo: "I consider quite the opposite." For *secus existimare,* cf. *Fam.* 3.6.6. Roman prowess in war is a seductive topic, and Cicero teases in promising to speak briefly, because the case does not depend on the issue. First he expands Cato's jibe to include Rome's wars with all, i.e., also mainland, Greeks starting with the invasion of Italy itself by Pyrrhus of Epirus (282–275 BCE), famous for his chivalry but also his tactics and the training of his disciplined forces.

derideatur . . . triumphus M'. Curi: here begins the enumeration of all Rome's great generals. Manius Curius (cos. 290, 274 BCE) defeated Pyrrhus at Malventum in 275 BCE. In this speech Cicero keeps to the orthodox enumeration of *triumphatores,* but in his senatorial invective against the Epicurean M. Calpurnius Piso (*Pis.* 58), Cicero offers a marvelously sarcastic variation mocking Piso's affectation of disdain for triumph with a series that begins *non est integrum Cn. Pompeio consilio iam uti tuo; erravit enim, non gustarat istam tuam philosophiam, ter iam homo stultus triumphavit.*

de Philippo T. Flaminini: Titus Flamininus (cos. 198 BCE) defeated Philip V of Macedon at Cynoscephalae in 197 BCE and proclaimed the liberty of Greece from Macedon at the Isthmian Games of 196 BCE.

de Aetolis M. Fulvi: Fulvius Nobilior (cos. 189 BCE), Ennius's patron, conquered Aetolia in 189 BCE

de rege Perse L. Pauli: Lucius Aemilius Paulus (cos. II 168 BCE) defeated Perseus of Macedon at Pydna in 167 BCE.

de Pseudophilippo Q. Metelli: Metellus "Macedonicus," as praetor in 146 BCE, defeated the uprising under a Macedonian pretender in that year and became consul in 143.

de Corinthiis L. Mummi: Lucius Mummius (cos. 146 BCE) defeated the Achaean league and conquered and destroyed Corinth in his magistracy.

cur Asiaticae nationes . . . contemnitur: Cicero implicitly acknowledges the Roman prejudice setting the Asian Greeks beneath those of the mainland.

ex veterum rerum monumentis: apart from the histories of Polybius we do not now have any of the Roman annals recording the war with Antiochus of Syria, in which L. Scipio won glory equal to that of his brother Africanus Maior (*aequa parta cum P. fratre gloria*).

quam laudem . . . nomine adsumpsit: just as Publius Scipio was acclaimed Africanus by his troops, so his brother Lucius took for himself the name Asiaticus. On Asiaticus's command and triumph, see Polybius 21.24.16–17 and Livy 37.1–4, 58.6–59.6. In fact, Lucius Scipio as consul in 190 BCE was eligible for the command, but recognizing that the Romans did not trust the inexperienced Lucius as commander, his elder brother Africanus offered to go as his legate with equal powers (alluded to by *aequa . . . gloria* above). On the process of formalizing such titles by the Senate when it decreed the victorious general a triumph, see Linderski 1995b.

prae se ferebat: carried before him, displayed proudly as in *Att.* 2.23.3 *prae se fert et ostentat*; *Tusc.* 5.50 *beata vita prae se ferenda est*.

32. virtus enituit egregia M. Catonis, proavi tui: Cicero answers Cato *ad hominem*; he will cite other actions of Cato the elder at §59 below. The great-grandfather of Cato the younger, M. Porcius Cato (234–149? BCE) was a newcomer from Tusculum who rose to be consul in 195 BCE and censor in 184 BCE after fighting in the second Punic war and later against Macedon. He was a feisty politician often opposed to the elite Scipio Africanus and famous for his rhetoric, especially in the cases he fought in his own defense. He would live to be well over 80 and trigger the third and last war against Carthage, though he may have died before its defeat and destruction. (He was also a writer of both a manual of agriculture and a seven-volume history of Rome and Italy, the *Origines*, Rome's first history composed in Latin.)

enituit: nicely assonant with *virtus*, is a metaphor of encomium; cf. impersonal *enituit*, *de Orat.* 2.125, *Brut.* 215.

Neque vero cum P. Africano . . . putaretur: see note in §31 above.

Atqui: "But still." The word *atqui* (not *atque*) is a strong adversative conjunctive.

si diligenter quid . . . antepones: this sentence prefaces the detailed outline of Rome's 25 years of war with Mithridates since his provocation of the massacre of Romans in Asia in 88 BCE.

RETROSPECTIVE OF THE NEWLY ENDED MITHRIDATIC WAR (§31–33)

Mithridates VI Eupator, King of Pontus, had ruled an expanding territory for over thirty years before his successes brought a significant conflict of interest with the encroachment of Rome's expanding empire in Asia Minor. In 88 BCE, Roman instigation of neighboring princelings to invade Pontus drove Mithridates to the ruthlessly organized simultaneous massacre of Italians in several Asian cities. Rome had been distracted by the urgency of the Social War, but was now ready to campaign against him. The first Mithridatic war was limited to Greece and ended when Sulla exploited his victories at Chaeronea and Orchomenos over Mithridates's general Archelaus, making a treaty with the king at the peace of Dardanus in 85 BCE so that Sulla could return to Italy and regain control there (see Hind, *CAH* IX ch.4). Murena's father then provoked new hostilities in search of glory and spoils in the so-called second Mithridatic war (84–81 BCE, cf. §12, note on father's campaigns), but this was followed by a lull for several years until Lucullus came out in 74 BCE to initiate new campaigns (on the latter part of the war, see Sherwin White *CAH* IX, ch.8a.)

Cicero outlines the war in eight phases. I offer a close paraphrase with running commentary.

(1) **32. L. Sulla . . . pugnax et acer et non rudis imperator:** Sulla's brutal reconquest of Rome and proscriptions had made him controversial. Cicero picks his epithets carefully.

invectum totam in Asiam cum pace dimisit: Mithridates had occupied the entire province. Sulla conceded this peace at Dardanus in 85 BCE because he needed to repatriate his army.

(2) **pater huiusce:** "father of my client." Murena's father started the "second Mithridatic war" the following year, 84 BCE (note the intensive alliteration of *vehementissime vigilantissimeque vexatum*) but the elder Murena only left the king substantially checked (*repressum*), not crushed (*oppressum*).

(3) **aliquot annis sumptis:** after taking some years to restore his forces, Mithridates gained the strength and confidence to believe he could unite the (Western) Ocean with the Black Sea and Sertorius's forces with his own (probably before 75 BCE). Sertorius (see Plut. *Sert.*) was the Marian rebel who formed a kingdom in Spain when Sulla seized power (first in 82, then from 80–73 BCE). Sertorius consistently defeated his opponents; after the death in battle of Domitius Calvinus (80 BCE), he inflicted defeats on Metellus Pius, commander from 79 BCE and even Pompey, who had been sent as proconsul to Hither Spain in 77. Sertorius was defeated only when betrayed in 73 BCE. Mithridates thought in global terms, and this alliance was an extraordinarily bold conception, but never implemented in action.

(4) **33. alterius res . . . L. Luculli vero res . . .:** when both consuls (M. Aurelius Cotta and L. Lucullus) were sent out in 74 BCE, one in pursuit of Mithridates, the other to protect Bithynia, the disastrous campaigns of the one (Cotta) greatly enhanced the king's wealth and reputation;

but (according to Cicero) his colleague Lucullus's achievements resulted in the successful conclusion of a war unrivalled in its magnitude and the skill and heroism with which it was conducted.

ad Cyzicenorum moenia: the siege of Cyzicus. When the thrust of the war had halted at Cyzicus (on the southern shore of the Propontis) and Mithridates had thought it would be his doorway to Asia (*effracta et revolsa* develops the image of gates broken open and forced back on their hinges), "Lucullus succeeded in the defense of our city of loyal allies and exhausted all the king's forces by the duration of the siege." (This was probably in the winter of 73/2 [cf. MRR 3.121–22] in which Lucullus arrived in Asia as commander over Asia, Bithynia, Pontus, and Cilicia.)

(5) **Quid? illam pugnam . . . commissam arbitraris?:** "Do you think the naval battle at Tenedos, when the enemy fleet was making for Italy at speed under forceful commanders, inflated with pride and confidence, was engaged in an ordinary struggle or a trivial combat?" Cicero avoids tedium by switching syntax and the mode from statement to question. For this battle compare *Imp. Pomp.* 21.

(6) **Mitto proelia, praetereo oppugnationes oppidorum:** *praeteritio*, i.e., a claim to pass over what one actually mentions. When Mithridates was finally (*tandem aliquando*) driven from his kingdom, he still prevailed so greatly by his strategy and authority that he could renew his power with new resources and troops in combination with the king of Armenia. According to Broughton's schedule in MRR 2.108 (as modified in 3.122), the king took refuge with Tigranes, his son-in-law, in 71 BCE at his newly founded capital of Tigranocerta.

plurima . . . non id agimus: another *praeteritio*. Murena did not participate in these last four or five years of campaigning by Lucullus.

(7) **34. Hoc dico:** this statement resumes the point from §32 (*si diligenter . . . consideraris*). Cicero reaches 67 BCE and Pompey's first maritime command against the pirates,

then in 66 BCE his take-over of Lucullus's old command in
Asia and the other provinces under the terms of the *lex
Manilia de imperio Gnaei Pompei*.

Si bellum hoc . . . ad Cn. Pompeium detulisset:
note the rhetorical elaboration of this climactic sentence:
the triple subject with anaphora *si bellum hoc*, *si hic hostis*,
si ille rex in the protasis, followed by the four parallel adverbial qualifiers in the apodosis neque tanta *cura* . . .
neque tot *annos*, neque tanta *gloria*, neque tanto *studio*.
The first clause deals with the Senate and people, then the
second clause including two qualifying phrases introduces
Lucullus; the final climax is the action of the *populus
Romanus* with its extended object *eius belli conficiendum
exitum*: "nor would the Roman people have entrusted to
Pompey the task of completing the outcome of the war."
Each clause is given resonance by the rhythmically
emphatic "past counterfactual" pluperfect subjunctives
putasset, *gessisset*, *detulisset* producing a ditrochaic
clausula in each case.

Besides the always delicate business of treating Lucullus
and his supplanter Pompey with (almost) equal respect,
note that Cicero attributes the war itself to both Senate and
people, but Pompey's superior command to the people
alone; we know from the surviving *Pro lege Manilia* that
Cicero supported Manilius's proposal to the assembly,
which carried it against the opposition of leading senators.
Here *eius belli conficiendum exitum* plays down Pompey's
assignment (and achievement) as if it were a mere mop-
ping-up operation.

**acerrima . . . illa quae cum rege commissa est et
summa contentione pugnata . . .:** Cicero calls Pompey's
defeat of Mithridates at the future site of Nicopolis (Magie
1950: 354) the fiercest and most urgent of all Pompey's
battles (i.e., from 83 BCE, supporting Sulla in Italy, Africa,
Sicily, and against Sertorius in Spain).

(8) **se ille eripuisset:** in the last phase Mithridates
escaped and fled to Panticapaeum on the Crimean

Bosphorus, which Pompey's army could not reach. Cicero's language turns the king's flight across the Black Sea into a personal pursuit culminating in his death. (Dio and Appian disagree about whether Mithridates committed suicide or was murdered by his son.)

Bosphorum confugisset: the bare accusative without a preposition is usual for towns, *domus*, *rus*, and small islands, here extended to the peninsula (A&G §427; W 8–9).

nomen tamen retinuit regium: with a slight anticlimax Cicero adds that even in his desperate misfortune, Mithridates kept his royal status of king.

illum vita expulit: ablative of separation (A&G §401; W 41.8).

Hunc tu hostem: simply reiterates the point that it was only with the recent news of Mithridates's death in the remote fortress that the war was seen to be over.

L. Murenam . . . cognitum esse defendimus: taking his last step back to his theme, Cicero reiterates his defense that Murena had been recognized as a hero of courage, strategy, and energy in this war.

hanc eius operam . . . habuisse: somewhat anticlimactically, Cicero notes that Murena's achievements had won no less dignity in earning the consulship than "our" (yours and mine, Servius?) efforts in the forum of civil life.

35. At enim in praeturae petitione: for *at enim* representing an imagined objection by the adversary, cf. *OLD* s.v. *at*, 4a and b. There is a deliberate anticlimax in Cicero's transition from the life-threatening war to the mechanics of politics and the praetorian elections for 65 BCE (in which Servius apparently got his majority of voting units ahead of Murena), and this anticlimax is reinforced by accusing Servius and Cato of arguing as if this were a matter of a civil contract (*syngrapha*, the Greek term for a contract or record of debt.).

Pergitisne: implies a perverse persistence by his adversaries.

Quod enim fretum, quem Euripum: electoral swings are often compared to shifting hurricanes (e.g., *turbulentissimae tempestates, de Orat.* 1.2; and *hac comitiorum tempestate populari* below, §36). I know of no other comparison with the swollen currents of the Euripus, the straits between Attica and Euboea, famous for its multiple shifts of tide by day and night, but cf. Cicero *De Natura Deorum* 2.19 *aestus maritimi fretorumque angustiae ortu et obitu lunae commoveri* for the association of tides and straits. On the Euripus, see Pomponius Mela 2.108 *Euripon vocant, rapidum mare, et alterno cursu septiens die et septiens nocte fluctibus invicem versis adeo immodice fluens ut ventos etiam et plena ventis navigia frustretur.*

quem Euripum: the Greek form is masculine, and the neuter of the manuscript tradition *quod Euripum* does not occur in Quintilian's quotation (8.6.49). Cicero maintains exact parallelism between *motus . . . agitationes fluctuum* and *perturbationes . . . aestus . . . ratio comitiorum.*

parva . . . aura rumoris: "the trivial breeze of popular favor"; cf. *Har. Resp.* 43 *aura popularis; Sest.* 10; *Mil.* 42.

aliud atque existimaris: "other than you'd expect." Compare the use of *ac* in *non secus ac, si* §10. *Existimaris* is the contracted form of *existima<ve>ris*, future perfect.

quasi . . . non ipse fecerit: "as if it had not made this happen." Cicero reinforces the idea of irrationality by representing the electorate as failing to understand its own behavior. The perfect subjunctive has been attracted into the mood of the preceding consecutive *admiretur* (A&G §593).

36. Nihil est incertius volgo . . . obscurius . . . fallacius: Cicero uses another tricolon to return to the irrationality of the electorate (*ratione . . . comitiorum*).

L. Philippum . . . Q. Catulum . . . M. Scaurum: Cicero illustrates his argument with three examples of distinguished statesmen defeated at the polls—and later elected. Marcius Philippus, defeated in 93 BCE by Herennius, although the latter was only a mediocre orator (Cic. *Brut*. 166) and Philippus was both nobly born and influential; he would become consul in 91 BCE. Q. Catulus, praised here for his culture and good judgment, was defeated by Mallius (responsible for the disastrous defeat in Gaul in 105 BCE) but finally elected in 102 BCE; and Aemilius Scaurus, the dominant elder statesman of his generation, defeated by Q. Maximus before his election for 115 BCE (see §16 above). Cicero could have added the high-principled Stoic Rutilius, who was defeated in the consular election of 115 BCE and had to wait until 106 BCE to get elected as consul for 105. See Broughton 1991.

ne . . . quidem: "not even after the event." The stress is again on irrationality.

certo aliquo caeli signo: these weather signs would be known to the more learned Romans from the third-century Hellenistic poet Aratus's *Phaenomena* and *Prognostica* (translated by Cicero in his youth and adapted in part in Virgil's first *Georgic*), but it was general knowledge even in Plautus's time a hundred years earlier that, e.g., the rising of Arcturus brought storms in November.

certo . . . signo . . . nulla ex certa ratione obscura aliqua ex causa: opposites repeating the language of the previous sentence.

hac comitiorum tempestate populari: for *tempestas* in political allegory compare *Mil*. 5 *equidem ceteras tempestates et procellas in illis dumtaxat fluctibus contionum semper Miloni putavi esse subeundas*, quoted by Quintilian at 8.6.48 just before his quotation of *Mur*. 35.

populari: literally "belonging to the people," also for a native of the same *populus*, had come to be used for policies that appealed to the common people rather than the senatorial elite.

esse videatur: Cicero rounds off his argument with his favorite clausula—resolved cretic + trochee; cf. §15.

37. si est reddenda ratio: Cicero's next move is to offer a calculation not of why Murena came ahead of the field in the recent consular election but why he had NOT done so in the praetorian election for 66 BCE.

duae res . . . Murenae profuerunt: *Murenae* is dative with *profuisse* (A&G §367). These favorable factors were missing not in Murena's praetorship itself but in the *petitio praeturae* (named later in this paragraph), which is meant to offer a clear contrast with his assets as candidate for the consulship.

exspectatio muneris . . . creverat: before Murena became a candidate for the praetorship, it is suggested, the people had been led by hostile rumors (*studiis sermonibusque competitorum*) to expect he would provide a *munus* (literally a "contribution" or "benefaction"). The word *munus* most often denotes a gladiatorial show or other spectacle, such as the popular *venatio* (wild beast hunt), but while politicians offering *munera* could rely on the generosity of friends to lend money or to provide stage properties, the show would usually put its impresario into debt.

The regular Roman *ludi* were financed either by one of the four aediles or the *praetor urbanus*. Note Cicero's enumeration in *Verr.* 5.36: as (plebeian) aedile, he had to celebrate the games of Ceres, then of Flora, and finally the *ludi Romani*. See Taylor 1939. Murena's appointment as urban praetor enabled him to win popularity by the lavishness of his *ludi*, marked by *scaenae magnificentia* (§38 below). Ryan 1995a shows that Sulla first suffered a praetorian defeat supposedly because the people preferred him to be aedile and give them a beast-hunt; then once elected praetor, he pressured the Senate to assign him the urban praetorship *extra sortem*, since it was customary for holders of that office to give beast-hunts. Individuals not holding office could present a *munus* (which might include theatrical performances) in memory of a kinsman, usually a deceased father. See §40 on *Antoni ludis* for a possible instance.

L. Luculli exercitus . . . comitiis L. Murenae praesto fuit: Cicero turns to the second factor favoring Murena's candidacy for the consulship. When Murena was seeking the praetorship, Lucullus's forces had not yet returned from Asia Minor. (These two factors are now repeated in reverse order. Murena gained from the presence of Lucullus's army awaiting celebration of his triumph and from his lavish *munus*.) This introduces the expansion on the political power of the political military in §38.

Lucullus himself, mentioned here for the last time before §69, was present in court on Murena's behalf (cf. §20n), but his support may have been a dubious asset. Murena was identified with Lucullus's interests and may have consciously committed himself to working for Lucullus's much contested triumph. Cicero too is Lucullus's friend, but for diplomatic reasons must balance his support with respect for Pompey; hence §33 *perfecta a L. Lucullo haec sunt omnia* and §34 *neque tanta gloria L. Lucullus* are balanced by *neque vero . . . exitum populus Romanus ad Cn. Pompeium detulisset*.

quod petitio praeturae . . . praetura restituit: a neat antithesis. Here *praetura* refers to his year of office at Rome itself rather than his extension as propraetor in Transalpine Gaul in 64.

38. voluntas militum: Cicero is trying to do too much in this sentence, linking three unequal clauses: (1) *cum per se valet multitudine*|(2) *cum apud suos gratia*|(3) *tum vero in consule declarando multum etiam apud universum populum Romanum auctoritatis habet*. This makes a triad of *per se . . . apud suos . . . apud universum populum Romanum*; overriding the normal construction of paired parallel *cum* and *tum* phrases; moving from *valere* with ablatives *multitudine* and *gratia*, to *habere* with the partitive genitive *multum . . . auctoritatis*; and shifting from the first opposition to the second contrast between *apud suos* and *apud universum populum Romanum*. F. X. Ryan suggests to me that a distinction is being made here between the soldiers of a given commander as numerous in themselves and their influence on fellow soldiers who had served under other commanders.

Num tibi haec parva videntur: again Cicero puts Sulpicius in the wrong by suggesting he has underrated the value of the army's goodwill not just in its own right (the sheer numbers, *multitudo*) but through their effect on popular feeling and the influence of military canvassing (*suffragatio*) over the entire community. And the purpose of the consular elections was still in this decade to appoint or choose promising commanders rather than statesmen, and certainly rather than diviners of language (*interpretes* may evoke here all or any of the four categories: jurisconsults, soothsayers, supervisors of priestly ritual, or readers of entrails).

'Me saucium recreauit': switching to vivid prosopopoeia (impersonation) of grateful soldiers, Cicero recalls the ideal general as unselfish, generous and skillful, even blessed or lucky (*felix*: cf. *Imp. Pomp.* §47–48 on Pompey's *felicitas* and *fortuna*). These values, insists Cicero, have unlimited influence on men's esteem (*fama*, the opinion they spread) and goodwill.

Hoc quanti putas esse: *quanti* is genitive of value (see §10n, above), as in *magni/tanti facio*.

omen . . . praerogativum: traditionally, elections of consuls in the *comitia centuriata* opened with the vote of a single unit chosen by lot (*praerogativum*), whose choice was commonly followed by later voting units out of respect for the supposed divine selection represented by the lot. The logical connection with the next sentence is that *felicitas* in a commander was also seen as a mark of divine support.

Sed si haec leviora . . .: again Sulpicius is reproached with underestimating important elements and with privileging the local "city" electoral support (*urbana suffragatio*) over that of soldiers, but this time in order to remind the audience of Murena's lavish games. Each year the four aediles and the urban praetor superintended theatrical performances at the public games, but theatrical and other contests could also be a *munus* of private persons (§37n). Curio never held either office; Antonius Hibrida was praetor with Cicero in 66 BCE, but we do not know he was urban praetor. However, as Cicero seems to imply at §40, rather than being copied by Murena, Antonius produced his silver proscenium when he was already seen as a rival of Cicero for the consulship, so his *scaena competitrix* may have copied Murena's gesture rather than been copied by him.

For the nexus of ideas, compare Cicero's letter to Curio during Milo's candidacy for the consulship in 53 BCE, listing the support of patriots, the gratitude of the masses for Milo's games, the support of the youth and influential men on account of Milo's own popularity and attentiveness (*diligentia*), and Cicero's activity in canvassing support, perhaps more influential because it is both right and due: *Habemus haec omnia, bonorum studium . . . vulgi ac multitudinis propter magnificentiam munerum liberalitatemque naturae, iuventutis et gratiosorum in suffragiis studia propter ipsius excellentem in eo genere vel gratiam vel diligentiam, nostram suffragationem . . . et iustam et debitam et propterea fortasse etiam gratiosiorem* (*Fam.* 2.6.3).

quid ego dicam . . .? Minus est mirandum: Cicero pretends to pass over the obvious fact that ignorant masses are enchanted with the games; once again Cicero claims there is nothing surprising in this since the elections belong to the masses. If lavish games give the people pleasure, there is nothing to cause surprise (repeated in the form *non est mirandum*) in the advantage they gave Murena with the people. The repetition implies Sulpicius's lack of initiative and recalls the glamor of Murena's successful games.

voluptati est: predicative dative (*dativus finalis*): a source of pleasure to the people.

39. Sed si nosmet . . . de multitudine indocta: "Even busy and responsible men like us enjoy the games; why would you be surprised at the ignorant masses?" (us = Cicero, or us = the judges?) Cicero takes it one step further, representing even his own busy life as being distracted by the pleasures of *ludi*, though he is more intellectual than the uneducated crowd (i.e., *docti*, the opposite of *indocta*).

40. L. Otho, vir fortis: whose law, apparently passed in his tribunate in 67 BCE, gave privileged seating at theatrical shows to the *equites*.

lex . . . omnium gratissima: according to Cicero, but it had in fact caused rioting during a recent performance in 63 BCE.

Cicero had been forced to suspend the show to hold a *contio* in defense of his colleague (cf. *Att.* 2.1.3 on the publication of this speech, of which only a tiny fragment survives: Crawford 1994: 209–14).

honestissimo ordini cum splendore: the judges of this trial were either senators or knights and *tribuni aerarii* from the next highest property class, complimented in traditional terms for their *splendor* and now recovering their enjoyment of pleasure. In Roman courtesies, both *honestus* and *splendidus* were conventionally applied to knights (cf. *Clu.* 198; *Verr.* 2.5.16; *Planc.* 12; and *De Natura Deorum* 3.74 *splendidus eques Romanus*).

nos quoque habuimus scaenam competitricem: *quoque* "like you." Cicero implies Sulpicius's disadvantage in competition with Murena's theatre. He remembers the discouragement he felt as candidate when he had the theatre of his rival Antonius as an opposing factor. Although Cicero had held three sets of games six years previously as aedile, he was still alarmed by Antonius's lavish games: contrast Sulpicius, who had offered no games. Did he not realize that Murena's silver stage damaged his interests? For *adversatam*, cf. *adversari* in §47.

trinos ludos: with naturally plural nouns like *castra*, *ludi*, the distributive (*bina*, *trina* etc.) is used instead of the cardinal number (A&G §137).

41. sint paria omnia: in a new refinement, Cicero makes a rhetorical concession (a concession in argument). Suppose all these elements in the competitors' records are equally valid, that work in the courts (*forensis*) is a match for military achievement (*militari* has dropped from this pairing in the manuscript tradition because of haplography with *militaris suffragatio* following), that the votes of the army are (only) equal to the civilian vote, and allow that there is no difference between offering the most glorious games and having provided none. Instead consider the rivals' actual activities in the praetorship.

sit idem: the neuter *idem* is parallel to *par*, "equal," "the same."

Huius sors . . . iuris dicundi: Murena had the happy lot of *iuris dicundi* (the phonetic shift from *dicundi* to *dicendi* was not complete in Cicero's time), laying down the law, a privilege that all Sulpicius's friends had wanted for him. (The imperfect *optabamus* marks the frustration of this hope.) Here Cicero alludes to the active legislative role of the *praetor urbanus*, whose edict each year incorporated new laws and refinements; the importance of this activity wins glory and the bestowal of justice (here *largitio* is a positive quality) earns goodwill. A wise praetor in this position can avoid offending by the consistency and fairness of his decisions, accruing goodwill from his mildness in judging.

aequitatis . . . aequabilitate: the two nouns are not synonyms. While *aequitas* was valued as the virtue of fairness, even making allowances as against the strict reading of the law, *aequabilitas* refers to consistency in judgment from one case to another. Cicero sees the highly desirable and influential urban praetorship as the best office (*provincia*) to earn a consulship, capping credit for fairness, integrity, and mildness with the pleasures of the public games.

42. Quid tua sors?: "What was the office that fell to your lot?" Cicero calls the *quaestio peculatus*, the new court established by Sulla to deal with embezzlement of public funds and other financial abuses by officials, "grim and ruthless" and stresses the tears and mourning (*squalor* was like sackcloth and ashes, a public gesture of mourning and sympathy for the defendant); it is less easy to give meaning to the manuscript tradition *catenarum et indicum*. Clark's Oxford Classical Text substitutes *accusatorum*, nicely parallel with *indicum* "informers." The *Sullana gratificatio* was Sulla's lavishing of confiscated property on his supporters, which would have to be reversed in this court. Cicero himself was fundamentally opposed to Sulla and a supporter of Marius, but he was influenced by his knowledge of Hellenistic history (e.g., his praise of Aratus's financial settlement for recalled exiles in *Off.* 2.81–82) into preserving the status quo as being less disturbing to society.

scriba damnatus: may refer to a recent episode, probably an unpopular judgment by Sulpicius himself, whose condemnation of this unknown scribe would offend the whole *ordo* or guild of scribes. On the status of scribes, not mere clerks but civil servants with expertise, see Badian 1989.

retinendi contra voluntatem: the jurors also had to serve beyond the actual verdict in a supplementary session, the *litis aestimatio*, determining the amount of restitution required.

lites severe aestimatae: as Lintott 1999: 158 points out, in this court the presiding officer may have consulted with the judges but took responsibility for the verdict (whereas juries/judges normally voted on this).

tu in provinciam ire noluisti: here Cicero is on delicate ground, since he, like Sulpicius, refused a province after his praetorship (as he declares) and has now declined a consular province. (He had it transferred to his colleague Antonius Hibrida.) But after 70 BCE many men refused a province: Pompey, because he was waiting for something altogether more grand (given by the *lex Gabinia* three years later); Crassus his colleague, perhaps for the same reason; Hortensius, consul of 69 BCE, knew that his wealth came from his service as an advocate at Rome; and Cicero (as he explained later in the *Pro Plancio*) had learned as a quaestor that men forgot him when he was out of Rome. He needed the unofficial but substantial proceeds of his courtroom activities. In 63 BCE it was a different case; it was not safe to leave Rome, and Cicero's gift of his allotted province, Macedonia, committed the shifty Antonius to at least the appearance of loyalty.

Habuit proficiscens dilectum: at the beginning of his governorship, Murena won goodwill and reputation from his levy in Umbria, where the modest number of recruits allocated to him let him be generous with exemptions and brought over to him the votes of many tribes with constituencies in Umbria. Roman tribes were originally strictly the four local ones in the city and 19 in the hinterland. As Rome came to dominate Italy, tribes were increased in

number to 35 and new areas were attached to existing tribes; again,
citizen colonies in other regions were assigned to specific tribes.

Ipse . . . perfecit: Murena also ensured that Roman businessmen
(*nostri* because Cicero is speaking to a jury largely composed of
businessmen) could extort monies they had lost hope of recovering
(*desperatas iam pecunias*). It is always possible that Murena
achieved this by fairness and scrupulous care, but Cicero learned
as governor of Cilicia in 51–50 BCE that high-principled colleagues
like Brutus and Appius Claudius used armed cavalry to recoup
their debts. The sum they demanded may have been legitimate; it
was more likely extortionate interest on enforced loans, like that of
Brutus to Salamis in Cyprus, which he recovered by besieging and
starving the town council. See Cic. *Att.* 5.21, 6.1 (in detail), 6.2 =
S. B. no. 114–16.

amicis praesto fuisti: *praesto* (cf. §37 above) is found only in this
fossilized phrase, regularly used of giving loyal support. It was
expected that a Roman would support his friends, but this represents a pretty limited interpretation of Sulpicius's office. Romans
also expected to share in the profit when their friends went to
govern a province (as Catullus voices his disappointment with
Memmius in Bithynia, e.g., Cat. 10) and had no incentive to
support a man who stayed home.

**43. Et quoniam ostendi . . . parem dignitatem . . . disparem
fortunam:** Cicero claims here to have shown that esteem due to
both candidates was objectively equal and lays stress on the unwelcome duties of Sulpicius's "provincial" assignment, holding *Fortuna*
responsible.

dicam iam apertius: Cicero is now moving to the most provocative and strongest of his arguments, and ostensibly softens its
effect with *meus necessarius*, reminding the jurors of his friendship with Sulpicius (cf. Craig 1981) and with his talk of private
warning.

**vobis audientibus amisso iam tempore quae ipsi soli re
integra saepe dixi:** *ipsi soli*, dative singular, "to him when alone,"

contrasts with *vobis audientibus*. The key phrases here are *amisso iam tempore* "now it is too late" and *re integra* "when the matter could have been put right" (cf. §8: *neque est integrum*). There was a time during the canvas when the outcome was open (*re integra*) and Sulpicius could have changed his attitude, as Cicero had warned him in private.

Petere consulatum nescire te, Servi, persaepe tibi dixi: with a powerful apostrophe and the damning verb (*nescire*), Cicero affirms that Sulpicius mishandled his candidacy. Reiterating Servius's responsibility for his threats, Cicero also emphasizes his point by repeating both the aggressive epithet *fortis* (three times) and his own warnings (*dicam . . . dicam . . . dixi*: reinforced by *persaepe* and then *solitus sum dicere*. Cf. *cotidie uti solebas* below, §43).

accusandi terrores . . . debilitant: Sulpicius had been acting vigorously but with the vigor of a prosecutor, not the wisdom of a candidate. His intimidating threats alienate the people from hope of his obtaining office and weaken the support of friends.

Nescio quo pacto: "somehow or other," not a literal admission of ignorance: *nescio* + *quis/quo* can be used in an indefinite adjectival sense equivalent of *aliquo* (A&G §575d).

simul atque candidatus . . . desperasse videatur: Cicero offers a politician's wisdom. The candidate, who seems or is seen to be planning an accusation, seems or is seen to have despaired of winning office. *Desper / asse videatur* (cretic + trochee), Cicero's favorite clausula.

accusationem meditari: the phrase closely resembles *Commentariolum* 56: *ut videaris accusationem iam meditari*, and is the first (see §44 and §47 below) of several phrases which show that one of these works was echoing the other; but which?

44. Quid ergo . . . aliud persequendi: the reiteration and contradiction of *non placet* by *immo vehementer placet* leads to a second contrast between *tempus petendi* and *tempus persequendi* (recalling the verbal contrast of §7–8 above). Romans saw both revenge and retribution of a wrong as duties. But this is not Cicero's real argument. Sulpicius may not have been able to produce his evidence against Murena before the last phase of the campaign, and it is true that if he did not prosecute before his rival entered office, he would forfeit the consulship and have to wait until Murena left office to prosecute him. Cicero's real point is that the position of a *competitor* is incompatible with a prosecution. Any other person could have prosecuted a candidate in order to convict him before the election. (Presumably Cato, too, would have prejudiced his standing as candidate for the tribunate by fronting a prosecution.) See Shackleton Bailey 1970, answered by Weinrib 1971.

magna spe, magno animo, magnis copiis: after the tricolon anaphora (cf. the triple anaphora of *magna* in §29), the element of battle persists and is reinforced by *campum*, here the Campus Martius but generally the battlefield.

Non placet mihi inquisitio . . . non testium . . . comparatio: cross-examination and witnesses. These processes belong with *minae* and *denuntiatio* (Adamietz [1989] prints *declamatio*—a harangue) as opposed to the proper aim of gathering votes, winning men over (*blanditiae*: cf. *Comm. Pet.* §42) and cordial greetings (*persalutatio*).

inquisitio: the formal interrogation required of a prosecutor to obtain evidence (*testium comparatio*) before starting the trial. We can get a clear picture of the tactical issues entailed from Asconius's introduction to his commentary on Cicero's *Pro Scauro* (the late-born son of Aemilius Scaurus). Here is an outline of Asconius's comment (17C):

> After his praetorship (56 BCE) Scaurus was governor of Sardinia and abused the provincials. Triarius and his sub-scriptores obtained 300 days for interrogation (*inquisitio-nis*) in Sardinia and Corsica but did not embark on their journey, explaining that the consular elections would take place during that time and Scaurus might buy the

consulship with the money he had extorted from the provincials, and enter office—as his father had done—before
he could be tried, and then go on to pillage other provinces before being held to account for his earlier governorship. So by staying in Rome the prosecutors
presumably hoped to prevent Scaurus becoming a candidate for the consulship.

This failed, as did the whole consular election in 53 BCE because
Scaurus's rivals were involved in an extraordinary scandal.

hoc novo more: was there a renewed curiosity about the expectations of candidates at this time. Did men scrutinize their expression (*ex voltu . . . coniecturam faciant*) to measure their confidence
and backing (*facultatis*)? What the statement does is give Cicero
an opportunity for *ethopoeia* (the imitation of character and behavior), a shift of personal focus, and the vivid colloquialisms of
sermocinatio.

omnes fere domos omnium concursent: the claim partly prepares the way for the account of Murena's huge escort in §69. Note
domos, accusative of destination without a preposition, the practice with *domus*, *rus*, and names of towns and small islands (A&G
§427.2; W 8–9).

**coniecturam faciant quantum quisque animi et facultatis
habere videatur:** both this phrase and *novo more* (above) recur
in the *Commentariolum Petitionis* §34, *coniectura fieri potuit
quantum sit . . . virium et facultatis habiturus*, and §35 *hac consuetudine quae nunc est*. Given several other echoes (see §47, §68–
73nn), Nisbet 1962: 84–87 raises the question whether *Pro Murena*
is imitating the *Commentariolum*, supposedly written in 64–63
BCE, or the author of the *Commentariolum* has borrowed from *Pro
Murena*.

45. iacet, diffidit, abiecit hastas: "he's ruined, lost his confidence, and thrown away his spears," typical comments from gladiatorial combat.

accusationem cogitare, inquirere in competitores, testis quaerere: the key words just now applied to Servius in §43–44 return.

'Alium fac iam': "Elect another now." *Iam* in Clark's redivision of the manuscript faciam seems ambiguous and its position after the imperative unidiomatic. I prefer Adamietz (1989), faciam, following earlier editors.

'quoniam sibi hic ipse desperat': compare §43 *honorem desperasse* "to despair of obtaining office." The dative here, analogous to the regular construction of *fidere/diffidere* (cf. *diffidit*, absolute in the preceding sentence, and *diffisum ingenio meo*, §63) denotes the person for whom despair is felt: since self-distrust is seen as unusual, Cicero stresses the anomaly with *ipse*.

amici intimi debilitantur: friends were crucial in this small oligarchy, but in the threat of a prosecution they will either abandon the enterprise or save their services and influence for the trial.

aut certam rem abiciunt: *totam* is the conjecture of Lambinus. Where manuscripts read variously *certam, textam,* or *testam,* Clark's reads *certam,* but this adjective in inappropriate for Sulpicius's sure failure. Again, with Adamietz (1989) I prefer Lambinus's *totam.* Halm's *desertam* is appealing but strains the verb in this context.

ipse candidatus . . . non possit ponere: even the candidate himself is distracted by the magnitude of his accusation.

exturbare, qui . . . defendatur: Cicero represents organizing a prosecution as uprooting (*exturbare*) from his country a man of wealth and power, such as would be defended (*defendatur*: generic or consecutive subjunctive) by his own resources, those of his friends and even of his enemies.

Omnes . . . in capitis periculis . . . praestamus: Cicero harks back to his claim in §8 that we should defend *etiam alienissimos* in the face of a capital charge. Cicero probably saw such political prosecutions as the Roman equivalent of ostracism, practiced in fifth-century Athens, when a motion was accepted by the assembly to vote on the desirability of expelling an individual for the good of the state.

46. petendi . . . defendendi . . . accusandi: comparing the quest for office with the pressure of courtroom speaking, Cicero notes that although defense advocacy is the more keenly felt obligation, the task of the accuser involves more effort, so that no candidate can carefully equip and organize (*adornet, instruat*) both his canvass and a prosecution.

Tu cum te de curriculo petitionis deflexisses: the metaphor is surely a chariot race, more obviously than, e.g., *Verr.* 2.173 *de curriculo vitae decedere*. Note the emphatic position of <u>*tu*</u>: "it is all YOUR fault!" Sulpicius's divided aim has distracted him, and he was wildly mistaken (*errasti = erravisti* "you have gone astray," whereas *deflexisses* implies a deliberate maneuver that might have succeeded).

istam accusandi denuntiationem: "that declaration of prosecuting of yours." The word *denuntiatio* does not mean denunciation, but is a technical term (a formal self-identification as accuser before the praetor) that puts the focus on the publishing of intent.

Legem ambitus flagitasti: even before §47, Cicero turns to Sulpicius's other misstep, his demand for a tougher bribery law.

erat enim severissime scripta Calpurnia: the *lex Calpurnia* of Piso (cos. 67 BCE; cf. MRR 2.142, Gruen 1974: 214f.) was already in place. It is not discussed in Crawford's *Roman Statutes* (1996) because no verbatim quotation is recognized.

Gestus est mos: *morem gerere* (cf. §67 below) is to humor what may be unreasonable, but Cicero presents this as homage to Sulpicius's stature.

petitioni . . . refragata est: a deponent with active force and the construction of, e.g., *resistere* "opposed your candidacy" (A&G §190). Compare Cic. *Phil.* 11.20.

47. Poena gravior: this paragraph is the fullest evidence for the contents of this law (on its application to candidates, see, e.g., *Har. Resp.* 56, where Cicero glosses *repulsi* in the reply of the Haruspices as *ii quos ad omnia progredientis, quos munera contra leges gladiatoria parantis, quos apertissime largientis non solum alieni sed etiam sui, vicini, tribules, urbani, rustici, reppulerunt*, implicitly identifying those rejected with practitioners of electoral corruption). The *lex Tullia* also imposed a heavier penalty on the poor who accepted pay as escorts.

tenuiorum: (opposite of *ampli*) is almost a class code for the poor (see §70 below, and compare, e.g., *Rosc. Am.*19 *Mallius Glaucia quidam, homo tenuis, libertinus, cliens et familiaris istius T Rosci*). The use of *tenuis* and *tenuior* is already found in Cicero's student work *de Inventione*.

in nostrum ordinem: the law imposed exile on candidates, who would all be senators, but the Senate gave way grudgingly (*non libenter*) to Sulpicius's demand for a harsher restriction on their ranks.

postulationi: like *flagitare*, this implies aggressive or unreasonable demands. The added penalty for those pleading sickness (either to postpone trial or, less likely, to escape jury service) offended many who either had to toil at the cost of their health or give up even other pleasant activities (this does not offer a clear sense). Thus even disregarding the clauses rejected by the Senate (*illa quidem quae mea summa voluntate senatus frequens repudiavit*, Servius's amendments alienated the poor, the senatorial class, and the wealthy municipal bourgeoisie (mostly knights).

Quid ergo? haec quis tulit?: Compare this to Cicero's use of *quid ergo* in §44 above. Cicero deliberately marks a new point, stressing his obligation to accept Sulpicius's proposal once it was accepted by a Senate majority (*auctoritati senatus*) and his lack of any personal benefit.

illa: distinguishes the clauses actually rejected by a full Senate, i.e., a session with a quorum. Compare §51 *frequenti senatu*.

In discussing these passages, Ryan 1998: 14 establishes that in Cicero's time, meetings such as this one introducing new legislative proposals required a quorum, probably of 200 senators.

mediocriter adversata tibi esse existimas?: compare this to §40 on the impact of Murena's silver *proscenium*.

Confusionem suffragiorum flagitasti: more technical and harder to interpret. The phrase may possibly have invoked random summoning of units from all classes, as suggested by Adamietz on the basis of the proposal made by Gaius Gracchus according to Pseudo-Sall. 2.8.3. Sulpicius demanded †*praerogationum legis Maniliae*† (several Mss read *prorogationem*, accusative); Mommsen suggested *perrogationem*. Scholars have certainly failed to make sense of *praerogationum*, or relate it to Manilius's law redistributing the votes of freedmen in §66. See MRR 2.153.

aequationem . . . suffragiorum: Zetzel translates this as "the equalization of influence, or prestige, of votes." What would it mean for Sulpicius to demand the leveling (cf. *Off.* 2.73) of votes? And why is *suffragiorum* repeated so soon in the same sentence? Cicero seems to blame Sulpicius for proposing the melding of equestrian and upper class voting groups, if we take Cicero's charge that the rejected clauses would alienate the influential men in the *municipia* (*honesti atque in suis vicinitatibus et municipiis grattosi*). For these local bigwigs, dominant in the regions and townships, cf. *Commentariolum* §24 (Appendix: I). They would be offended to see a man like Sulpicius fighting to remove the gradations of rank and influence which fueled their self-esteem.

esse pugnatum: the impersonal perfect passive infinitive, "should have been fought."

Idem editicios iudices esse voluisti: "yet (adversative) you also wanted the jurors to be determined by the accuser (*editicius* from *edere* 'to publish') so as to unleash against the property of all respectable men the hidden resentments of citizens which are now controlled as silent disagreements." But with what is *editicios* contrasted? These jurors would be taken from men listed on the panel; the only difference is that as *editicii* named by the accuser they could not be challenged by defending counsel.

optimi cuiusque: literally, "of each best man."

48. Haec omnia . . . adipiscendi obsaepiebant: the same clauses that built up your access to prosecution obstructed your path to obtaining office. *Munire* (cf. §23 above) is to construct a road; the less common *obsaepire* (to hedge off, put a *saepes* or barricade around it) takes its specific reference from the preceding context. Note the persistent stress on the personal pronoun *tibi, petitioni tuae.*

ab homine ingeniosissimo et copiosissimo, Q. Hortensio: Cicero shared this defense with his senatorial seniors, Hortensius (cos. 69 BCE), a showy Asiatic orator (*ingeniosissimus* is a mixed compliment), whose style is described vividly at *Brut.* 320–27, and M. Crassus (cos. 70 BCE), whose impact came from his wealth and social prominence, showing accuracy rather than talent. See Appendix: II, quoting *Brut.* 233. Cicero knows he is repeating topics handled by the older men who spoke before him.

quoad possum . . . vestrae satietati: in fact Cicero makes this overlap with an excuse for bypassing arguments and inconvenient factual details in favor of larger issues.

quam te securim putas iniecisse: note the *-im* accusative of *securis*, an i-stem like *sitis* and *turris* (A&G §67). Instead of an indirect question, *quantam securim inieceris*, Cicero substitutes *putas*, introducing an accusative and infinitive with *te* as subject and *securim* as object, "what kind of axe do you think you threw?" Sulpicius has shot himself in the foot! The preceding allusion to *plaga* makes it easier to introduce this rustic metaphor, found also in Plautus. A more common version uses *ascia*.

cum . . . adduxisti: the temporal *cum*-clause retains the indicative when it merely describes the time an action took place (A&G §545; W 231.)

in eum metum adduxisti ut . . .: here as in §9 (*eiusmodi*), the demonstrative stands for *talis/tantus*, and so can introduce a result clause.

48–53. ne consul Catilina fieret: Earlier (§8), Cicero introduced Catiline as bent on destruction, *exitium . . . molientem*. Fear that Catiline might be elected consul had driven conservatives like the senators and *equites* of this jury to elect Cicero in 64; in fact Cicero's best weapon for Murena's acquittal was to play on their fear of Catiline, and the five sections (§48–53) that set up his character as a dangerous desperado are designed to begin and end with the risk of his becoming consul: cf. §53 **Catilinae subitam spem consulatus adipiscendi**. Cicero represents Catiline as a tragic villain, first by characterizing his state of mind (*alacrem atque laetum . . . inflatum*), then by a physical description of his appearance (rhetorical *notatio*) to convey his passionate nature: *voltus . . . plenus furoris, oculi sceleris, sermo adrogantiae*. But §49 also incorporates two other dangerous features—Catiline's following of frivolous youths, *choro iuventutis*, and a growing army of dispossessed veterans and peasants *spe militum. . . . exercitu*. The next paragraph (§50) introduces his alleged threats (*voces*), reflected in the report of his private *contio* (see below), then §51 cites two metaphorical aphorisms: first his challenge in the Senate debate of November 8, on the nation's two bodies: the conservatives lacked a head, but he was ready to put himself at the head of the dispossessed; but before that his retort to Cato's threat of prosecution, that he would quench any conflagration of his fortunes not with water but with demolition.

§52–53: record Cicero's countermeasures and recall Catiline's burning ambition *spe et cupiditate . . . inflatum*, and his behavior that triggered the public alarm and shift of political support (*repentina inclinatio*) transferring electoral votes from Sulpicius to Murena.

Three of these features demand separate notes.

1. Cicero's moral characterization is elaborately developed by Sallust's two-phase portrait of Catiline. Catiline's *animus* is *audax, subdolus, varius . . . ardens . . .* also *vastus . . . ferox* (Sall. *Cat.* 5); and his devices to corrupt young men are listed in §14 and reprised in §16. Seven years later, in 56 BCE, Cicero would present a much more nuanced portrait of Catiline, in order to defend one of Catiline's *adulescentes*, M. Caelius Rufus. (On this see Cicero *Pro Caelio* 12–14.)

2. **stipatum choro iuventutis:** middle-aged conservatives, many with growing sons, would dread this aspect of Catiline, as corrupter of the young. Sallust harped on this theme in his portrait at *Cat.* 14.5 *maxime adulescentium familiaritates adpetebat . . .* 16.1 *iuventutem quam . . . inlexerat multis modis mala facinora edocebat.* For *stipare* (cf. *stipatores* "bodyguards"), compare Sallust's metaphor in the same passage, *omnium flagitiorum atque facinorum circum se tamquam stipatorum catervas habebat.* The word *chorus*, however, is an unusual choice; its associations were with poetry and the stage and the nearest parallel is perhaps Lucilius 92 (Warmington, *Remains of Old Latin* 3, 87–93 p. 30), where the group of lictors around a Roman magistrate actually behaves like a dramatic *chorus*, saluting the magistrate in unison.

3. **quas habuisse in contione domestica dicebatur:** since a *contio* is either a public assembly addressed by a magistrate in Rome or a military assembly, where the general's speech to men under his command is also a *contio* or *allocutio* (Pina Polo 1995), the phrase *domestica contio* is an oxymoron, drawing attention to the lack of proper authority. This is made clear by the consul's speech in Liv. 39.15–16, reiterating the official nature of a *contio* and damning the Bacchanal sessions as a *contio nocturna*. Catiline's speech to his followers was both unauthorized and private.

Cicero had already offered portraits of Catiline in action in his first two Catilinarian speeches, 1.6–7 and 2 passim. Here he contrasts Catiline's aggressive confidence and many supporters with

the gloom of Sulpicius and his friends (*tristem . . . maestos*). Catiline is encouraged both by expectation of military backing and by
the promises that he claimed he had received from Antonius (*tum
conlegae mei . . . promissis*). Cicero enlarges on the theme of Catiline's army (no Roman had the right to command an army within
Italy) drawn from the Sullan veterans in the new colonies of Arezzo
and Fiesole. This is already a mixed crowd, a *turba*, associated with
violent rioting, but Cicero expands even this rabble by including
the disfranchised Marians ruined by the disasters of Sulla's
dictatorship.

49. te inquirere videbant . . .: people saw Servius's preoccupation with interrogations and conferences with his secondary prosecutors (*subscriptores*) with anxiety and fear that Catiline,
confident in his rabble of supporters, would be elected.

quibus . . . obscuriores videri solent: this next phrase seems
to add a general comment that such proceedings made the
aspect of candidates seem more ambiguous. But the wording is
troubled. After *testificationes* (the formal evidence of witnesses),
the phrase *seductiones testium* seems gratuitous and an unpar-
alleled usage, but the phrase serves a rhetorical purpose, making
a neat pair with intransitive *secessiones*. Could *testificationes* be
a gloss?

**Catilinam interea (sc. animadvertebant) alacrem atque
laetum:** in contrast with Sulpicius's party, *tristem ipsum, maestos
amicos . . .*

sic ut ei iam exploratus et domi conditus: "as if the consulship
was already tracked down (*exploratus* like game) and bagged and
put in his home larder" (*domi*, locative: A&G §427; W 51). The
verb *condere*, a compound of *con + dare*, should not be confused
with *condire* (fourth conjugation) at the end of §66. Catiline
showed contempt for Murena and saw Sulpicius as merely an
accuser (this was when Sulpicius was still uttering general threats
of prosecuting bribery) rather than a rival.

50. si ille factus esset: "if Catiline had been elected."

nolite . . . velle: this sentence works backward from its last words. *Quibus rebus* refers to the previous sentence, and stands in the ablative as cause or instrument of *qui timor iniectus sit quantaque desperatio . . .* an extended indirect question (hence the subjunctive verb *sit*) depending on *a me commoneri*, itself dependent on *nolite . . . velle*: the earliest example of this pleonasm in Cicero (cf. *Cael.* 79, *Balb.* 50, *Phil.* 7.25).

illius nefarii gladiatoris voces . . .: "the boasts of that abominable gladiator." Cicero had already used *gladiator* of Catiline at *Cat.* 1.29 and 2.24 and will use it repeatedly for Clodius in the speeches *post Reditum* (*Dom.* 48, *Sest.* 55, *Pis.*190) and for M. Antonius at *Phil.* 2.6 and 13.15 *unus furiosus gladiator cum taeterrimorum latronum manu contra patriam gerit bellum.* He only applies this extreme insult to these three men, his *bêtes noires*.

in contione domestica: this must refer to the speech recreated by Sallust in *Cat.* 20.2—ending *in abdita parte aedium*—and Cicero's claims of knowing even secret communications at *Cat.* 1.8.

negasset inveniri posse . . . non oportere: in complex oratio oblique, *negare* sometimes loses its force, and so *non* is inserted to maintain the negation (cf. Cic. *Fin.* 1.18.61).

integrorum . . . promissis . . . credere non oportere: continued oratio obliqua. *Credere* takes the dative of the person or utterance trusted (A&G §367).

quid ipse deberet, quid possideret: Cicero focuses Catiline's words on recovering lost possessions, and his own debts and losses as guarantee that he had the daring needed to serve as leader and standard bearer.

calamitosum . . . calamitosorum: compare *Quinct.* 95, *calamitosum est bonis euerti, calamitosius cum dedecore.* The word originates in agricultural disaster (hailstorms and other acts of god) and is rather a favorite in this speech.

qui esset futurus: "the man destined to be."

dux et signifer: this may be the first metaphorical use of *signifer*. Compare *Planc.* 74 *duces et quasi signiferi* and *Att.* 2.1.7 (60 BCE).

51. referente me: ablative absolute, "when I was presiding," as one would expect since Cicero was the consul presiding over that meeting.

ne postero die comitia haberentur: this proposal belongs to the eve of the elections in July. The insertion of *si quid uellet* into the request *de his rebus iussi dicere* echoes an official formula.

de his rebus . . . quae ad me adlatae essent: these phrases should be taken together as the object of *dicere*. *Si quid vellet* probably suggests that Cicero is giving Catiline the floor to exonerate himself (compare the modern judge's "Does the prisoner have anything to say in his defense?").

non se purgavit sed indicavit atque induit: "far from excusing himself Catiline declared himself . . ." But what is the meaning of *induit* here? Zetzel translates this as "gave evidence against himself and *took on his own guilt*." That is, he wrapped himself in guilt, as in *Verr.* 2.106 *dum expedire se vult, induat*.

Tum . . . dixit duo corpora esse rei publicae: the body of the elite was weak with a feeble head (*infirmo capite:* who? Cicero?), but the sturdy (*firmum*) body of the people was without a head. Plut. *Cic.* 14 has "two bodies, one lean and wasted but with a head (not what Cicero has reported) and the other headless but strong and large."

Infirmo capite: ablative of description (cf. §13 *ista sis auctoritate:* A&G §415; W 43.5 and 83).

se vivo non defuturum: *se vivo*, ablative absolute. *Esse* should be supplied with the participle *defuturum*, forming the future infinitive as in *restincturum* below.

Congemuit senatus frequens: "the full Senate groaned collectively" (*con* + *gemere*), but it passed a mild decree because some saw no cause for fear while others feared every possibility. Clark has supplemented *omnia*, providing contrast with *nihil*.

si quod esset . . . incendium: *si quod* serves as an indefinite adjective, "if any," almost "whatever."

Erupit e senatu triumphans gaudio: compare *Cat.* 2.1 *abiit, excessit, evasit, erupit.* Catiline's earlier retort to Cato was that he would put out any conflagration of his fortunes not with water but by (wholesale) demolition. This was the behavior of a homeowner in a desperate situation, since demolition would extend the damage to others and threaten adjacent properties.

52. lorica, non quae me tegeret: the relative clause stands for Cicero's purpose in adopting the breastplate and so takes the subjunctive. Cicero's countermeasures: his adoption of a bodyguard and military breastplate were not in self-defense but to draw everyone's attention so that they would rush to give aid and protection to their consul. Mark Antony did the same after Caesar's assassination, according to Appian *B.C.* 2.131.

caput et collum solere petere: the comment on Catiline's fighting habits is meant to imply his ruthless and impatient nature, he "goes in for the kill"; cf. Regulus in Pliny *Ep.* 1.20.14 *iugulum statim video, hunc premo.* We may sense some embarrassment on Cicero's part at the possibility of being thought a self-dramatizing coward since no crisis actually materialized, but the comment is more pointed for listeners, who had witnessed or heard about Catiline's brutality during the Sullan prescriptions, when he openly killed many, including Marius Gratidianus. Compare Ascon. 90C (from *In toga candida*) *quod caput etiam tum plenum animae et spiritus ad Sullam usque ab Ianiculo ad aedem Apollinis manibus ipse suis detulit.*

te, Servi, remissiorem: it was once again Servius's fault, through his apparent indifference to his candidacy (cf. §48 end), which led patriots to attach themselves to Murena.

illam . . . pestem: for Catiline as a scourge or disease of the community, cf. *Cat.* 1.30 *haec tam adulta rei publicae pestis.*

53. honestissimo patre . . . petisset diligenter: in addition to Murena's admirable parentage, well-behaved youth, successful service as lieutenant, and the threefold achievements of his service both as praetor in the city (as judge and provider of public entertainment) and his successful, popular command as propraetor in Transalpine Gaul, Murena has now proved himself a conscientious candidate for office, not distracted by a private feud like Sulpicius.

et ita . . . minaretur: Cicero does not add that most electors would have felt Murena had the military support to oppose Catiline if it came to violence. Once again, there is no mention of Silanus.

ad virum bonum: this is Murena, whose birth, character and career showed him to be manly and stable, not yielding to threats or (like the villain Catiline) making them. *Huic* resumes all this. It should be no surprise that Catiline's sudden optimism (recalling *et spe et cupiditate inflammatum* in the previous sentence) was a great asset (*magno adiumento*, predicative dative) to this fine fellow.

53. Catilinae subitam spem consulatus adipiscendi: *spes* is qualified by both the possessive genitive *Catilinae* and the objective gerundive phrase, literally, "of the consulship to be obtained."

§54–75 THE THIRD DIVISION OF THE SPEECH:
CRIMINA AMBITUS

Two charges, information given by Murena's *divisores* and mysterious money set aside probably by the same *divisores*, have been reduced to mere rubrics (see below). By stressing the thorough treatment of these topics by his co-advocates (*perpurgatus ab eis qui ante me dixerunt*) Cicero puts the jury off guard, deliberately giving the impression that this is only a recapitulation (the rhetorical term *retractare* is more common in letters and treatises than in formal oratory). But responsibility shared is responsibility shirked: Crassus and Hortensius may have been equally summary.

54. C. Postumo, familiari meo: Cicero treats with courteous respect this subsidiary prosecutor C. Postumius, *praetorius candidatus*, so a man around 40, the age when candidates competed for the praetorship. (The gentile name is more likely than the form Postumus preserved in the Mss.) Postumius is a *paternus amicus . . . vetus vicinus ac necessarius* (§56) for whom this trial offers a chance of publicity, but the edited speech deals with him rapidly, postponing the allegations of the young Ser. Sulpicius about tampering with the equestrian centuries (§72–73). Cicero is subordinating this material to his comprehensive promise (cf. §56, 58–60) to answer Cato's account of his accusation, the Senate's decree and matters of high state.

de divisorum indiciis: technical and highly relevant material on the information provided by the agents.

de deprehensis pecuniis: along with the preceding comment, this seems to imply money concealed for under-the-counter payment. The evidence must have included lists of names (supposedly unpaid volunteers) and money set aside. Candidates' staffs (slaves and free agents) will probably have kept any list of supporters well apart from the monies set aside to recompense them.

55. pauca . . . prius de L. Murenae fortuna conquerar: with the semi-technical *conqueror* Cicero steps back and changes to a highly emotional tone as if he were choking with sorrow . . . *ita sum animo adfectus ut nequeam . . . huius euentum fortunamque miserari*. He has often envied men who put aside ambition, and Murena's unwarranted endangerment from prosecution (implied by *tantis tamque improvisis periculis*) has made it impossible for him to show sufficient pity to our common misfortune and Murena's victimization. Compare this allusion to a personal fortune to §51 on the fire set alight to Catiline's *fortunae*. *Fortuna* is most often used of misfortune seen as undeserved, but here it is designed to intensify the contrast of present misfortune witth the excellent good fortune *veteris fortunae*. Cicero comments in his letter *Fam.* 5.12.4 on the emotional and dramatic appeal of depicting extreme changes of fortune: *temporum varietates, fortunaeque vicissitudines*.

gradum dignitatis: this entire section suggests that Murena's candidacy was a legitimate attempt to advance one step beyond his family's achievements, which now risks penalties out of proportion to his ambition. Modern readers may find this line strange: do we think the sons of leading statesmen, say George Bush or Justin Trudeau, have more right to supreme office than a self-made politician? Do the Japanese, who systematically elect sons to fathers' parliamentary seats, believe their fathers have earned this for them, or that heredity will make the young men wiser statesmen? Perhaps the key is the unexpressed prejudice of the elite that Murena, like Cicero himself, is an intruder in their closed shop.

venit in periculum. . . . ne . . . amittat: *periculum* carries the notion of fear or anxiety and so can be followed by *ne* with the subjunctive to denote the events feared (A&G §564; W 188–90).

studium novae laudis: from Cicero's point of view, Murena risks losing the honor he had inherited because of his desire for a new level of glory. The love of glory was in Roman thinking laudable and the mark of a future leader. Although only the nominative and vocative of *gloria* are metrically admissible in hexameters, Virgil's young warriors, and even his race horses, feel the aspiration: G. 3.101 *gloria palmae*; *Aen.* 5.138 *laudumque arrecta cupido* and 394 *non laudis amor nec gloria cessit/pulsa metu.*

56. studio accusandi . . . descenderint: Romans were strongly prejudiced against accusers as malicious careerists. Worst of all (*acerbissimum*), each of the prosecutors (*accusat* will be three times repeated; see below) is identified as having no cause to attack Murena; they are not driven by wrongs he has inflicted (*non iniuria . . . permotum*) or any regular feud (*simultatis*), something Romans thought a justification for prosecuting, but have been lowered by their passion for accusing into creating this feud; cf. §44.

inimicitiarum . . . inimicitias: the word, suggesting committed hostility, goes beyond the immediate context of the trial.

ut omittam: a *praeteritio*. The *ut* is probably best explained as concessive, "even though I leave out." *Quem intelligo . . . permotum* should be treated as a parenthesis, before continuing the list of accusers.

Accusat Ser. Sulpicius: young Servius's talent should have been exercised as a defense counsel, increasing the security of all his father's associates. Shackleton Bailey sees *sodalis filius* (Mss have either *fil*- or *fili*) as excluding the possibility that this Servius is the plaintiff's son. Certainly it would be proper piety for the plaintiff's son to use the courts to avenge wrong done to his father, but membership in a *sodalitas* also bound men (and perhaps their sons?) not to prosecute but to defend their *sodales*. Compare Cicero's gentle handling of young Atratinus at *Cael.* 2 with his more ironic treatment of the subscriptor Herennius, said at *Cael.* 26 to be Caelius's *sodalis* and faulted for violating the supposed loyalty of *sodales* and for lacking *humanitas*.

Accusat M. Cato: Cato had no reason for estrangement from Murena in any matter, but this man was born in our society so that his power and talent could serve as protection even for those with no connection to him, not as a source of harm See §58n below

inimico esse deberet: the motif of *inimicitiae* returns.

Ea condicione nobis erat . . . natus ut: compare §48 *in eum metum ut*. The construction is consecutive: *nobis* is dative of advantage or perhaps a freer "ethical" dative, "as far as we are concerned."

57. quasi desultorius: Cicero deals briefly with Postumius by imputing his participation to the preposterous ambition of a mere show-jumper to take part in the high-prestige chariot race. *Desultores* (cf. Sen. Rhet. *Suas.* 1.6 on Dellius as *desultor bellorum civilium*) were trick riders who worked with a pair of horses, either leaping from the back of one to the other or bestriding both together. Compare the denarius of C. Censorinus (Crawford 1974: 346/1a) intended to commemorate the games of 212 BCE. Suet. *Jul.* 39.2 distinguishes *quadrigas bigasque* from *equos desultorios*. Postumius is aspiring out of his league.

dignitati . . . aliquis largitus est: apparently Postumius had abandoned his candidacy out of respect for the stature of his competitors, or perhaps one of them bribed him to withdraw, which makes him a desirable friend ready to pursue another man's wrong rather than his own. This can only be an ironic attempt to discredit poor Postumius, before Cicero's text abridges what may have been incriminating evidence to the following rubrics.

DE POSTVMI CRIMINIBVS, DE SERVI ADVLESCENTIS: on the charges of Postumius, and the young Servius, note Pliny's comment in *Ep.*1.20 . . . *Ciceronis pro Murena, pro Vareno in quibus brevis et nuda quasi subscriptio quorundam criminum solis titulis indicatur ex his apparet eum permulta dixisse, cum ederet omisisse.*

§58–81 ANSWERING CATO'S ACCUSATIONS

58. Venio nunc ad M. Catonem, quod est firmamentum: the relative pronoun takes the gender of the predicate, not its antecedent.

firmamentum ac robur: while *firmamentum* is a technical rhetorical term for the main argument (*Inv.* 1.19; *Part.* 59, 103) Cicero has already adopted the combination *firmamentum ac robur* to describe Pompey in *Imp. Pomp.*10. Hence although the manuscript tradition supplies *fundamentum*, humanist and later editors have preferred *firmamentum*. Such was Cato's prestige and reputation for searching out and denouncing corruption, demonstrated only three years before in his service as quaestor, that his role as accuser was one of the strongest factors militating for Murena's conviction. Cicero had to walk a tightrope between demonstrating his respect for the man and showing up his Stoic principles as unworldly and impractical. On Cicero's technique in arguing against Cato, see Craig 1986.

primum illud deprecabor . . . ne quid L Murenae dignitas illius . . . noceat: *nocere* like its near synonym *obesse* takes the dative (*L. Murenae*) of the person harmed (A&G §367), while *quid* (three times) serves as internal accusative (A&G §390c; W 12–15), "that it does no harm/does not harm at all." Cicero's procedure will be to cite Scipio (Aemilianus) and Cato's own great-grandfather as foils to Cato, and open and close this section with Scipio as his model. But first he praises Cato for his prestige, his forthcoming tribunate (he would enter this on 10 December) and the impressive brilliance (*splendor et grauitas*) of his life so far. He then rephrases this as *ea . . . bona quae ille adeptus est ut multis prodesse possit* "those merits that he acquired in order to benefit many."

Bis consul fuerat . . .: this Africanus, born son of Aemilius Paulus and adopted by the elder Africanus's delicate son, earned this title in his own right by his conquest of Carthage in 146 BCE and went on to conquer Numantia, capital of the Spanish rebels, in the following decade (133 BCE).

in *eo* summa eloquentia: Scipio's eloquence and moral probity were as great as the power of Rome itself, which was maintained by his services (*illius opera tenebatur*). But when he prosecuted L. Cotta (Cic. *Brut.* 81, see Alexander 1990: #9), the jurors did not want it to seem that anyone was overwhelmed by the excessive power of his adversary. As Alexander notes, Cicero is in error here and elsewhere when he describes Scipio as already twice consul at the time of the trial, 138 BCE. It went through eight hearings before Cotta was acquitted.

maiores natu: *natu* is ablative of the supine, used as an ablative of respect (A&G §510; W 12–15).

sapientissimi homines qui tum . . . iudicabant: Cicero uses the wise judgment of our ancestors (*maiores natu*) to convince the jurors of the advisability of resisting the influence of a respected and prominent prosecutor. In answering Cato, he makes play with the Stoic concept of the *sapiens* (§61–63) and contrasts Stoic absolutism with the *humanitas* (§65–66) of mercy, so that when the jurors (*delecti . . . atque sapientissimi viri*, §83) come to their verdict, they will have the merciful approach of their ancestors as a model.

59. Ser. Galbam: reverting to a cause célèbre associated with the origin of the standing court on provincial abuses, Cicero describes the offence of Servius Sulpicius Galba, whom his political enemies tried to destroy, but the Roman people enabled to escape prosecution (see Cic. *Brut.* 89–90, Alexander 1990: #1). There is some dispute about the procedure involved. According to *Brut.*, the tribune Libo proposed a law, backed by Cato, to set up a *quaestio extraordinaria* to investigate Galba's treacherous massacre of surrendered Lusitanians, but Richardson 1987: 2 n12 suggests the occasion of Cato's speech was almost certainly a *contio* held by Galba in his attempt to pass a popular bill establishing this *quaestio*.

traditum memoriae *est*: Cicero's source was in fact Cato's own report in his *Origines* fr.109 Peter.

populus universus . . . iudices restiterunt: keeping the goodwill of all classes, Cicero maintains that both the common people and educated men (*sapientes*) and the jury itself resisted the excessive power of prosecutors. So now Cicero rejects the abuse of an accuser's power and force and authority in court and speaks for the defendants. Let the accusers' might prevail for the survival of the innocent, support of the powerless, and aid for the afflicted; but these merits should be rejected when aimed at the ruin (*pernicies* opposed to *salus* as in *de Orat.* 2.35) of fellow citizens.

Nolo . . . adferat: Cicero commonly uses a subordinate subjunctive after *nolo* without *ut* (A&G §442b).

60. si quis hoc forte dicet . . .: Cato's prosecution is treated as a potential *praeiudicium*, but Cicero argues (by way of introducing the *Paradoxa Stoicorum*) that Cato tended to introduce philosophical issues alien to the immediate circumstances. Certainly Cato provoked popular resentment, according to *Fin.* 3.7–8, by his obsession with reading even when waiting for the Senate to gather formally in the curia.

Catonem descensurum . . . fuisse, nisi prius de causa iudicasset: this hybrid future-in-the-past infinitive, followed by a conditional pluperfect subjunctive, is the conventional grammatical sequence for a past counterfactual in indirect speech (A&G §584; 272d). *Descendere* is a fine double entendre, denoting a literal "coming down" (i.e., to the forum) where cases were pleaded and also a "stooping" to an unworthy action.

iudicium . . . pro aliquo praeiudicio: Cicero distinguishes the accuser's personal judgment from a formal *praeiudicium*, that is a relevant previous court verdict. Clearly this was legally necessary, but most people are informally influenced by a prosecutor's reputation. Cicero now proposes not to criticize Cato's decision but perhaps (*forsitan*) to reshape and correct some details.

'Non multa peccas . . . sed peccas; te regere possum': "your mistake is trivial, but it IS a mistake and I can guide you."

ille fortissimo viro senior magister: Quint. 8.6.29–30 notes the figure of *antonomasia*, substitution of descriptive terms for naming. This dictum seems to have been a saying from *Chironos Hypothekae* ("Chiron's Treasury"), the collection of school maxims credited in Hellenistic tradition to Achilles's old teacher, the centaur Chiron. The analogy puts Cato in the position of Achilles, assuming for himself, Cicero, the status of older teacher (*senior magister*).

At ego non te: Cicero contrasts his own position; of course he would never claim Cato needed to be corrected rather than lightly redirected.

esse videare: a consecutive present subjunctive. Note the clausula.

natura . . . doctrina: using standard rhetorical categories (cf. *Brut*. 112) Cicero contrasts Cato's *natura* of integrity, restraint, generosity, and all the virtues with the effect of *doctrina* (theory), which he stigmatizes as too rough and harsh for reality or nature to allow.

61. haec oratio habenda . . . disputabo: Cicero compliments the urbanity of his jury in order to speak more freely about education (*de studiis humanitatis*), something he treats as familiar and pleasing to his hearers. He would himself be instrumental in developing the ideal of enlightened concern for society and makes a similar point in speaking of poetry in the nearly contemporary *pro Archia*. But when Cicero refers back to the case of Murena in *Fin.* 4.74, he treats the jurors of 63 BCE as uneducated in comparison with his readers: *non ego tecum iam ita iocabor ut isdem his de rebus, cum L. Murenam te accusante defenderem. Apud imperitos tum illa dicta sunt, aliquid etiam coronae datum* (concessions to the casual bystanders.) Again he contrasts Cato's innate moral superiority with the deficiencies that are blamed on his teacher.

haec bona . . . ipsius scitote esse propria: *scitote* is the future imperative generally reserved for legal texts (cf. the English future imperative "you/he/she/they *shall* return the stolen property") and proverbial expressions (A&G §163; W 126n), which Romans preferred to *scite*, as they preferred *scito*, singular, to *sci*, which is not found. Compare *resistito* in §64 and the regular forms *memento*, *mementote*. Cato's wisdom is not divine but self-imposed. Cicero first extends his argument to the most general axioms of the Stoic school (§60–66), then supplies examples from Roman political life (§62) before returning to the specific charges made against Murena's canvass.

There are two ways of approaching Roman Stoicism in Cicero's time: one is in terms of contemporary Greek Stoic "house-philosophers" teaching orally in private (like Cicero's blind Stoic protégé Diodotus); the other comes later, in the form of Roman adaptations into Latin like that of Cicero: but Cicero was exceptional, because he had attended lectures of Posidonius while in Rhodes studying rhetoric with Molo in the 70s BCE. The two phases are treated separately in, e.g., Rawson 1985.

Zeno: Zeno of Citium founded his school around 300 BCE, and his successor, Diogenes of Babylon, came to Rome from Athens as one of three heads of philosophical schools chosen as ambassadors in 155 BCE. The following generation saw Panaetius as private adviser to Scipio, and in the next generation, men like

Rutilius Rufus (cos. 105 BCE) and Q. Aelius Tubero (see below §75) took instruction from Stoics. At *Brut.* 113–14, Cicero claims Rutilius studied with Panaetius, and according to Rawson (1985: 207n) even Servius himself may have learned dialectic from Diodotus.

Huius . . . praecepta eius modi: Cicero (distancing himself from adherence) serves up simplified versions of Zeno's sayings and instructions, which rigorously assert that the wise man is never moved by personal favor and never forgives a man's error; that only the foolish and frivolous feel pity, whereas a real man is neither softened nor appeased. These are some of the so-called Stoic Paradoxes, which Cicero worked up into mini-declamations in his *Paradoxa Stoicorum* of 45 BCE.

1. *quod honestum est id solum bonum esse.* Only what is honorable is good.
2. *in quo virtus sit ei nihil desse ad beate vivendum.* A man possessed of virtue lacks nothing to attain a blessed life.
3. *aequalia esse peccata et recte facta ("nullum in delictis esse discrimen, aeque peccare si priuatis ac si magistratibus manus afferat").* All wrongdoing and good actions are of equal value; there is no distinction between offences, and a man offends as much whether he offers violence to private citizens or to magistrates.
4. *omnem stultum insanire.* Every fool is a madman.
5. *solum sapientem esse liberum et omnem stultum servum.* Only the wise man is free, and every fool is a slave.
6. *solum sapientem esse divitem.* Only the wise man is wealthy.

In *Pro Murena* Cicero bypasses the indisputable 1 and 2 and concentrates on two of the paradoxes—the equality of all offences great and small and the wise man's monopoly of beauty, liberty, wealth, and authority. Zeno supposedly claimed that wise men, even at their most ugly, were the only handsome fellows. They alone were wealthy even if they were beggars, and kings even if they were enslaved.

Dixisti quippiam: this is the neuter singular form of the indefinite pronoun *quispiam*, a synonym of the more common *quisquam*, *quaequam*, *quicquam* (A&G §151d).

distortissimi: the superlative from the past participle of *distorquere* is exceptional.

servitutem serviant: a normally intransitive verb can take an internal (or cognate) accusative in *figura etymologica* (on which see Quint. 7.3.26). This doubling is an archaic and comic turn of phrase, suggesting Cato's own old-fashioned manner.

scelus . . . nefarium: compare this to the language of §62 below, *sceleratus et nefarius, exorari scelus, misereri flagitium*. The almost archaic extravagance of these reiterated denunciations reinforces their incongruity.

qui gallum gallinaceum . . . sententiam mutare numquam: Cicero takes last the supposed equal wickedness of all offences, putting the man who kills a chicken without need on a par with a father-killer. Only the wise man has knowledge and does not entertain opinions: he regrets nothing, is never deceived, and never changes his judgment.

62. homo ingeniosissimus, . . . auctoribus eruditis inductus: *ingeniosissimus* (cf. §48 on Hortensius) suggests cleverness but a lack of common sense, while the learning (*eruditio*) of Cato's authorities removes him further from the common sense of the Roman juror.

adripuit . . . sed ita vivendi: worse, Cato did not just seize (*adripuit*) on these moral notions for the purposes of abstract argument, but for practice in real life, *vivendi* (sc. *causa*).

Petunt aliquid publicani: this is the first of a series of general political issues showing how Cato's response would be inappropriate. We know, in fact, from *Att.* 2.1.8 that Cato caused a major political breach by his obstinacy in resisting requests for concessions from the Asian tax companies, which had overbid on their contracts and were now asking for a remission that would protect their profits. In a letter to Atticus, Cicero admitted that this was unjustified, but it was politically essential to retain their goodwill. But that letter dates from two years after *Pro Murena* (June 60 BCE). It is possible that this sentence was added in a revision of the speech, but it is just as likely that Cato was already quarrelling with the *publicani* in 63 BCE.

Supplices . . . calamitosi: on *calamitosi* see §50 above. This group is harder to identify, but suggests the children of the proscribed, whose appeal for restoration Cicero had reluctantly led the Senate to turn down this year.

sceleratus . . . fueris, si . . . feceris: two future perfects in an open condition, which is backed up by the more general claim that forgiving whoever asks for pardon is wicked, even if their offence is minor.

fixum atque statutum: if you say that something "is definite and resolved," "you have been misled by opinion," and we are told that "the wise man does not hold opinions." If you were mistaken, he treats this as an insult.

Hac ex disciplina nobis illa sunt: is Cicero actually quoting Cato? This is *sermocinatio*, an imagined conversational exchange. "I said in the Senate I would lay charges against a consular candidate." "Perhaps you said it in anger?" He answers that the wise man never gets angry. "Perhaps you were reacting to circumstances." "NO," he says, "only a wicked man misleads with a falsehood: to change one's mind is shameful, to be appeased is a crime, to feel pity a scandal."

63. Nostri autem illi: "those great teachers of ours." Cicero poses as an older man who went through Cato's phase of seeking formal teaching from mistrust of his own judgment. The followers of Plato and Aristotle from the Academy and the Peripatos were moderate men who allowed for exceptions, with different levels of penalty for different offences. The prime difference between Stoics and Peripatetics was that Peripatetics permitted and saw the usefulness of anger. So the consistent man made room for pardoning and might err in anger, then calm down, changing his mind. Peripatetics believed that all virtues were a form of moderation or mean. This is the theme applied in detail to various virtues in books 4 and 5 of Aristotle's *Nicomachean Ethics*.

64. Hos ad magistros: with *hos*, Cicero contrasts the inferior quality of present-day teachers with the great men of old (cf. §63 above, *illi*). If Cato had let Nature direct him to these teachers, he would not have been more virtuous (brave, restrained, and just) but more inclined to *lenitas*. (This is Greek *epieikeia*, the mildness that tempers justice with understanding.)

neque enim esse potes: these plain words could be understood in two ways: first, "you cannot be better and braver and more moderate and just" because your virtue is already superlative, and second (if less obvious), "you are incapable of being better" etc. This may influence our understanding of *si potuisses* below, an otherwise unlikely qualification. Understand "you either would not have uttered [your atrocious threat in the Senate]" or "you would have interpreted it more mildly, if you had been capable of it." Cicero sees prosecution as only justified by feuding (*inimicitiae* §64, cf. §56 above) or wrongs inflicted (*iniuria*). Indeed, since Fortune had put Cato and Murena into office together (*eiusdem anni custodia* "protecting the same year"), Cato would have felt bound by this civic bond, and not uttered those outrageous words in the Senate—presumably the threats to lay charges against a consular candidate—or interpreted them more mildly.

potuisses: seems an unlikely qualification. The manuscript reading *seposuisses* is probably influenced by *posuisset* above. While the compound verb *seponere* is Ciceronian, it usually means setting aside as a category, without dropping or rejecting. Thus Cato would have kept these words from utterance on that occasion.

65. ego opinione auguror: Cicero ventures to believe Cato is simply angry, excited, or inflamed by his philosophical studies.

concitatum . . . elatum . . . flagrantem: the last adjective is very strong (as in *flagrantem odio, infamia*). Cato's instructors had carried their definition of duty further than Nature wished, that is, as if we stopped when we should, when we had disputed to the intellectual limit of the argument *ad ultimum animo contendissemus.*

'Nihil ignoveris.' Immo aliquid, non omnia: the perfect subjunctive after the negative *nihil* is a form of prohibition (A&G §450). Cicero quotes the Stoic prohibitions, modifying each one.

resistito . . . permaneto: the future generalizing imperatives are typical of legal usage and perhaps intended to color the order with archaic or legal force. See §61n above.

gratiae, cum officium et fides postulabit: and so puts the strong moral forces of duty and truthful loyalty on the side of yielding.

'. . . commotus ne sis': the prohibition on pity is accepted if it weakens severity but offset by the glory and credit due to merciful behavior.

humanitatis: "mercy," as in §6 above, *lenitatis . . . misericordiae . . . ad humanitatem* (cf. §9 *inhumanitatis*).

sententia alia vicerit melior: sticking to one's decision is good unless a superior decision replaces it. *Sententia* with a political as well as moral force again refers back to Cato's original threat of prosecution.

66. Huiusce modi: the fossilized phrase *huius modi* = "of this kind," i.e. *talis.*, For the - *ce* enclitic, cf. §26.

Scipio ille fuit: Cicero marks the approaching end of this section by returning to Scipio Aemilianus, who behaved like Cato and lived with the learned (Stoic) Panaetius as Cato kept a learned man in his house. He claims that Panaetius's instruction made Scipio not harsher but milder. Still softening up the jury, Cicero praises the good humor of Scipio's associates, above all Laelius, whom these studies made more pleasant, weightier, and wiser; or (Furius) Philus or (Sulpicius) Galus.

sed te domum iam deducam tuam: Cicero will "help Cato" by returning him to his family (sc. history). Compare the social practice of *domum deducere*, an act of respectful loyalty.

Est illud quidem exemplum . . .: "you have that model set before you within your family, but the resemblance to his nature could have reached you more easily than it reached each and every one of us." *Potuit* may be again ambiguous, between the factual "was able to reach" and counterfactual "could have reached." Cicero may have already begun to shape in his mind the liberal personality he would create for Cato the Censor in *de Senectute* more than 15 years later.

asperseris: Cicero, with that in mind, introduces the metaphor of seasoning food. For a parallel use of *aspergere*, cf. *Orator* 87 *huic generi orationis aspergentur etiam sales*. If Cato can sprinkle his ancestor's generosity onto his own severity, it will not improve his own qualities, excellent as they already are, but they will be more agreeably seasoned.

condita: for *condire* of making the personality more palatable, cf. *Brut.* 177, *de Orat.* 2.212.

67. ut ad id . . . revertar: Cicero is ready to return to his main theme.

tolle mihi . . . remove . . .: *mihi* is an ethical dative (cf. above §21n). These second person imperatives seem to return directly to Servius, unless we treat them as mere general figures. Now that the impact of Cato's reputation—*nomen, vim* (cf. §59 *vim maiorem*) *auctoritatem*—has been removed, he suggests that he and Servius focus on the actual charges.

Quid accusas . . . Calpurniam factum videri: this is a brief recapitulation of the first issue treated in the speech, that Cicero should not defend the offence he punished by law.

quod idem defendam quod lege punierim: the verbs are subjunctive in subordinate clauses of indirect speech after *reprehendis*. But Cicero set a penalty for bribery, not for innocence: he is ready to join Sulpicius in accusing bribery. There are three clauses in the Senate decree of amendment proposed by Cicero: if men were hired for pay to meet the candidates, if hired men escorted them around (these were called *sectatores*), and if seats for Murena's gladiatorial show were handed out randomly to whole tribes and likewise meals offered randomly, then these actions were deemed in violation of the *lex Calpurnia*.

issent: = *ivissent*, pluperfect subjunctive, "had gone to meet him."

si conducti sectarentur: some manuscripts read *conducti*, others *corrupti*: hence Adamietz excises the participle as a gloss.

volgo . . . tributim: the two nouns do not contradict each other, but define allocations of seats (with *locus* understand *datus*, parallel to *prandia* "meals" . . . *data*) dished out unselectively (*volgo*) and to all tribes (not just the candidate's own). What is Cicero's point? That his opponents are arguing about what behavior is illegal, instead of investigating whether it actually took place.

candidatis morem gerit: the Senate is passing an unnecessary decree to oblige the candidates. *Morem gerere* (cf. §46 above) normally denotes humoring an unreasonable demand, unnecessary since what urgently needs investigation is whether this happened, but if so (*sin factum sit*) no one can doubt that such behavior violates the law. Technically, Cicero is reasserting that the case is one of fact—NOT GUILTY (the *status coniecturalis*)—not of quality or definition.

§68–73: The paragraphs dealing with *adsectatio* contain a number of verbal coincidences with *Commentariolum* §34–38. As Nisbet 1961: 84–87 says, "if we acknowledge a relationship between the two works (and most scholars would) we must admit that *Mur.* 68–73 had a particularly close relationship with the *Commentariolum*: either Cicero when he wrote *Mur.* 68–73 had the *commentariolum* very much in mind or else the author of the *Commentariolum* had made a close study of *Mur.* 68–73." So for example, *Mur.* 69 *omitto clientis vicinos tribulis* corresponds to *Comm.* 17 *ut tribules* *ut vicini ut clientes*. But it could be argued that these were standard categories. Cicero argues that it is ridiculous to leave what is at issue uncertain but to pass judgment on the undisputed general principle decreed at the request of all the candidates in such a way that no one can tell from the decree for or against whom it was passed (and it may indeed have been aimed not at Murena but at Catiline). What matters is whether Murena committed these infringements: if so Cicero will allow that they are in violation of the law. The whole burden of this section is to write off as normal practice what may on this occasion have gone beyond the normal degree. Now he quotes the prosecutors' accusations, which offer an important outline of Roman society and the relationship between patron and client.

68. obviam prodierunt . . . decedenti: the participle stands for the noun; to him, Murena, departing from his province. The dative is used after *obviam ire, prodire* (A&G §370c).

eccui . . . non proditur reuertenti: "is there anyone whom men don't go out to meet on his return?" *Eccui* is the dative of *ecquis, ecquae, ecquod*; *proditur* is a generalizing impersonal passive.

'Quae fuit ista multitudo': Cicero feigns the prosecution's surprise at the attending crowd, but Cicero makes a point from enumerating who constituted the crowd. If Cicero cannot give an account of the crowd, this is nothing to cause surprise; indeed, even the prosecution's supporters (Postumius) showed up, because it would be more surprising if a large number did not show up.

quid habet admirationis: the subject of *habet* is the accusative and infinitive phrase. **admirationis:** is partitive genitive with *quid* (A&G §346.3; W 77 ii).

69. rogatos: unlike other verbs of asking, *rogare* can take two objects, the request and the person asked, so the passive participle is regularly used. Cicero's sentence supposes that many were actually invited, something not alien to Roman practice. The next two paragraphs turn the alleged hired meeters and greeters into the Roman norm.

infimorum . . . filios: Rome is a community where we regularly come to escort nobodies (or their sons, born in the lowest class) often leaving the furthest part of the city when it is still night; so is it an offence (*criminosum*) or surprising if men are willing (*non gravantur*) to appear on the Campus Martius at the third hour (i.e., eight or nine AM), especially if they are invited on behalf of such a distinguished man? Cicero is building up the argument that this is normal and not limited to the political class.

deductum venire: the supine is regularly used after a verb of motion to convey purpose.

societates: "whole business partnerships came to greet Murena, including many who are now sitting as jurors (on this actual jury) and many of the most distinguished men in the Senate (*nostri ordinis*), and the whole obsequious tribe (*natio*) of candidates who will not let anyone enter the city unhonored, even the accuser Postumius and his crowd."

dignitati: summing up, and returning to the allegation of hiring greeters, Cicero adds that no man ever lacked *frequentia gratuita* to match both his *dignitas* and his aspirations.

cum bene magna caterva: the use of *bene* as an intensifier is colloquial.

per eos dies: "over a period of days." *Per* distinguishes time within which from the simple accusative of duration.

70. sectabantur multi . . . sectatoribus . . . adsectationem: Cicero stresses the opponent's allegation that many followed the candidate around. But this is only an offence if they did so for pay. Sulpicius challenges the need for followers (*sectatores*, cf. *Comm. Pet.* §34). But this service (*opera*) and personal attendance has always been Roman practice; it is the only opportunity for humble men (*tenues*) to earn or repay a favor. As Cicero points out, speaking both from the viewpoint of an attending senator and of a candidate, senators and *equites* cannot be expected to trail around after their associates all day long: we candidates think ourselves

paid due respect if they throng our house and escort us from time
to time or honor us with a turn around in the basilica.

ad forum deducimur: compare §66 *domum deducere.*

unum habent . . . locum, hanc . . . operam: *hanc* etc. stands in
apposition to *locum.*

uno basilicae spatio: basilicas were long and shady, so one turn
along (or inside) a basilica would be a symbolic gesture as part of
the public ritual. There were two main basilicas in the forum: the
Basilica Porcia and the Basilica Aemilia (damaged but restored
after this date by the consul of 50 BCE).

tenuiorum . . . non occupatorum: the assumption is that persons
of low status did not have duties and obligations and should be
able to pay attentions to candidates. *Tenuis* can be taken conde-
scendingly or sympathetically. Contrast the *homines tenues et
egentes* of *Cat.* 2.20 with Horace's *me libertino patre natum et in
tenui re, Epist.* 1.20.20.

71. eripere hunc inferiori . . .: Cato should not deprive the
humble of the benefits of their service, but leave them some way
of repaying us (the senators and *equites* in the jury) for their
dependence on us. In Roman society, the client system meant that
anyone without money or influence depended on the protection of
his patron, either a former owner, if the man had been his slave
before becoming a freedman, or perhaps a military officer under
whom he had served. They were zealous to protect their right to
these services.

eripere: literally, "to rob." In Plautus's time we find bourgeois
figures acting in court on behalf of their humbler clients.

suffragium: if humble men are reduced to their votes, they have
no effect in the *comitia centuriata* used for consular elections,
since the voting units of the lower census classes were not normally called to vote if the elite units agreed in their support. In
addition, there were so many poor citizens in each of these lower
census classes that the individual's vote would count for nothing

even within his own unit. "They cannot speak for us in court or guarantee us in business (*spondere*) or invite us to their homes. Not being able to do these favors they think the favors we do them can only be repaid by their personal service" (*opera*).

legi Fabiae: like *consulto*, the dative is used after *restiterunt*. The *lex Fabia* limited the number of followers (we know nothing further about this law).

L. Caesare consule: in 64 BCE. Adamietz notes that this *senatus consultum* must have existed before the *lex Fabia*, and comments that Cicero seldom names a year by only one of its consuls. Shackleton Bailey 1979: 259 proposes inserting the second consul, *C. Figulo* with the plural *coss.*, but Adamietz can point to exceptional instances in Cicero's speeches and philosophical writings where only a single consul is named.

instituto officiorum: Cicero claims that no penalty can be used to exclude the loyal respect of the humble from what is an ancient practice.

72. At spectacula sunt tributim . . .: the third objection is to seats distributed by tribe for shows and dinners. Cicero's reply is that Murena did not do this himself, but his friends did on a modest scale (*more et modo*). Cicero does not try to defend this practice, but represents any restriction of such hospitality as politically counterproductive. Servius's protests in the Senate have cost us (meaning you, Servius, and others) many votes; there has never been a time within our fathers' memory in which there has not been this currying of favor or generosity, of giving seats at the Circus and in the forum (i.e., for chariot races and gladiatorial *munera*) to friends and fellow tribesmen. These are the rewards which humble men earned, lavished by their fellow tribesmen.

73.***: editors agree that a substantial passage is missing here. Syntactically and logically we expect (1) a charge about seats distributed, and (2) the beginning of Cicero's counter-objection.

Praefectum fabrum . . . dedisse: *fabrum* is a contracted genitive plural like *deum* for *deorum*. This official was supervisor of engineering and artillery in a military force, a position that brought wealth through contracts and confiscations to notorious figures like Caesar's *praefectus fabrum* Mamurra, mocked by Cat. 30. See Welch 1995. Although the main verb governing *praefectum . . . dedisse* is lost, it was obviously an allegation by one of the prosecutors. Cicero blames their excessive scrupulousness for all the charges mentioned in the last three sections (also those explicitly omitted) and claims Murena is still protected by the senatorial motion (but note it is only an *auctoritas*, not a *senatus consultum*, so the motion was not carried).

num obviam prodire crimen putat?: once again a distinction between going to meet a candidate and doing so for pay, between many followers and hired followers. Similarly, is it an offence (*crimen putat*) to provide seats for the show or an invitation to a dinner? No, only indiscriminately.

volgo, passim: "men *en bloc*," but clearly this has happened, and Pinarius Natta, Murena's son-in-law, has been lavishing seats in order to earn himself a position among the centuries of the elite.

in equitum centuriis: the eighteen centuries of the elite. Cicero claims this is no reason to treat young Natta's exercise of influence as a deceit or offence by his father-in-law Murena in this service between kinsmen by marriage. Again, if Murena's relation and kinswoman, the Vestal Virgin, made a present to him of her seat at the gladiatorial show (which would be in a privileged position at the front) this is simply an act of family loyalty, so that Murena is innocent of responsibility. Cicero dismisses these acts on the three grounds he has already invoked: as services by kinsmen, as the perquisites of the humble, and as gifts offered by candidates.

id erit eius vitrico fraudi aut crimini: *crimini*, like *fraudi*, is predicative dative, "shall this be treated as a fraudulent act or offense of his stepfather," but *vitrico* is in fact dative of disadvantage. For a similarly constructed sentence, see §12n, *magno adiumento*.

74. agit mecum austere et Stoice . . .: the puritanical side of Stoicism was always strong at Rome, and Cicero sees the banquets through Cato's eyes as using food to entice goodwill, since men's judgment in appointing to office should not be corrupted by pleasure.

adlici benivolentiam cibo . . . voluptatibus: the accumulation of strong sensual vocabulary like *adlicere* and *delenire*, associated with pleasure, reinforces the contrast between the solemn metaphor of *gubernacula* and the image of the pander appealing to susceptible young men.

Quippe . . . tu mihi: ethical dative (cf. *tu mihi fueris* §21). Again Cicero impersonates Cato: "I suppose then that you would aim at the highest office and authority at the helm of the state by indulging men's senses, soothing their spirits, and applying pleasures to them?" "Were you seeking to pander to a flock of pampered youth, or seeking command over the world from the Roman people?"

Horribilis oratio: *horribilis* "shudder-making" belongs in letters rather than oratory, but cf. *Cat.* 2.15 *horribilis belli periculum.*

Lacedaemonii . . . Cretes: Cicero parades his knowledge of Greek history. The military messes of the Spartans and Cretans were models of mythical austerity: the Spartans sitting on bare wood, the Cretans eating without reclining. But they were not more successful than the Romans, who divided their time between toil and indulgence. The latter were destroyed by a single Roman assault (Cicero refers to Metellus Creticus's recent campaigns in Crete in 69–67 BCE), while the Spartans (in a formally recognized alliance with Rome since the subjugation of Achaea in 146 BCE) only preserve their discipline and code of laws under the protection of our Roman empire.

75. maiorum instituta: compare *vetere instituto* §72. It follows that Cato's excessively severe speech is condemning Rome's ancestral customs (cf. *maiorum instituta* with *vetere instituto* §72) sanctioned by the duration of her empire.

Q. Tubero . . . homo eruditissimus ac Stoicus: Cicero cites the
cautionary example of Q. Aelius Tubero (RE Aelius 155), like Sulpicius a jurist of high birth. In fact, Cicero rounds off this anecdote
with a reminder of his noble family: *L Pauli nepos, P Africani
sororis filius*. L. Pauli is Aemilius Paulus, his grandfather, victor at
Pydna over Perseus of Macedon (cf. §31 above, *triumphus de rege
Perse L. Pauli*). Aemilius, as Plut. *Aem.* 35 reports, "had four sons
of whom two . . . had been adopted into other families, namely
Scipio and Fabius; and two sons still boys, the children of a second
wife . . . one of these, aged 14 years, died five days before Aemilius
celebrated his triumph, and the death of the other, who was 12
years of age, followed three days after the triumph." Cicero calls
the adopted sons Q. Maximus and P. Africanus because after adoption they became P. Cornelius Scipio Aemilianus (awarded the
honorific title Africanus from his conquest of Carthage) and
Q. Fabius Maximus Aemilianus (RE 109), elected consul in the
year of his brother's victory.

   Why did Aemilius place his older sons for adoption? There
are three probable motives: he could not afford to rear and
further the political careers of four sons, he had divorced the
mother of the older sons some 15 years before, and he had
remarried. The adoptions would certainly strengthen the family
bond with his friends, P. Cornelius Scipio and Fabius Maximus;
probably neither man had a natural son. Polyb. 31.26 tells us
that Aemilius Paulus also married his sister Aemilia to the older
Scipio Africanus, the victor of Zama. All three families reinforced their connections both by adoption and by marriage. So
Cicero reports here that Fabius Maximus Allobrogicus (cos. 121
BCE), son of Fabius Maximus Aemilianus and so Scipio Aemilianus's nephew by birth, organized Aemilianus's funeral games
and public feast (as the two of them had honored their father
Paulus's death in 160 BCE with funeral games, which included
two comedies by Terence.)

patrui sui: Aemilianus was the *patruus* (paternal uncle) not of
Tubero but of Allobrogicus. We learn a lot more about Tubero and
his failed career from Cicero's later account in *Brut.* 117, which

shows Tubero destroying his own political future: Cicero reports
that Tubero as tribune voted that augurs could not be exempted
from their duties against the witness of his uncle Aemilianus.
Tubero was a conservative, a *constans civis* and harassed Tiberius
Gracchus (as a speech of Tiberius reveals), but a poor speaker and
a rigorous Stoic, severe (*durior*) and in his life *durus, incultus, horridus*. It sounds as though he had damaged his own prospects even
before the funeral, but it suits Cicero's argument here at *Mur.* 75
to suppress Tubero's uncompromising political actions before the
episode of the funeral feast.

ut triclinium sterneret: that is to provide the equipment (set the
table) for a unit (nine persons?) at his uncle's funeral feast.

pelliculis haedinis lectulos Punicanos: note the contemptuous
diminutives for Tubero's stingy furnishings of plain Punic benches,
goatskins, and (plain earthenware) Samian pottery for the funeral
feast. The form *Punic-anos* rather than *Punicos* distinguishes a
special type of bench from benches that were actually from Punic
Carthage. Diminutives are rare in formal oratory, and tend either
to evoke comedy or imply contempt. Cicero does not mention
here or in *Brutus* that the Aelii Tuberones were exceptionally poor
and may have found it necessary to mask their poverty in Stoic
principles. Thus described, Tubero makes a splendid precedent for
Sulpicius's defeat. No doubt the Roman people deeply resented
his incongruous philosophical principles, when they withheld their
votes in the following praetorian election from a man so nobly
born that he could have been expected to have a brilliant career on
genus alone (§76). (Sumner 1973 dates this political defeat to soon
after the death of Aemilianus in 129 BCE.)

privatam luxuriam, publicam magnificentiam: *magnificentia,*
"expenditure," was last used of Murena's aedilician display in §38
and *magnificentissimos . . . fecisse ludos*, §41. Cicero contrasts
private luxury with the grand public displays cherished by the
Roman people, who understand the proper alternation of toil and
pleasure (cf. Hor. *Od.* 2.15.13–14 *privatus illis census erat brevis; /
commune magnum*). The analogy with Servius is obvious.

76. vicissitudinem laboris ac voluptatis: a repetition with variation of §74 *tempora voluptatis laborisque.*

Haec omnia . . . largitionem: by an agile leap back to §75, Cicero returns to the claim that the common people should not be robbed of their reward of games, gladiators, and feasting, which the ancestors secured, nor should candidates be deprived of a kindness, which is more a matter of generosity than bribery.

sordis et inhumanitatem: an interesting transfer of both physical *sordes* (economic shabbiness, regularly plural) and *inhumanitas* (meanness, abusive treatment, see §9 above) to mere social disrespect or lack of courtesy.

§76–77 summa est dignitas: Cato claims men should only be moved to entrust office by the candidate's *dignitas* (personal merit, the preoccupation of §15–53 above), but Cicero reproaches him with inconsistency; since he has immense *dignitas*, why does he ask any man for his support (as Cato must have done when seeking the tribunate earlier this year)? The argument challenges the whole notion of how to seek office. Switching from third to the more immediate first and second person, he asks why one should have to ask to be put in authority: "Should I be requested for this favor by you, Cato, rather than requesting you to take on toil and risk on my behalf?"

postea quam es designatus: the tribune-elect, as Cato now was.

eos notiores esse servo tuo quam tibi: isn't it shameful that your slave should know men better than you, his master? Cicero lists a series of paradoxes marked by *tamen*: "if you know your fellow-citizens but still need a reminder(er) to address them, you ask for their name if it is uncertain. But when you are reminded you greet them, (*tamen*) as if you yourself knew them. Why do you greet the same men more casually once you are elected?" Cicero claims all these acts would be correct by the standards of society, but would be felt as vicious if carefully measured (*perpendeas*; cf. §3 above of Cato *diligentissime perpendenti*) against your code. Cicero returns to the rules of Cato's discipline (*sin perpendere . . . velis*, cf. §3), by whose standards these actions are rotten.

nec plebi Romanae eripiendi fructus isti sunt: *plebi* is a dative of separation after *eripere* and not the dative of the agent with the gerundive construction. Compare the dative of separation in *candidatis adimenda* below.

78. At enim te ad accusandum res publica adduxit: *at enim* often introduces an imaginary objection or counterargument that Cicero wants to refute. He acknowledges Cato's good faith but argues that he has slipped inadvertently (*imprudentia*).

Audite, audite consulem . . .: with the emphatic anadiplosis of *audire* Cicero shifts gear into a more urgent and melodramatic mode, urging his audience to listen to a consul who thinks of the state both day and night (cf. Antonius's self-mockery in *de Orat.* 2.28 *audite vero, audite . . .*). In contrast to Cato's claims, Cicero now declares he is acting not only for the dignity of his friend Murena, but for public peace and leisure, for the harmony and life and well-being of all his hearers. The increased urgency is needed to rouse his audience before it is too late.

§78–85 L. Catilina: This is the second extended presentation of Catiline. Where §48–53 covered what had already occurred, these sections focus on the imminent and ubiquitous danger from inside, indeed the heart of the community, and from the army gathering outside. Thus §79 moves from Catiline's contempt for the state to the rot within, the *equus Troianus* and conspirators who had not deserted Catiline but stayed behind to welcome him. In §80 and again §84 Cicero's countermeasures are followed by the bloodcurdling identification of the enemy within, citizens and, he will reveal, senators here in our midst. Worse still (§81–82), more enemies are waiting to enter office (on 10 December), like the tribune Metellus, and challenge Cato himself, as incoming tribune, as well as the current and outgoing consuls. The terror motif alternates with allusions to Catiline's approaching army of irregulars (§85) and a picture of every part of the city in panic, with an army (Catiline's force; cf. §79) on the Campus Martius, where regular armies were levied and mustered. The main theme of Catiline has returned.

§78–79: Cicero now argues that Catiline only left Rome with a token band of supporters. He would not have expected to overwhelm (*oppressurum*, cf. *opprimemini* below) the city with so small a force. Rather, the trouble is still there in the city, even in the Senate itself. The infection has spread (*latius patet*) and the Trojan horse is already inside Rome (anadiplosis of *intus*), but he, Cicero, is not afraid, and has taken steps to ensure that citizens are not caught sleeping while he is their consul (and only six or seven weeks now remain before he steps down). He has moved from past accusations into the immediate future and is spreading alarm and suspicion.

Intus, intus, inquam, est equus Troianus: compare *Cat.* 2.11 *intus insidiae sunt*. This maintains the melodramatic tenor with the anadiplosis of *intus* (cf. *audite* above, §78). Cicero uses the motif of the enemy in our midst to frame this section (cf. below, §84 *hostis est enim . . . in urbe, in foro . . . in ipsa curia non nemo hostis est*) and puts his audience on red alert against the unnamed terrorists left behind.

79. copias illius quas hic video: is *hic* "here at Rome" or "here in this court in the forum"? Cicero holds back, reserving for his climax in §84 the revelation that Catiline's fellow conspirators are in the Senate itself.

in speculis: from *specula* (*-ae*) not *speculu*, this is metaphorical (cf. *Verr.* 1.46, *nunc autem homines in speculis sunt*; *Deiot.* 22, *semper in speculis esse*), "on the watch" rather than in the actual rooftop loggias of Roman (and medieval Italian) palazzi.

in capite atque in cervicibus: *capite* is a natural collective, whereas *cervices* is the regular plural usage, as at *Fam.* 12.23.2 *in cervicibus nostris conlocare*; *Sulla* 28 *quos ego a vestris cervicibus depuli*.

integrum consulem et bonum imperatorem . . . volunt: Murena has been presented as an experienced general, which his colleague Silanus is not; is it also implied that Silanus is not *integer*? It must either mean unimpaired, undamaged, or as in §3 above, honest.

deici: commonly used of dislodging the defender of a stronghold. In contrast, Cicero calls his own reaction a defensive thrust, *reieci*.

reieci . . . debilitavi . . . compressi: in a tricolon Cicero claims to have driven the enemy away from the election field (when he appeared in his shining breastplate), weakened them in the forum (probably in a *contio* like *Cat.* 2 delivered in the Comitia), and frequently checked their attacks at his home (but there was only one known assassination attempt).

his vos si alterum consulem tradideritis: this picks up *quorum* in the relative clause opening the sentence. Again the jury would become tools of the armed enemy, who would gain far more from the jury vote than from their own armed action.

Magni interest . . . esse Kalendis Ianuariis . . . duo consules: Cicero reminds the jurors of the proximity of the change of consulship.

80. Nolite arbitrari . . .: Cicero's point is that the political enemies are not the usual radicals relying on popular legislation or ruinous extravagance. Since Gaius Gracchus, politicians had won the people of Rome by providing cheap or free grain rations, something Cato himself would do as tribune in 62 BCE.

***eos* uti:** the sentence as transmitted is incomplete, and Clark supplements with *eos*, changing the manuscript reading *aut* to *uti*.

consilia . . . urbis delendae: the enemy's plots provide a leitmotif. But why would the radicals backing Catiline destroy Rome or its population or put an end to the name of Rome? Worse, these plans have been dreamed up by fellow citizens.

Atque haec cives, cives, inquam . . .: another anadiplosis, doubly dreadful since Roman citizens have planned this destruction of their state, and a situation creating a constitutional crisis when Cicero had to refer to the Senate the proposal for executing these Roman citizens, a penalty that by Gaius Gracchus's *lex Sempronia* could only be inflicted by the Roman people acting as a court or a court constituted by the people. **occurro** . . .

debilito . . . resisto: another tricolon reiterates Cicero's continued success.

In exitu . . . vicarium: Cicero's consulship is approaching its end (about six weeks remain). As Cicero's successor and representative, Murena is not strictly speaking a *vicarius*, who was a slave employed by another to fulfill his duties (cf. *Sull.* 26 *cuius vicarius qui velit esse, inueniri nemo potest*). Condemning Murena would rob Cicero of the successor whom he needs to defend the state.

81. tempestatem: now Cicero adds another danger, a crisis (*tempestas*) in the coming year of Cato's tribunate.

designati tribuni: this is Metellus Nepos, newly elected tribunician colleague of Cato, who had begun to denounce Cicero. It was known that Cato had not planned to stand for this office, but had been urged to it by conservative fellow citizens (Plut. *Cato min.* 20). As far as we know, Metellus's political aim (and that of Caesar, praetor in 62 BCE and allied with him) was to denounce Cicero so as to stir up public demand for the recall of Pompey to deal with Catiline.

ab eo tempore . . .: by 63 BCE there was a growing belief that Catiline had conspired in 65 BCE (*per hoc triennium*) to stage a coup d'état against the incoming consuls (here exaggerated as the Senate), along with a junior magistrate, Cn. Piso, since assassinated. Cicero claims this conspiracy is about to break out in these days and months, and his own survival up to now has only been achieved through divine guidance by night and day. What the enemy wants is not the killing of Cicero in his own right but the removal of a vigilant consul from his protection of the state (cf. §79 *de urbis praesidio* and §82 end *sine praesidio*).

82. me meo nomine . . . sed vigilantem consulem: the ablative *meo nomine* specifies the aspect involved, i.e., "me, on my personal account" as opposed to Cicero, the magistrate.

Nec minus vellent . . . te quoque . . . tollere: now Cicero claims common cause with Cato and takes the opportunity to praise him for his courage, intellect, and authority (back to the theme of §58 above). Cicero conjures up an unlikely scenario in which the power of Cato's tribunate will be weakened by the removal of the patriotic consul. This would assume that the remaining body of tribunes (9 out of 10) would be unanimous.

Ne sufficiatur consul non timent: Cicero eliminates one contingency, viz. that there would be time before 1 January to elect a substitute consul (*suffectus*). Instead, the conspirators hope to have D. Silanus without a colleague and Cato without a consul.

D. Silanum, clarum virum: the only reference to Silanus in the whole speech, and it could not be more tepid. All other individuals named have been graced with complimentary epithets, whereas *vir clarus* is not even a superlative. Silanus's vote in the Catilinarian debate is recorded in neutral terms by Cic. *Cat.* 4.7 and Sall. *Cat.* 50.4 (cf. Caesar's honorific reference at Sall. *Cat.* 51.16). Cato had declared he would not allow a prosecution of his brother-in-law Silanus (Plut. *Cato min.* 21.2–3), and we may surmise that being himself too young to be a candidate, he wanted an alliance of Ser. Sulpicius and Silanus to implement his principles. Was Cicero hostile because of this, or did he simply despise Silanus (a man with no record of achievement)? We have no evidence of Silanus's activity apart from his vote opening the Catilinarian debate, the vote which he tried to rescind.

83. est tuum . . . consulem non cupidum: with his lavish compliment that Cato was born for his country's sake, Cicero makes it Cato's role or duty to save Murena as his ally (*adiutorem*) as a consul appointed by fortune to embrace public peace (a new claim, cf. §79 *et natura et fortuna cum rei publicae salute coniunctum*), but by his expertise to wage war and by his spirit and experience to take on any task.

huiusce rei . . . vos gubernatis: Cicero flatters the jury with their importance and insists that Catiline would condemn Murena if he could pass a verdict, or even kill him. It is Catiline's interest to deprive the state of its parent (*orbare* "to orphan") to reduce the number of its commanders, and by driving off his rival to give the tribunes a greater chance to stir up rioting and discord.

Idemne . . . ille importunissimus gladiator?: for Catiline as *gladiator*, cf. §50 and the abusive *latrocinium* (§84): he had been declared a *hostis* weeks before.

84. In discrimen extremum venimus: *vēnimus* (perfect, like *lapsi*). This is the crisis point, in which we need to add reinforcements, not reduce our backing.

Hostis est enim non apud Anienem: the Anio, a tributary of the Tiber within walking distance of Rome, was, according to Livy, the nearest Hannibal brought his camp in 211 BCE in preparation for attacking the city (*inter haec Hannibal ad Anienem fluvium tria milia passuum ab urbe castra admovit. Ibi stativis positis ipse cum duobus milibus equitum ad portam Collinam usque ad Herculis templum est progressus atque unde proxume poterat moenia situmque urbis obequitans contemplabatur*, Liv. 26.10.3). Now the enemy is inside (cf. §78 *intus est equus Troianus*), not just in the forum but in the heart of the state.

illo sacrario rei publicae: *sacrarium* ("shrine"), which Cicero had previously used only of actual Sicilian shrines, is a highly rhetorical designation for the senate house. Sall. *Cat.* 17.3 lists 11 men of senatorial status among the conspirators, but Ryan 1994 has shown that only two were certainly senators in 64 BCE, with five non-senators and four of dubious status. Cicero reports in the fourth Catilinarian the arrests and confessions on 5 December of P. Cornelius Lentulus Sura (RE 240), consul in 71 BCE but expelled from the Senate by the censors of 70 BCE; he had resumed his career and was currently again in office as praetor. C. Cornelius Cethegus (RE 89) was also a senator, as was L. Cassius Longinus, now absent from Rome.

Di faxint: *faxint* is an early sigmatized optative equivalent of *faciant* found in wishes and prayers (A §183.3; W. 115n i).

Meus conlega: Cicero and his audience all knew that Antonius had been Catiline's ally and would be reluctant to act against him; they probably also knew that Cicero had bribed Antonius into neutrality by offering him the proconsular governorship of Macedonia, which he took up in 62 BCE. Given Antonius Hybrida's poor record and former alliance with Catiline, this may represent more a wish than any expectation. In fact, Antonius was given a military command against Catiline but experienced a convenient illness, which left the battle at Pistoia under the command of his subordinate.

85. redundarint: *redundare* is used of waves bounced back onto the shore (*de Orat.* 1.3). If there is only one consul, he will be kept busy getting a suffect consul elected (*in sufficiendo conlega*).

sint * illa pestis . . . qua po *** minatur:** the text is damaged, and there is no way to link the lucid *illa pestis immanis importuna Catilinae prorumpet* with the main subject, the man who will be able to obstruct him, i.e., the sole consul Silanus. The other fragmented clause surely identifies the places from which Catiline threatens and on which he was marching, from Etruria to the outskirts of Rome (*suburbanus*, cf. *suburbanum rusticum et amoenum*, *S. Rosc.*133), which will be engulfed in a fivefold disaster: frenzy in the *comitium* (place of popular assembly and therefore superior to Halm's *urbe*), panic in the Senate, conspiracy in the forum, an army in the Campus Martius (whose army? that of Catiline's deputy Manlius?), and devastation across the land. Cicero must have spoken this defense only a week or so after his first speech against Catiline in the Senate and the second Catilinarian addressed to the Roman people.

furor . . . timor . . . coniuratio: compare *Cat.* 1.18; 2.25–26, where the State personified warns him of *timor*, and 1.27, 30, 31. As for *coniuratio*, we are accustomed to hearing about the "conspiracy of Catiline," but the use of *coniuratio* for a domestic plot was still a fresh image at this time. The *ferrum flammamque* of §85 are echoed in Cicero's admission of exploiting the theme: *Att.* 1.14.3 *totum hunc locum quem ego varie meis orationibus . . . soleo pingere, de flamma, de ferro . . . pertexuit.* But all these threats can be wiped away if the state is well-defended by both official and private action.

sede ac loco: compare *sede ac domo, Verr.* 5.187; *tectis ac sedibus suis, Agr.* 2.90.

quae iam diu comparantur: "which have long been in preparation." With adverbs like *iamdiu, iampridem,* the present tense represents events continuing from past time into the present (A&G §471b).

§86–90: we have come to the part of the *peroratio* often called *miseratio,* from the verb *miserari,* to invoke pity, as in §55 *non queam satis . . . huius eventum fortunamque miserari.* It is marked by words like *supplex, fidem obtestatur, misericordiam implorat.* This will be developed in §87–88 with *misericordiam, miseranda, quo se miser vertet, matrem quae misera . . .,* and §89: *ibit igitur in exsilium miser? quae si acerba, si misera, si luctuosa sunt, si alienissima a mansuetudine et misericordia vestra . . . conservate populi Romani beneficium.*

86. Quae cum . . . nova lamentatione obruatis: the long period opening §86 is articulated in two blocks: (1) the political: *primum rei publicae causa . . . moneo . . . pro auctoritate consulari hortor . . . obtestor . . .;* and (2) the personal: *deinde idem et defensoris et amici officio adductus oro atque obsecro.* The chief purpose of this section is to trade on the jury's enjoyment of power and pride in the magnanimity that makes them saviors of the state. Cicero divides his supplications between pleas on behalf of the state and for his friend, that the jurors should not burden with new lamentation the recent congratulation of poor Murena.

ut ne . . . obruatis: the two conjunctions sometimes replace the use of *ne* alone (without change of meaning) in an indirect command.

corporis morbo . . . confectus morbo: was Murena physically ill, as Cicero's words declare twice in this paragraph?

nunc idem . . . vestras opes intuetur: next Cicero plays on the "reversal of fortune" motif, that the man who seemed so fortunate, newly glorified with Rome's greatest honor, as first to bring the consulship into his old-established family and ancient community, should now be clad in mourning and worn out by sickness. Murena has become a suppliant, dependent on the jury's protection (*fides*) mercy, power, and resources.

87. per deos immortalis! iudices: the gods are invoked as a last emotional appeal (cf. §1, *precatus a dis immortalibus sum, iudices*). The jury should not deprive Murena of his earlier sources of honor (the plural *honestatibus* is exceptional) and all his rank and fortune along with the achievement that he believed would make him more honored.

orat atque obsecrat: Murena himself is begging for a place for moderation, a refuge for the humble (*demissis*), and support for his decency. These three abstractions correspond loosely to his inoffensive personal behavior (*ethos*), doing unjust harm to no man, refraining from offence to anyone's ear or intention, and shunning the alienation of anyone in civilian life or military service. To be stripped of the consulship should provoke great compassion, since everything else is being snatched away with it.

sit apud vos modestiae locus, sit . . . perfugium, sit auxilium . . .: the three subjunctives are hortatory/jussive (A&G §439; W 109).

invidiam . . . habere consulatus ipse nullam potest: a new point, "there is nothing to envy in a position isolated and exposed to the harangues of traitors, the treachery of conspirators, the weapons of Catiline, and every kind of danger and injustice." But *invidia*, whether referring to the envy felt by others or the unpopularity felt by its victim, was a major theme and source of argument in rhetoric, like its Greek counterpart, *phthonos*. This is discussed in some detail by Aristotle *Rhet.* 2.10, analyzing the sources of envy that the accusing speaker (or political rival) can provoke, the aspects of a defendant's life that are open to envy, and the use that can be made by defending counsel of charges of envy against his client. For Cicero's own adaptation of the Aristotelian theory of *psychagogia*, ("manipulating the emotions") see *de Orat.* 2.177, 206–10.

88. in hoc praeclaro consulatu: "this glorious consulship," surely ironic when contrasted with the pitiable experiences obvious to Cicero and his audience.

quo se miser vertet?: this rhetorical figure (*dubitatio*) had a long and famous history. The background to Gaius Gracchus's cry of despair when he was attacked as a traitor by a body of senators is filled in by Cicero in *de Orat.* 3.213–14. When Gracchus asked where he could turn in his time of affliction, rejecting his home and every alternative, he was already echoing Medea's question in Ennius's and Euripides's tragedy.

domumne . . .: Cicero considers and rejects first Murena's own home, where he will see his father's image so recently covered in the laurels of victory.

An ad matrem . . .: for *an* introducing an alternative question, often ironic in tone, see §11 above. His unhappy mother will be terrified to see him stripped of all his rank. This was also an element in Gracchus's famous lament.

89. nova poena legis: in Murena's case, the newly stiffened law is robbing him of house and home and the sight of all his family.

Ibit igitur in exsilium miser?: Murena cannot travel to exile in the East, scene of his successful warfare, or to the West, where Transalpine Gaul, where he governed so successfully, would see him mourning. His brother is a legate in part of this province, but how great will be his distress at the perversion of fortune if after the fresh news of election Murena suddenly appears as messenger of his own disaster.

gratulatum Romam concurrerent: the accusative of the supine *gratulatum* is the purpose and *Romam* (as usual without a preposition) the destination.

90. Quae si acerba . . . mansuetudine et misericordia vestra: Cicero had taken pains early in his speech to stress the virtue of *mansuetudo* and *misericordia* (§6). Now his appeal treats Murena's election as the gift of the Roman people (begging the question whether the vote was obtained by bribery) and the man himself as the possession of the state.

date hoc . . . honestissimo: Cicero invokes the jury in the name of Murena's family, dead and alive, and of his hometown Lanuvium.

quod . . . frequens maestumque vidistis: which the jury can see represented by a large and grieving delegation. Such local delegations were an expected feature of defense proceedings.

a sacris . . . facere necesse est: *facere* stands for *sacra facere*, to perform rites of sacrifice. Milo would attend the same ritual.

Iunonis Sospitae: Lanuvium held the chief shrine of the warrior goddess *Juno Sospita* (the savior), whose image in her goatskin helmet is found on many Roman coins. While *sacris patriis* suggests that Murena's family held priesthoods in Juno Sospita's cult, it may only develop the idea of Murena's birthplace (*domesticum et suum consulem* is emphatic, "her own local consul"). Her cult was well known: Propertius 4.7 describes Cynthia going on a pleasure trip to view the ritual at Lanuvium, in which a virgin was sent into Sospita's grotto to feed a sacred serpent. Ovid adds in *Fasti*. 6.60 that Lanuvium called the month of June Iunonius in its calendar.

At Rome coins were struck about this time by L. Roscius Fabatus. (Crawford 1974: #412 dated them to 64 BCE, early enough to have influenced Cicero's text, but they have now been downdated to 59 BCE). The obverse shows Juno Sospita in her distinctive goatskin helmet. Crawford also suggests that two of the moneyers of 62 BCE, L. Aemilius Lepidus Paulus and L. Scribonius Libo, had the Catilinarian conspiracy (and its failure) in mind when they chose the legends *CONCORDIA* and *BONUS EVENTUS*.

Quem ego vobis . . .: in his last sentence, Cicero recalls his own role as consul, now entrusting Murena to the jury's wise mercies and promising and guaranteeing to them that he will be peace-loving (*ut cupidissimum oti*, where *ut* is only read by some manuscripts) and devoted to good conservatives (*bonorum*), but fierce against disloyalty (*seditionem*), gallant in war (*in bello*), and most hostile to the conspiracy that is now trying to undermine the state (*huic coniurationi* . . . etc).

promittam et spondeam: we might compare the personal guarantee for Caelius that rounds off the *Pro Caelio* (§80): *quem si nobis, si suis, si rei publicae conservatis, addictum deditum obstrictum vobis ac liberis vestris habebitis . . . vos potissimum, iudices, fructus uberes diuturnosque capietis.*

Appendix: *Related Texts*

I. THE *COMMENTARIOLUM PETITIONIS* ATTRIBUTED TO QUINTUS CICERO FOR CICERO'S ELECTION CAMPAIGN OF 64 BCE (TEXT FROM D. R. SHACKLETON BAILEY, LCL, CAMBRIDGE, MA, 2002).

This "Handbook of Electioneering" ascribed to Quintus Cicero was preserved with the collection of Cicero's *Ad Familiares*, but absent from the oldest and most reliable manuscript, the codex Mediceus 49.9. To be useful to Cicero, this handbook would need to have been circulated in 64 BCE, but it seems to contain echoes of both Cicero's speech *In Toga Candida*, composed late in 64, and the *Pro Murena*. There are also local inconsistencies, such as the claim that Cicero was already *patronus consularium* and had defended Gallius. So the piece itself could be a learned exercise depending on the published works of Cicero. It is worth noting that while the pamphlet repeatedly refers to Pompey (5, 14) it does not mention Lucullus or other conservatives from the 60s. Even so, its coincidences with *Pro Murena* are informative. I offer here a selection of excerpts from Shackleton Bailey's text: *Cicero Letters* . . . vol. 28, Loeb Classical Library (2002).

A. *The Consulship and Cicero's Personal Situation*

(2) Civitas quae sit cogita, quid petas, qui sis. Prope cottidie tibi hoc ad forum descendenti meditandum est; **novus sum, consulatum peto, Roma est**. Nominis novitatem dicendi gloria maxime sublevabis. Semper ea res plurimum dignitatis habuit. Non potest qui

dignus habetur patronus consularium indignus consulatu putari. . . . (3) Deinde fac ut amicorum et multitudo et genera appareant. Habes enim ea quae <non multi homines> novi habuerunt: omnis publicanos, totam fere equestrem ordinem, multa propria muni- cipia, multos abs te defensos homines cuiusque ordinis, aliquot col- legia, praeterea studio dicendi conciliatos plurimos adulescentulos, cottidianam amicorum adsiduitatem et frequentiam. (4) Haec cura ut teneas commonendo et rogando et omni ratione efficiendo ut intelligant qui debent tua causa, referendae gratiae (*sc.* tempus) qui volunt, obligandi tui tempus sibi aliud nullum fore, etiam hos multum videtur adiuvare posse novum hominem hominum nobil- ium voluntas et maxime consularium; prodest, quorum in locum ac numerum pervenire uelis, ab iis ipsis illo loco ac numero dignum putari, (5) ii rogandi omnes sunt diligenter et ad eos allegandum est persuadendumque est iis **nos semper cum optimatibus de re publica sensisse, minime popularis fuisse; si quid loqui pop- ulariter videamur nos eo consilio fecisse ut Cn Pompeium nobis adiungeremus** ut eum qui plurimum posset aut amicum in nostra petitione haberemus aut certe non adversarium. (6) Praeterea adulescentis nobilis elabora ut habeas, uel ut teneas studiosos quos habes; multum dignitatis adferent si plurimos habes, perfice ut sciant quantum in iis putes esse: si adduxeris ut ii qui non nolunt cupiant, plurimum proderunt.

Consider what kind of community this is, what you are aiming for and who you are. You must reflect daily as you go down to the forum: **I am a newcomer, I am competing for the consulship, and this is Rome**. You will best mitigate the newness of your name by the glory derived from your eloquence. This skill has always had the greatest prestige. The man who is thought to be a worthy defender of men of consular rank cannot be thought unworthy of the consulship. (3) Next make sure the number and quality of your friends is obvious. For you have something few new men have had—all the tax-companies, virtually the whole eques- trian class, many communities on your side, many men of every class defended by you, some colleges and besides a great many young men won over by their enthusiasm for oratory as well as the daily attentions and company of your friends. (4) Make sure that you keep these friends by reminding them and asking them and ensuring that your debtors who want to return thanks realize that they will have no other occasion to oblige you. It is also seems that the goodwill of noblemen and that of former consuls in particular is to your benefit, that is the men whose rank you wish to reach, that you should be thought worthy of that rank and class by the men themselves. (5) All of these should be solicited and we must ally ourselves with them **and persuade them that we always sided with the elite in politics and were least of all populists. If we seem to be speaking in popular fashion we did this in order to win over Cn Pompeius**, so as to have this man of enormous power either as a friend in our canvassing or at least not an antagonist. (6) Besides this, work so as to have young nobles or keep the devotees you already have. They will contribute much prestige, if you have as many as possible. Be sure they know how important you think them. If you persuade those not unwilling to be eager on your behalf, they will be very useful.

The division of politicians into Optimates and Populares was somewhat clouded by the association of being popularis with support for Pompey. I have printed in bold Cicero's main statement of political allegiance.

B. Cicero's Rivals

(7) P Galbam et L. Cassium summo loco natos quis est qui petere consulatum putet? Vides igitur amplissimis ex familiis homines, quod sine nervis sint, tibi paris non esse: (8) at Antonius et Catilina molesti sunt. Immo homini navo, industrio, innocenti, diserto, gratioso apud eos qui res iudicant, optandi competitores ambo a pueritia sicarii, ambo libidinosi, ambo egentes. Eorum alterius bona proscripta vidimus, vocem deinde audivimus iurantis se Romae iudicio aequo cum homine Graeco certare non posse et senatu eiectum scimus optimorum censorum existimatione, in praetura competitorem habuimus amico Sabidio et Panthera, cum ad

tabulam quos poneret non haberet . . . in petitione autem consulatus omnis caupones compilare per turpissimam legationem maluit
quam adesse et populo Romano supplicare (9) alter, vero, di boni!
Quo splendore est? Primum nobilitate eadem [qua Catilina] num
maiore? Non, sed virtute quam ob rem? quod **Antonius umbram
suam metuit, hic ne leges quidem**, natus in patris egestate edu-
catus in sororiis stupris, corroboratus in caede ciuium.

Who is there who believes P. Galba and L. Cassius, men nobly
born, are seeking the consulship? So you see that men of the most
distinguished families are not your equals because they lack vigor.
(8) But Antonius and Catiline are troublesome. No, for a man who
is energetic and industrious, honorable, eloquent, and influential,
they are desirable rivals, both cut-throats, both lecherous, both
needy. We saw the auction of one man's property, and heard his
words as he swore that he could not compete at Rome on equal
terms with a Greek and we know he was rejected from the senate
by the judgment of excellent censors. We had him as our rival in
the praetorship with Sabidius and Panther as friends, when he did
not have any other slaves to put up for auction. Now in his candidacy for the consulship he preferred to rob all the innkeepers in a
most shameful journey rather than stay here and supplicate the
Roman people. (9) As for the other, by the gods, what sort of
glamor is his? Firstly of the same nobility as Catiline. Or perhaps
greater? No but in excellence, just as Antonius was afraid of his
own shadow, this man is not even afraid of the law, born with an
impoverished father, reared in incest with his sisters, and hardened
by the slaughter of citizens.

C. The Importance of the Consulship

(13) Quoniam quae subsidia novitatis haberes et habere posses
exposui, nunc de magnitudine petitionis dicendum videtur. Consulatum petis quo honore nemo est quin te dignum arbitretur, sed
multi qui invideant; petis enim homo ex equestri loco summum
locum civitatis, atque ita summum ut forti homini, diserto,

innocenti multo idem ille honos plus amplitudinis quam ceteris adferat. noli putare eos qui sunt eo honore usi non videre, tu cum idem sis adeptus quid dignitatis habiturus sis, eos vero qui consul-aribus familiis nati locum maiorum consecuti non sunt suspicor tibi: nisi si qui admodum te amant, invidere, etiam novos homines praetorios existimo nisi qui tuo beneficio vincti siint, nolle abs te honore superari.

Now since I have set out the assets your newness possesses and might possess, it seems I should speak about the grandeur of your goal. You are seeking the consulship, of which no one doubts you are worthy, but many are jealous of you, since you are born of an equestrian rank but seeking the highest position in the state, one so high that for an eloquent and honorable man this same honor brings much more distinction than to others. Don't think that men who enjoyed this rank do not see how much dignity you will have when you have the same achievement, while I suspect that men born of consular families who have not achieved their ancestors' position are jealous of you, unless they are very fond of you; I think even the new men of praetorian rank are reluctant to be outdone in office by you unless they are bound by kindnesses from you.

D. Lesser and Household Associates

(17) ut quisque est intimus ac maxime domesticus, ut is amet <et> quam amplissimum esse te cupiat valde elaborandum est, tum ut **tribules ut vicini, ut clients ut denique liberti postremo etiam servi tui;** nam fere omnis sermo ad forensem famam e domesticis emanat auctoribus.

As each man is close to you and of your household, you must toil vigorously for him to love you and desire your importance, also so that **your tribesmen and neighbors and clients and freedmen**, finally even your slaves, since almost all gossip about reputation in public life emerges from household sources.

E. Associations of Friends

(19) nam hoc biennio **quattuor sodalitates** hominum ad ambitionem gratiosissimorum tibi obligasti C. Fundani, Q. Galli, C. Corneli, C. Orchivi, horum in causis ad te deferendis quid tibi eorum sodales receperint et confirmarint scio, nam interfui.

For in the last two years you have bound **four associations** to you through the aspirations of their most influential men, C. Fundanius, Q. Gallius, C. Cornelius, and C. Orchivius. I know what their colleagues took on and confirmed in passing on their cases to you, since I was involved.

F. Local Magnates

(24) Sunt enim **homines in suis vicinitatibus et municipiis gratiosi**, sunt diligentes et copiosi qui, etiam si antea non studuerunt huic gratiae, tamen ex tempore elaborare eius causa cui debent aut volunt facile possunt: his hominum generibus sic inserviendum est ut ipsi intelligant te videre quid a quoque exspectes, sentire quid accipias, meminisse quid acceperis.

In fact there are **men of influence in their districts and towns**, attentive and well-funded men who, even if they did not previously devote themselves to this influence, can still easily toil for the sake of a man whom they owe debts and wish well. You must devote yourself to these men so that they realize you see what to expect from each one, know what you are receiving, and remember what you have received.

G. Election Friends

(25) In ipsa petitione **amicitiae permultae ac perutiles** comparantur; nam ceteris molestiis habet hoc tamen petitio commodi: potes honeste, quod in cetera vita non queas, quoscumque velis adiungere ad amicitiam, quibus cum si alio

tempore agas ut te utantur, absurde facere videare . . . modo ut intelligat te magni se aestimare, ex animo agere, bene se ponere, fore ex eo non brevem et **suffragatoriam** sed firmam et perpetuam amicitiam.

In the actual canvass many very valuable friendships are obtained, for amid the other troubles canvassing has this advantage, which you cannot claim in the rest of life, that you can bind whomever you choose to your friendship, men whom it would seem foolish for you to encourage to keep you company at any other time. Just let the man realize that you value him highly, are acting sincerely, and he is investing his effort well; then from him you will develop not a short **voting friendship** but one strong and lasting.

H. The Working Class and Voters Outside Rome

(29) Quam ob rem omnis centurias multis et variis amicitiis cura ut confirmatas habeas et primum, quod ante oculos est, senatores equitesque Romanos ceterorum ordinum omnium navos homines et gratiosos complectere. **Multi homines urbani industrii multi libertini in foro gratiosi navique versantur . . . deinde habeto rationem urbis totius, collegiorum montium pagorum vicinitatum;** ex his principes ad amicitiam tuam si adiunxeris per eos reliquam multitudinem facile tenebis. **postea totam Italiam fac ut in animo ac memoria tributim discriptam comprehensamque habeas, ne quod municipium coloniam praefecturam, locum denique Italia** ne quem esse patiare in quo non habeas firmamenti quod satis esse possit (31) . . . homines municipales et rusticani si nomine nobis noti sunt in amicitia te esse arbitrantur.

So see that you have all the voting units strengthened by many different friendships, first, as is obvious, senators and Roman equestrians, and embrace vigorous and influential men of all ranks. **There are many town-dwellers who are productive and**

many freedmen capable and influential in public life . . . finally take the whole city into account, its colleges, hill-communities, villages, and districts. If you win the alliance of the leading men from among these groups, you will easily control the crowd. **Finally make sure you have all of Italy organized by tribes and in your grasp, not allowing a town or colony or region or place of Italy** in which you do not have sufficient support. (31) Townsmen and country folk will believe they enjoy your friendship if they are known to us by name.

In the city there were different types of associations, business, social, religious, and regional; there were similar associations on the old "hills" of Rome, and in outlying villages. Roman tribes were originally local and focused on one place, then with added territories they developed separate districts; a map would show which tribes were concentrated in any given area. The old Italian communities usually had status as municipalities with their own internal administration; colonies were either Latin or full Roman citizens; prefectures served as administrative foci for scattered communities.

I. Ordo Equester

(33) Iam **equitum centuriae** multo facilius mihi diligentia posse teneri videntur. Primum cognosci equites oportet (pauci enim sunt) deinde appeti (multo enim facilius illa adulescentulorum ad amicitiam aetas adiungitur) deinde habes ex iuventute optimum quemque et studiosissimum humanitatis . . . studia iuvenum in suffragando in obeundo in nuntiando in adsectando mirifice et magna et honesta sunt.

Now it seems to me that **the voting units of equestrians** can be kept loyal much more easily by careful attention. First you must get to know the equestrians (for they are few), then approach them (and the age of young men is won over to friendship much more easily), then you have all the best members of the younger generation and those most devoted to culture. The enthusiasm of young men is both great and honorable in canvassing, in meeting people, in reporting, and in attending on you.

> *The* **ordo equitum** *was composed of three main categories of men: country landowners; municipal leaders and businessmen; and the sons of senatorial families still too young to be enrolled in senatorial magistracies. Cicero used these last as bodyguards during the elections.*

J. Adsectatores

(34) Et, quoniam adsectationis mentio facta est, id quoque curandum est ut cottidiana cuiusque generis et ordinis et aetatis utare; nam ex ea ipsa copia coniectura fieri poterit quantum sis in ipso campo virium ac facultatis habiturus. Huius autem rei **tres partes sunt: una salutatorum [cum domum veniunt], altera deductorum, tertia adsectatorum**.

And now that I have mentioned attendance, you must take care to have it daily, from all sorts and ranks and ages, for the very number will give an idea of the resources of strength you will have at the poll itself. This category falls into three parts: **the first, callers at your house; the second, escorts from your house; the third, attendants in general**.

> *Quintus divides public escorts into salutatores, who came to the candidate's home; deductores, who escorted him down to the forum, and* **adsectatores**, *the adsidua adsectatorum copia who are either voluntary or under an obligation (as courtroom clients); if they cannot follow the candidate they should send their dependents to do so.*

K. Election Promises

(47) C. Cotta in ambitione artifex dicere solebat se operam suam, quod non contra officium rogaretur, polliceri solere omnibus, impertire iis apud quos optime poni arbitraretur, ideo se nemini negare, quod saepe accideret causa cur is cui pollicitus esset non uteretur . . . deinde esse extremum ut irascatur is cui mendacium dixeris . . .

C. Cotta, that expert in electioneering, used to say it was his habit to promise to everyone any support that was not contrary to his obligations, but that he would carry it out only for those with whom he thought it was best placed. So he refused no one because often there was a reason why the man receiving the promise did not take it up. . . . Finally the worst case would be that the man to whom you uttered a falsehood would get angry.

L. Reprise of First Two Opening Maxims

(54) Tertium restat; "**Roma est**," ciuitas ex nationum conventu constituta in quae multae insidiae, multa fallacia, multa in omni genere vitia versantur, multorum adrogantia multorum contumacia multorum malevolentia multorum superbia, multorum odium ac molestia perferenda est. video esse magni consili atque artis in tot hominum cuiusque modi vitiis tantisque versantem vitare offensionem, vitare fabulam, vitare insidias, (55) esse unum hominem accommodatum ad tantam morum ac sermonum ac voluntatum varietatem. Qua re etiam atque etiam perge tenere totam istam viam quam institisti; excelle dicendo; hoc et tenentur Romae homines et adliciuntur et ab impediendo ac laedendo repelluntur et quoniam in hoc vel maxime est vitiosa ciuitas quod largitione interposita virtutis ac dignitatis oblivisci solet, in hoc fac ut te bene noris, id est ut intelligas eum esse te qui iudici ac periculi metum maximum competitoribus adferre possis . . . (56) atque haec ita te volo illis proponere <non> ut videare accusationem iam meditari, sed ut hoc terrore facilius hoc ipsum quod agis consequare . . . video

nulla comitia tam inquinata largitione quibus non gratis aliquae centuriae renuntient suos magno opere necessarios . . . **si competitoribus iudicium proponimus sequestribus metum inicimus, divisores ratione aliqua coercemus**, perfici potest ut largitio nulla fiat aut nihil valeat.

The third maxim is left. Rome is a community composed from the assembling of nations; in it we must endure many traps, much deception, and many vices of every kind, the arrogance and abusiveness and ill will and pride of many men, and their hatred and obstructiveness. I can see it requires great judgment and art when moving among so many great vices to avoid giving offence, gossip, and treachery, (55) to be the single man adjusted to such a variety of behavior and talk and attitudes. So persist again and again in holding to the path your have embarked upon; excel in speaking, since this is what keeps Romans loyal and attracts them and fends them away from hampering and harming. Since the community is most vicious in forgetting virtue and dignity when bribery is introduced, see that you know yourself well and realize you are the man who can impose the greatest fear of prosecution and condemnation on everyone. (56) Indeed I want you to present this to them not so that you seem to be already planning your accusation, but so as to achieve your intention more easily through fear of this. . . . I can see that no elections are so corrupted by bribery that some voting units will not vote for their closest associates. **If we set a trial before our rivals and put fear into the bribery agents and control the distributors** in some way, it is possible there will either be no bribery, or it will be ineffectual.

> *In this coda-like accumulation of parallel phrases Quintus introduces for the first time at §56–57 the issue of election bribery* (comitia inquinata largitione) *and laying charges* (accusationem meditari) *familiar from the context of Sulpicius's charges against Murena.*

II. MURENA'S ADVOCATES (CF. INTRODUCTION I.2)

(A) M. Licinius Crassus: [Crassus] mediocriter a doctrina instructus, angustius etiam a natura, labore et industria et quod adhibebat ad obtinendas causas curam etiam et et gratiam, in principibus patronis aliquot annos fuit. In huius oratione sermo Latinus erat, verba non abiecta, res compositae diligenter, nullus flos tamen neque lumen ullum, animi magna, vocis parva contentio, omnia fere ut similiter atque uno modo dicerentur. (Cic. *Brutus* 233, 46 BCE)

Crassus was only moderately equipped by education, and even more grudgingly by nature. Through toil and diligence and because he also applied both care and influence to his cases, he counted among the leading advocates for some years. His speech employed good Latin and refined diction, his material was carefully assembled but without ornament or highlight; he employed strong force of argument but little voice, so that everything was uttered in the same way and style.

Nam ut iis qui honeste rem quaerunt mercaturis faciendis, operis dandis, publicis sumendis, intelligimus opus esse quaesito, sic qui videt domi tuae pariter accusatorum atque indicum consociatos greges, qui nocentes et pecuniosos reos eosdem te actore corruptelam iudicii molientes, qui tuas mercedum pactiones in patrociniis, intercessiones pecuniarum in coitionibus candidatorum, dimissiones libertorum ad defaenerandas diripiendasque provincias; qui expulsiones vicinorum, qui latrocinia in agris, qui cum servis, cum libertis, cum clientibus societates, qui possessiones vacuas, qui proscriptiones locupletium, qui clades (LCL caedes) municipiorum, qui illam Sullani temporis messem recordetur, qui tot testamenta subiecta, qui tot sublatos homines, qui denique omnia venalia, dilectum decretum, alienam suam sententiam, forum, domum, vocem silentium; quis hunc non putet confiteri sibi quaesito opus esse? (Cic. Paradoxa Stoicorum VI.46, composition date uncertain; declamatory portrait of Crassus as politician)

For just as we understand that men who seek wealth honorably by trading, providing labor and taking on public taxes need to make money, so consider someone who sees the thronging crowds of accusers and informers at your home, who sees the same guilty and moneyed defendants contriving the corruption of a court, who sees the bargains of your profits in functioning as patron and the expenditure of money on agreements between candidates, who sees freedmen sent out to strip provinces with usury and plunder: when he recalls the evictions of neighbors, the brigandage in the countryside, gangs formed from slaves, freedmen, and clients, and sees empty properties, the proscription of the wealthy, the ruination of townships and the harvest of profit of the Sullan period; when he sees wills foisted on the dead, so many men eliminated, and in short everything up for sale, levies, decrees, his own vote, or another man's, public life, his home, his speech or silence, who would not think such a man is acknowledging that he needs to make money?

(B) Q. Hortensius Hortalus: (325) Si quaerimus, cur adulescens magis floruerit dicendo quam senior Hortensius, causas reperiemus verissimas duas. Primum quod genus erat orationis Asiaticum adulescentiae magis concessum quam senectuti. Genera autem Asiaticae dictionis duo sunt; unum sententiosum et argutum, sententiis non tam gravibus et severis quam concinnis et venustis . . . Aliud autem genus est non tam sententiis frequentatum quam verbis volucre atque incitatum, quale est nunc Asia tota, nec flumine solum orationis sed etiam exornato et faceto genere verborum. (326) haec autem . . . genera dicendi aptiora sunt adulescentibus, in senibus gravitatem non habent. Itaque Hortensius utroque genere florens clamores faciebet adulescens. Habebat enim et Meneclium illud studium crebrarum venustarumque sententiarum in quibus . . . erant quaedam magis venustae dulcesque sententiae quam aut necessariae aut interdum utiles; et erat oratio cum incitata et vibrans tum etiam accurata et polita . . . (327) erat excellens iudicio vulgi et facile primas tenebat adulescens. etsi enim genus illud dicendi auctoritatis habebat parum, tamen aptum esse aetati videbatur, Et certe quod et ingeni quaedam forma elucebat et exercitatio perfecta verborum astricta comprehensione, summam hominum admirationem excitabat. Sed cum iam honores et illa senior auctoritas gravius quiddam requireret, remanebat idem nec decebat idem. Quodque exercitationem studiumque dimiserat, quod in eo fuerat accerrimum, concinnitas illa crebritasque sententiarum pristina manebat, sed ea vestitu illo orationis qua consuerat ornata non erat. (*Brutus* 325–27, excerpted)

(325) If we ask why Hortensius was more successful in speaking as a young man than when older, we will find the two most likely explanations. First because his style was Asiatic, more suited to youth rather than age. For there are two kinds of Attic style, one full of apophthegms and point, with apophthegms less weighty and severe than neat and elegant. Then there is the other style, less packed with apophthegms than with words, swift and excited, such as there now is all over Asia, not just in the flow of its speech but in its ornate and charming language. (326) These styles are better suited to young men, but lack weight in older speakers. So Hortensius, successful in both styles, won applause as a young man. For he had that enthusiasm for packed and elegant apophthegms, among which some were more elegant and pleasing than either necessary or useful, and his diction was both excited and vigorous as well as precise and polished. (327) As a young man he excelled in the judgment of the crowd and easily won first place. For even if his style carried too little authority, it still seemed appropriate to his age. Certainly because the form of his intellect shone through and his practice, perfected and controlled by the shapeliness of his phrasing, he stirred up men's highest admiration. But when office and his authority as an older man needed a more weighty element, he stayed the same, but it did not suit him as well. And because he had let go his practice and diligence, which was his strongest merit, his abundance of apophthegms persisted, but it was no longer adorned with its customary dress of style.

III. THE LETTER ATTRIBUTED TO MITHRIDATES IN
SALLUST *HISTORIES* 4

This fictional letter of Rome's enemy composed by Sallust in the decade after Cicero's death was preserved out of context as a model political speech. It is addressed to King Arsaces of Parthia, here called Persia (but the Parthian king in the 60s was Phraates II, father-in-law of Tigranes the younger). The dramatic date of this letter should probably be soon after Pompey's arrival in Anatolia: compare Plutarch's report of negotiations between Pompey and Phraates in *Pompey* 33. Mithridates solicits an alliance, explaining away his previous lack of success. He puts a negative interpretation on Roman dealings with Philip V of Macedon, Antiochus of Syria, Perse(u)s of Macedon, Eumenes of Pergamum, Aristonicus, and now himself.

Sallust *Histories* fr. 69 pp. 198–201 in L. D. Reynolds ed. *C Sallusti Crispi Catilina, Iugurtha, Historiarum Fragmenta Selecta Appendix Sallustiana*, Oxford Classical Text 1991.

(1) Rex Mithridates regi Arsaci salutem.[1] Omnes qui secundis rebus suis ad belli societatem orantur considerare debent liceatne tum pacem agere, dein quod quaesitur satisne pium tutum gloriosum an indecorum sit. (2) Tibi si perpetua pace frui licet, nisi hostes opportuni et scelestissumi, egregia fama si Romanos oppresseris futura est, neque petere audeam societatem et frustra mala mea cum bonis tuis misceri sperem. (3) atque ea quae te morari posse videntur, ira in Tigranem[2] recentis belli et meae res parum prosperae, si vere aestimare voles, maxume hortabuntur. (4) Ille enim obnoxius qualem tu voles societatem accipiet, mihi fortuna multis rebus ereptis usum dedit bene suadendi et, quod

---

[1] *Arsaci* may be a corruption of *Arsacidi*, since this king was of the Arsacid dynasty. Phraates II, successor to the monarchy of Antiochus, was father-in-law of Tigranes's son (also called Tigranes). His capital was Seleucia in Mesopotamia.

[2] The elder Tigranes, king of Armenia, was son-in-law of Mithridates, who took refuge with him in 73.

florentibus optabile est, ego non validissimus praebeo exemplum quo rectius tua componas.

(5) Namque Romanis cum nationibus populis regibus cunctis una et ea vetus causa bellandi est, cupido profunda imperii et divitiarum. Qua primo cum rege Macedonum Philippo bellum sumpsere,[3] dum a Carthaginiensibus premebantur amicitiam simulantes. (6) Ei subvenientem Antiochum concessione Asiae per dolum avortere. Ac mox fracto Philippo Antiochus omni cis Taurum agro et decem milibus talentorum spoliatus est.[4] (7) Persen deinde, Philippi filium,[5] post multa et varia certamina apud Samothracos deos acceptum in fidem callidi et repertores perfidiae, quia pacto vitam dederant, insomniis occidere. (8) Eumenen, quoius amicitiam gloriose ostentant, initio prodidere Antiocho pacis mercedem; post, habitum custodiae agri captivi, sumptibus et contumeliis ex rege miserrumum servorum effecere,[6] simulatoque impio testamento filium eius Aristonicum[7] quia patrium regnum petiverat, hostium more per triumphum duxere, Asia ab ipsis obsessa est. (9) Postremo Bithyniam Nicomede mortuo[8]

---

[3] Hard pressed by Hannibal during the second Punic War, Rome made an alliance with Philip V of Macedon at Phoenice in 205, which did not result in any collaboration. Instead, within two years of defeating Carthage, Rome declared war on Philip and sent Flamininus as commander against him. Flamininus defeated him at Cynoscephalae in 197 and went on to proclaim the liberation of Greece.

[4] Discontented with living under Roman control, the Aetolians and Athenians invited Antiochus to liberate them, but his campaign was unsuccessful. In 189 BCE, Rome sent out an expedition under Lucius and Publius Scipio, which defeated Antiochus at the battle of Magnesia. The war was ended by the treaty of Apamea (188 BCE), which forced Antiochus to withdraw from Anatolia south and west of the Taurus Mountains.

[5] Rome favored Philip's son Demetrius to be his successor and victimized his brother Perse(u)s after his defeat at Pydna (167 BCE), capturing and leading him in triumph.

[6] After the defeat of Antiochus, the most important state in Asia Minor was the Attalid kingdom of Pergamum. Rome initially treated its king, Eumenes II, as an ally, but then turned against him in favor of his brother Attalus. Attalus left his kingdom to Rome on his death in 137 BCE to protect it from further warfare.

[7] Eumenes's supposed son Aristonicus led a rebellion against Rome, which was defeated in 133 BCE. Pergamum then became the new province of Asia.

[8] Nicomedes of Bithynia, the guest-friend of Julius Caesar, died in 75 BCE, and the Romans claimed he had bequeathed his kingdom to them. So, in 74 BCE both Roman consuls were sent to Anatolia, Cotta to Bithynia, Lucullus to Pontus. As Cicero notes (*Mur.* 32), Cotta suffered serious losses in a naval battle, but Lucullus was more successful, raising the siege of Cyzicus and driving Mithridates out of Pontus to take refuge with his son-in-law Tigranes of Armenia. Lucullus then captured Tigranes's new capital of Tigranocerta.

diripuere, quom filius Nysa, quam reginam appellauerat, genitus haud dubie est.

(10) Nam quid ego me appellem? Quem diiunctum undique regnis et tetrarchiis ab imperio eorum, quia fama erat divitem neque serviturum esse, per Nicomedem bello laecessiverunt, sceleris eorum haud ignarum et ea quae accedere testatum antea Cretensis, solos omnium liberos ea tempestate, et regem Ptolemaeum. (10) Atque ego ultus iniurias Nicomedem Bithynia expuli Asiamque, spolium Regis Antiochi, recepi et Graeciae dempsi grave servitium. (12) Incepta mea postremus servorum Archelaus[9] exercitu prodito inpediuit, illique quos ignavia aut prava calliditas, ut meis laboribus tuti essent, armis abstinuit acerrimas poenas solvent, Ptolemaeus, pretio in dies bellum prolatans, Cretenses impugnati semel iam neque finem nisi excidio habituri. (13) Equidem quom mihi ob ipsorum interna mala dilata proelia magis quam pacem datam intelligerem, abnuente Tigrane, qui mea dicta sero probat, te remoto procul, omnibus aliis obnoxiis, rursum tamen bellum coepi, Marcumque Cottam Romanum ducem apud Calchedona terra fudi, mari exui classe pulcherrima.[10] (14) Apud Cyzicum magno cum exercitu in obsidio moranti frumentum defuit, nullo circum adnitente; simul hiems mari prohibebat. Ita sine vi hostium regredi conatus in patrium regnum naufragiis apud Parium et Heracleam militum optimos cum classibus amisi. (15) Restituto deinde apud Caberam exercitu et variis inter me atque Lucullum[11] proeliis inopia rursus ambos incessit. Illi suberat regnum Ariobarzanis[12] bello intactum, ego vastis circum omnibus locis in Armeniam concessi; secutique Romani non me, sed morem suom omnia regna subvortundi, quia multitudinem artis locis pugna prohibuere, inprudentiam Tigranis pro victoria ostentant.

[9] In the so-called first Mithridatic war, Mithridates's general Archelaus accepted the invitation from Athens to invade Greece. He was besieged by Sulla and defeated. Sulla and Mithridates signed an interim peace at Dardanus in 85 BCE.

[10] Lucullus's campaigns in Armenia suffered from long chains of supply and the disloyalty of his legate Clodius, which caused disaffection among his soldiers. He was relieved of Bithynia and replaced as commander-in-chief by Pompey in 66 BCE.

[11] Lucullus apparently had support from Ariobarzanes of Cappadocia.

[12] After Sulla's peace treaty with Mithridates, Sulla's legate, Murena's father, provoked the renewal of hostilities in 83 BCE, being awarded a triumph (which he did not live to celebrate) for some dubious successes.

(16) Nunc quaeso considera nobis oppressis utrum firmiorem te ad resistundum an finem bello futurum putes. Scio equidem tibi magnas opes virorum, armorum et auri esse et ea re a nobis ad societatem, ab illis ad praedam peteris. Ceterum consilium est Tigranis regno integro, meis militibus <belli prudentibus> procul ab domo parvo labore per nostra corpora bellum conficere, quoniam neque vincere neque vinci sine tuo periculo possumus. (17) An ignoras Romanos, postquam ad occidentem pergentibus finem Oceanus fecit,[13] arma huc convortisse, neque quicquam a principio nisi raptum habere, domum coniuges agros imperium. Convenas olim sine patria parentibus, peste conditos orbis terrarum, quibus non humana ulla neque divina obstant quin socios amicos, procul iuxta sitos, inopes potentesque trahant excindant, omniaque non serva, et maxume regna, hostilia ducant?[14] (18) Namque pauci libertatem, pars magna iustos dominos uolunt; nos suspecti sumus, aemuli et in tempore vindices adfuturi. (19) Tu vero, quoi Seleucea, maxuma urbium, regnumque Persidis inclutis divitiis est, quid ab illis nisi dolum in praesens et postea bellum expectas? (20) Romani arma in omnis habent, acerruma in eos quibus victis spolia maxuma sunt; audendo et fallundo et bella ex bellis serundo magni facti: (21) per hunc morem extinguent omnia aut occident, quod haud difficile est si tu Mesopotamia, nos Armenia circumgredimur exercitum sine frumento, sine auxiliis, fortuna aut nostris vitiis adhuc incolumem. (22) Teque illa fama sequetur, auxilio profectum magnis regibus latrones gentium oppressisse. (23) quod uti facias moneo hortorque, neu malis pernicie nostra tuam prolatare quam societate victor fieri.

(1) King Mithridates sends greetings to King Arsaces.[1] All men who are solicited for alliance in war when their own affairs are prospering should consider whether they are free to keep the peace, and then whether their aims are sufficiently pious, safe, and glorious, or improper. (2) If you are free to keep undisturbed

---

[13] Mithridates alludes to the Roman conquest of Spain where he himself was seeking alliance with the Roman rebel leader Sertorius as late as 75 BCE, just before Sertorius was betrayed and assassinated.

[14] The universal summing up of Rome's abuse of her competitors.

peace, except for enemies both convenient and wicked, you will have a distinguished reputation provided you overcome the Romans, and I would not dare to seek alliance now and hope futilely to combine my misfortunes with your advantages. (3) But the very factors which seem able to deter you, your anger against Tigranes[2] over the recent war and my failures, if you want to assess them fairly, will encourage you most to action. (4) For being vulnerable he will accept alliance on your terms, and with the deprivation of many of my resources Fortune has made me experienced in persuasion and—something desirable for successful men—I in my weakness provide an example to help you arrange your affairs more wisely. (5) For the Romans have from the beginning only one original motive to wage war on nations, peoples, and all kings, their deep desire for empire and wealth. In this they first took up war against King Philip of Macedon[3] under the guise of friendship as long as they were hard pressed by the Carthaginians. (6) When Antiochus came to his aid they turned away his hostilities by granting him Asia, but as soon as Philip had been broken Antiochus was stripped of all his territory beyond the Taurus and of 10,000 talents.[4] (7) Then these clever devisers of treachery killed Perses son of Philip when he had been taken under the protection of the Samothracian gods, causing his death by depriving him of sleep because they had granted his life by an agreement.[5] (8) As for Eumenes, to whom they paraded the offer of friendship, they first betrayed him to Antiochus as his reward for the peace, then keeping him under guard in captured territory, they reduced him by extortionate demands and insults to become the most wretched of slaves,[6] and by a false and impious will led in triumph his son Aristonicus,[7] who had sought his father's kingdom while Asia was taken as their possession. Finally when Nicomedes died they plundered Bithynia,[8] although his son had undoubtedly been born to Nysa whom he had called his queen.

(10) Why should I call on my own example? I was separated on all sides from them by kingdoms and tetrarchies, but because it was rumored that I was wealthy and would not be a slave they provoked me to war through Nicomedes, who was hardly unaware of

their crime, and had witnessed what had happened to the Cretans, the only free people at that time, and to King Ptolemy. (11) And so I avenged these wrongs by expelling Nicomedes from Bithynia and recovering Asia, stripped from King Antiochus, and I rescued Greece from a grievous enslavement. (12) That worst of slaves Archelaus forestalled my enterprises by betraying the army.[9] And those whose worthlessness or perverted cleverness kept from warfare so that they would be safe through my efforts, suffered the most bitter of penalties. Ptolemaeus by paying to postpone the war from day to day while the Cretans were punished at the first attack, expecting no end except to be taken by storm. (13) When I realized that because of their internal strife battles had been postponed rather than peace conferred, Tigranes, who now late in the day approves my warnings, refused help. You were far away and everyone else was vulnerable, but I none the less renewed the war and routed Marcus Cotta the Roman leader near Calchedon on land and stripped him of a splendid fleet in a sea battle.[10] (14) At Cyzicus I ran out of grain delaying with my huge army in the siege, when no one nearby supported us and winter kept us from supply by sea. So attempting to return to my ancestral kingdom without enemy attack, I lost my best soldiers and their fleet in shipwrecks near Parium and Heraclea.[11] Finally when I had reconstituted my army at Cabera, after indecisive battles between me and Lucullus, starvation again attacked both forces. He had the support of Ariobarzanes's kingdom untouched by war,[12] but since everywhere around was devastated, I retreated to Armenia, and the Romans followed not me but their own practice of subverting all kingdoms; and because they prevented my large forces from engaging in battle by occupying constricted spaces, they now parade Tigranes's improvidence as a victory.

(16) Now please consider whether once we are overwhelmed you will be in a stronger position to resist or there will be an end of the war? I know you have great resources in manpower, munitions, and gold, and for this reason are being sought by us as an ally and by them as spoils. But my plan is while Tigranes's kingdom is undamaged, to finish the war with my experienced soldiers far from home at small cost, with our own manpower, since we cannot

either conquer or be conquered except at risk to you. (17) Or don't
you know that the Romans, once the ocean put a stop to their
advance to the west, turned their forces toward us, and that in the
beginning they had nothing except by theft, their home, wives,
lands, and empire?[13] Long ago as a random assembly without
native land or parents, created to be ruin of the world, whom no
power human or divine prevents from plundering and destroying
allies and friends, far and near, poor and powerful, the Romans
think all nations that are not enslaved, especially kingdoms, are
their enemies?[14] (18) For few peoples want freedom, mostly only
fair masters; we are suspect as rivals and in due course avengers.
As for you, who possess Seleucia, greatest of cities, and the
kingdom of Persia with its renowned wealth, what can you expect
from them except immediate treachery, and after that war? (20)
The Romans have forces arrayed against everyone, but most sav-
agely against those whose defeat will provide the best spoils; by
daring and cheating and contriving one war after another they
have become great. (21) In this fashion they will destroy everything or perish—which is not impossible if you in Mesopotamia
and we in Armenia surround their army, caught without grain supplies and without reinforcements, that army which has so far been
unharmed though luck or our own weaknesses. And this renown
will follow you, that in setting out to aid mighty kings you overwhelmed these brigands or all nations. (23) I urge you and warn
you to do this, and not to prefer using our ruination to postpone
your own, rather than to become victor through alliance with us.

Bibliography

A&G = J. H. Allen and J. B. Greenough, *New Latin Grammar*. Focus Publishing, 2001.

MRR = T. R. S. Broughton, *Magistrates of the Roman Republic*, 3 vols. APA Publications, Atlanta, 1968–86, New York, 1991.

OCD = *Oxford Classical Dictionary* ed. 3, 2003.

W = E. C. Woodcock, *A New Latin Syntax*. Cambridge, MA, 1959.

Adamietz, J., ed. 1989. *Marcus Tullius Cicero* Pro Murena *mit einem Kommentar*, Wissenschaftliche Buchgesellschaft, Darmstadt.

Alexander, M. C., 1990. *Trials in the Late Roman Republic 149–50 BC. Phoenix Supplement* 26, University of Toronto Press, Toronto.

———. 2002. *The Case for the Prosecution in the Ciceronian Era*, University of Michigan Press, Ann Arbor.

———. 2009. "The *Commentariolum Petitionis* as an Attack on Election Campaigns." *Athenaeum* 97: 31–57, 369–95.

Astin, A. E. 1967. *Scipio Aemilianus*, Oxford.

———. 1978. *Cato the Censor*, Oxford.

Badian, E. 1989. "The *Scribae* of the Roman Republic." *Klio* 71: 582–603.

Broughton, T. R. S. 1991. "Candidates Defeated in Roman Elections; Some Ancient Roman Also-rans." *Transactions of the American Philosophical Society* 81:1–18.

Brunt, P. A. 1982. "*Nobilitas* and *Novitas*." *Journal of Roman Studies* 72: 1–17.

———. 1988. *The Fall of the Roman Republic*, Oxford.

Craig, C. P. 1981. "The *Accusator* as *Amicus*: An Original Roman Tactic of Ethical Argumentation." *Transactions of the American Philological Association* 111: 31–37.

———. 1986. "Cato's Stoicism and the Understanding of Cicero's Speech for Murena." *Transactions of the American Philological Association* 116: 229–39.

———. 1993. *Form as Argument in Cicero's Speeches: A Study of Dilemma*, American Philological Association, Atlanta.

Crawford, J. 1994. *M. Tullius Cicero: The Fragmentary Speeches*, 2 ed. Atlanta.

Crawford, M. H. 1974. *Roman Republican Coinage*, Cambridge.

———. 1978. *The Roman Republic*, Harvard University Press (reprinted Fontana Books).

————. 1996. *Roman Statutes*, 2 Vols. BICS Supplement 64, London.

David, J-M. 1992. *Le Patronat judiciaire au dernier siècle de la République romaine*, Rome. Paris, Les Belles Lettres.

Douglas, A. E., ed. 1967. *M. Tulli Ciceronis Brutus*, Oxford.

Edwards, C. 1993. *The Politics of Immorality in Ancient Rome*, Cambridge.

Fantham, E. 2004. *The Roman World of Cicero* De Oratore, Oxford.

Gardner, J. 1987. *Women in Roman Law and Society*, London.

Gelzer, M. 1962. *The Roman Nobility*, tr. Robin Seager, Oxford.

Gildenhard, I. 2003. "The 'Annalist' before the Annalists: Ennius and his *Annales*," in *Formen römischer Geschichtsschreibung von den Anfängen bis Livius*, ed. U. Eigler et al., Wissenschaftliche Buchgesellschaft, Darmstadt. 93–114.

Gruen, E. S. 1968. *Roman Politics and the Criminal Courts, 149–78 BC*. Cambridge, MA.

————. 1974. *The Last Generation of the Roman Republic*, Berkeley.

Haffter, H. 1967. "Die römische *Humanitas*," in *Römische Wertbegriffe*, ed. H Oppermann, Darmstadt. 468–82.

Henderson, M. I. 1950. "*De Commentariolo Petitionis*." *Journal of Roman Studies* 40: 8–21.

Hoffer, S. 2007. "Cicero's Stomach: Political Indignation and the Use of Repeated Allusive Expressions in Cicero's Correspondence," in *Ancient Letters*, ed. R. Morello and A. D. Morrison, Oxford. 87–106.

Kennedy, George A. 1968. "The Rhetoric of Advocacy." *American Journal of Philology* 89: 419–36.

————. 1988. *The Art of Rhetoric in the Roman World*, Princeton.

Leeman, A. D. 1982. "The Technique of Persuasion in Cicero's Pro Murena," in *Éloquence et rhétorique chez Cicéron*, Geneva. 193–228.

Linderski, J. 1995a. "Buying the Vote: Electoral Corruption in the Late Republic," in *Roman Questions: Selected Papers 1*. Stuttgart.

————. 1995b. "The Surname of M. Antonius Creticus and the *cognomina ex victis gentibus*," in *Roman Questions I*. Stuttgart. 436–43.

Lintott, A. W. 1990. "Electoral Bribery in the Roman Republic." *JRS* 80: 1–16.

————. 1999. *The Constitution of the Roman Republic*, Oxford.

————. 2008. *Cicero as Evidence. A Historian's Companion*, Oxford.

Lloyd, G. E. R. 1967. *The Development of Aristotle's Thought*, Cambridge.

Long, A. A. 1995. "Cicero's Plato and Aristotle," in *Cicero the Philosopher*, ed. J Powell. Oxford.

Magie, D. 1950. *Roman Rule in Asia Minor to the End of the Third Century after Christ*, Princeton.

May, J. M. 1988. *Trials of Character: the Eloquence of Ciceronian Ethos*, University of North Carolina Press, Chapel Hill.

McGing, B. C. 1986. *The Foreign Policy of Mithridates VI Eupator, King of Pontus*, Princeton.

Millar, F. 1998. *The Crowd in Rome in the Late Republic*, University of Michigan Press, Ann Arbor.

Mitchell, T. N. 1979. *Cicero: The Ascending Years*, New Haven.

Morstein-Marx, R. 2004. *Mass Oratory and Political Power in the Late Roman Republic*, Cambridge.

Nisbet, R. G. M. 1961. "The *Commentariolum Petitionis*: Some Arguments against Authenticity." *Journal of Roman Studies* 51: 84–87.

Otto, A. 1890. *Die Sprichwörter und sprichwörtlichen Redensarten der Römer*, Berlin.

Pina Polo, F. 1995. "Procedures and Functions of Civil and Military *Contiones* in Rome." *Klio* 77: 203–16.

Powell, J. and J. Patterson, eds. 2004. *Cicero the Advocate*, Oxford.

Ramsey, J. T. 1984. "Cicero *pro Murena* 29: The Orator as Citharoedus; the Versatile Artist." *Classical Philology* 79: 220–25.

———. 2007. Sallust: *Bellum Catilinae*, 2 ed. APA, New York.

Rawson, E. D. 1975. *Cicero: A Portrait*, London/Cornell University Press, Utica, NY.

———. 1985. *Intellectual Life in the Late Roman Republic*, Johns Hopkins University Press, Baltimore, MD.

Reynolds, L. D., ed. 1983. *Texts and Transmission: A Survey of the Latin Classics*, Oxford.

Richardson, J. S. 1987 "The Purpose of the *Lex Calpurnia de Repetundis*." *Journal of Roman Studies* 77: 1–12.

Riggsby, A. M. 1997. "Did the Romans Believe in Their Verdicts?" *Rhetorica* 15: 235–51.

———. 1999. *Crime and Community in Ciceronian Rome*, Austin, TX. [For *Pro Murena* see pp. 28–38 passim.]

———. 2010. *Roman Law and the Legal World of the Romans*, Cambridge.

Rüpke, J. 2011. *The Roman Calendar from Numa to Constantine: Time, History, and the Fasti*, Wiley-Blackwell, Chichester and Malden.

Ryan, F. X. 1994. "The Quaestorship of Q. Curius and C. Cornelius Cethegus." *Classical Philology* 89: 251–61.

———. 1995a. "The Second Praetorian Campaign of Sulla (Plut. *Sulla* 5.104)." *Maia* 47: 399–403.

———. 1995b. "Two Senators in 73 B.C." *Zeitschrift für Papyrologie und Epigraphie* 108: 306–8.

———. 1998. *Rank and Participation in the Roman Senate*, Historia Einzelschrift, Stuttgart.

Shackleton Bailey, D. R., ed. 1965–70. *Cicero's Letters to Atticus*, 7 Vols., Cambridge.

Shackleton Bailey, D. R. 1970. "The Prosecution of Roman Magistrates Elect." *Phoenix* 24: 162–65.

———. 1971. *Cicero*, London.

———. 1979. "On Cicero's Speeches." *Harvard Studies in Classical Philology* 83: 237–45.

———. 1986. "Nobiles and Novi Reconsidered." *American Journal of Philology* 107: 255–60.

Sherwin White, A. N. 1994. "Lucullus, Pompey and the East." *Cambridge Ancient History* 9: 229–54.

Staveley, E. S. 1972. *Greek and Roman Voting and Elections*, London.

Sumner, G. V. 1966. "Cicero, Pompeius and Rullus." *Transactions of the American Philological Association* 97: 570–82.

———. 1973. *The Orators in Cicero's* Brutus: *Prosopography and Chronology. Phoenix Supplement* 11, Toronto.

Tatum, W. J. 1999. *The Patrician Tribune: Publius Clodius Pulcher*, University of North Carolina Press, Chapel Hill.

———. 2003. "Alterum est tamen boni viri, alterum petitoris: The Good Man Canvasses." *Phoenix* 61: 109–35.

Taylor, L. R. 1939. "Cicero's Aedileship." *American Journal of Philology* 60: 194–202.

———. 1966. *Roman Voting Assemblies*, University of Michigan Press, Ann Arbor.

Treggiari, S. M. 2003. "Ancestral Virtues and Vices: Cicero on Nature, Nurture and Presentation," in *Myth, History and Culture in Republican Rome: Studies in Honour of T. P. Wiseman*, ed. D Braund and C. Gill, Exeter University Press, 139–64.

Weinrib, E. J. 1971. "The Prosecution of Magistrates Designate." *Phoenix* 25: 145–50.

Welch, K. E. 1995. "The Office of *Praefectus* in the Late Republic." *Chiron* 25: 131–45.

Wiseman, T. P. 1966. "The Ambitions of Q. Cicero." *Journal of Roman Studies* 56: 118–25.

———. 1971. *New Men in the Roman Senate, 139 BC–AD 14*, Oxford.

———. 2011. *Remembering the Roman People*, Oxford.

Yakobson, A. 1999. *Elections and Electioneering in Rome: A Study in the Political System of the Late Republic. Historia Einzelschriften* 128, Stuttgart.

Zetzel, J. E. G. 1994. Rev. of Craig 1993, *Bryn Mawr Classical Review* 94.01.05, 4.446–51.

———. 2009. *Cicero: Ten Speeches*, Indianapolis.

Index of Persons and Places

Person are listed alphabetically **by gentile name**; **references are given by unit numbers of the speech**. Each Roman is provided with his entry number under the (capitalized) gentile name of his clan: for example, CORNELIUS Scipio with his reference number as listed in Paulys *Real-Encyclopedie* (RE).